365 New Testament

Devotions
FOR KIDS

by Mark Littleton

Standard
PUBLISHING

Cincinnati, Ohio

Published by Standard Publishing, Cincinnati, Ohio
www.standardpub.com

Copyright © 2010 by Mark Littleton

Printed in: United States of America
Project manager: Carla Crane
Project editor: Dawn Korth
Cover design: MTWdesign
Interior design: Andrew Quach

Scripture taken from the Holy Bible, *New Living Translation,* copyright © 1996, 2004. Used by permission of Tyndale House Publishers, Inc., Wheaton, Illinois 60189. All rights reserved.

Published in association with the literary agency of Schiavone Literary Agency, Inc., 236 Trails End, West Palm Beach, FL 33413-2135.

ISBN 978-0-7847-2375-3

Library of Congress Cataloging-in-Publication Data

Littleton, Mark R., 1950-
 365 New Testament devotions for kids / by Mark Littleton.
    p. cm.
  ISBN 978-0-7847-2375-3
  1. Bible. N.T.--Meditations. 2. Christian children--Prayers and devotions. 3. Devotional calendars--Juvenile literature. I. Title.
  BS2347.55A15 2010
  242'.62--dc22
                                    2010004791

15 14 13 12 11 10   1 2 3 4 5 6 7 8 9

To Elizabeth, child of my old age, joyful daughter of my own joy and happiness: May you be blessed all the days of your life. And if, perchance, you read this book, may God give you the insight and help from it that you will need to live and survive and triumph in this world.

Table of Contents

You'll probably read this book starting with Week 1 and going through the New Testament from Matthew to Revelation. If you want to read devotions from a specific New Testament book, this table of contents will help you.

This devotion book goes through the whole New Testament, focusing on interesting, insightful, important, and even fun Bible verses that I hope will instruct and guide you. When you find a verse that means a lot to you, memorize it. Put it on a card and read it every day to get it deep in your brain and in your heart.

There are five elements to each devotion: the title, the Bible verse (from *The New Living Translation*), the "Extra Mile" (if you want to read more from the Bible), the devotional reading, and a prayer. You can use the prayer as a starting point for talking to God after you read the devotion.

Take the devotions as you find them. Some are meant to teach you. Some are examples of how you can live out the Scripture in your life. Some are stories to inspire you to do better and greater things. I'm confident that reading these every day for a year will prepare you for the battle you will face every day as a Christian. There are enemies out there. I hope this book will help you win.

Most of all, remember that God is with you. No matter how low you go, or how high you rise, he's there. In trouble and out of trouble, in good times and bad, he will be there. Let him know every day you're listening, open to his guidance and leadership, and that you worship him as your God and greatest friend.

I commend you for choosing this book. May God bless you on every page.

Mark Littleton
October, 2009

Congratulations! If you're trying to use this book to develop a habit of spending time with God and his Word every day, you're off to a great adventure! It's an effort that will help you grow spiritually, and it will please God.

To help you keep track of your progress, there's a Devotional Journal at the end of this book. It starts on page 375. Use it to keep track of what you've read in this book and the Bible. Also, use the spaces provided to write down what you pray for, and note when God answers. At the end of the year, celebrate what you've accomplished, and praise God for answered prayer.

Where It All Started

Matthew 1:1: This is a record of the ancestors of Jesus the Messiah, a descendant of David and of Abraham.

The Extra Mile: Matthew 1:1-17

Glenda showed her mother the Web site. "See," she said. "You can go back to all kinds of people. Who knows who's in our line?"

"Why don't you go see, honey? I'd like to know myself."

Glenda began searching various databases. Soon she found someone who fought in the Civil War on her father's side. Then she located a long lost ancestor who was in Congress in the early 1800s. It was fun uncovering these great people and finding out that her family weren't a bunch of "losers," as one kid at school had said about his family.

As Glenda compiled the genealogy entries, she began to see more and more how spread out her family was. She had relatives from Greece, France, and Canada. The truth about her family encouraged her to want to excel in her life too. She realized she was one of a long line of people who left their stamp on history.

In the same way, Matthew opens his story of Jesus with Jesus' genealogy. Look down this list and you'll see many famous people from Israel's history, including Abraham, Isaac, Jacob, King David, and King Solomon. There are also some stunning bad guys in the midst of the list too. Can you figure which ones they are?

Everyone has a history. We all came from somewhere, going back literally to Adam and Eve. God values you and your family. And one day, you'll meet them all.

Prayer: Lord, help me remember that no matter who is behind me, I'm the next one to do great things for you.

She's Our Ancestor?

Matthew 1:5: Salmon was the father of Boaz (whose mother was Rahab).

The Extra Mile: Matthew 1:18–25

Jesus was perfect. He never committed a sin. He never made a mistake. He never spoke or thought a wicked word. He wasn't 99.44 percent pure like Ivory Soap. No, he was 100 percent. The real thing. Perfection personified.

But that doesn't mean some of his ancestors were the best people going.

Take Rahab. According to Joshua 2:1, she was a prostitute. She sold her body to wicked men to use sexually however they wished.

It's a hard way to live. And it displeases God. But Rahab also had something else: faith. When the Israelite spies came to Jericho, she helped them. Why? Because she probably knew of the miracles done in Israel and she chose to believe in their God. For that, she was saved from the fall and destruction at Jericho. For that, she would also marry a Jew and become one of the great, great ancestors of Jesus!

Isn't it amazing that a person like Rahab would be in Jesus' line?

No, when you think about it, it's just like God, isn't it? Doesn't he always bring good out of bad? God has used all sorts of people, including sinners, to work in his plan.

Do you ever feel like you're too messed up for God to use you? Look to Rahab. She reminds us: God loves us and can give us a great mission, if we'll only ask.

Prayer: Thank you, Lord, for reminding me that you can make a great believer of me no matter what I've done in the past.

What Could Anyone Possibly Give to God?

Matthew 2:11: They entered the house and saw the child with his mother, Mary, and they bowed down and worshiped him. Then they opened their treasure chests and gave him gifts of gold, frankincense, and myrrh.

The Extra Mile: Matthew 2:1–12

When the wise men traveled west to find Jesus, they must have thought long and hard about what to bring him. Their gifts reveal tremendous insight about Jesus.

Gold—a gift for a king. Jesus was to become the King of kings! The wise men must have realized Jesus would rule the world, and therefore they should honor him.

Incense—a gift for a priest. Jesus became our priest to teach us what God is like. In this way, they saw that he would represent them to God the Father.

Myrrh—a gift for someone who would die. Jesus died for our sins. The wise men saw somehow that Jesus would be the Savior of the world.

When we bring gifts to God, we usually think of giving money in church. But there are many gifts you can give to God: praise—for God's greatness; loving others—just as he loved you; helping your friends, family and others—this pleases God; obeying God even when it's hard—this brings God's blessing; praying for others—asking God to help them.

There are many good gifts you can bring to God today. What will you give him that shows you understand what his heart is like—as the wise men did long ago?

Prayer: God, let me give you a heart that pleases you.

The Devil Almost Stops the Show

Matthew 2:16: Herod was furious when he realized that the wise men had outwitted him. He sent soldiers to kill all the boys in and around Bethlehem who were two years old and under.

The Extra Mile: Matthew 2:13–23

God and the devil are fighting a huge war. The battleground is earth. Satan will do anything to hurt God. He does this by trying to make God's people sin, or give up, or even reject God.

One of the greatest battles God and Satan fought was the one that brought Jesus into the world. Satan knew Jesus was coming, so he took steps to try and derail his birth. King Herod, a vicious, paranoid person who killed members of his own family to protect his throne, spoke with the wise men about Jesus. When he learned what they'd seen in the stars, he told them to find Jesus and then report back to him. He wanted to come and worship Jesus too.

But it was a plot. Herod wanted to kill Jesus and make sure he couldn't take over Herod's throne.

But God always finds ways to defeat people like Herod, who are inspired by Satan. God warned Joseph, the earthly father of Jesus, that Herod wanted to kill the baby. Joseph awoke in the middle of the night and headed off for Egypt, where they would be safe. Some say the gifts of the wise men, especially the gold, paid for them while they remained in Egypt without a job or anything else. Herod the murderer killed many little boys in Bethlehem, but Jesus was saved. One day, he would save the whole world by dying on the cross.

There are times in our lives when Satan appears to be winning. But God is always in charge. Nothing happens that he hasn't planned for ahead of time.

Do you think all is lost? Do you want to give up? Take a word from the story of Herod and Jesus: no matter how bad it looks, God is still in control.

Prayer: Lord, don't let me ever give up on you. No matter how bad things look, I choose to trust you and your plan.

How to Prove You're a Believer

Matthew 3:8: Prove by the way you live that you have repented of your sins and turned to God.

The Extra Mile: Matthew 3:1-10

Erik stood on the basketball court with his friends, ready to wing the ball to the basket. He shot and missed. The game went on. He would have more chances, but he made a big mistake when he missed that one shot. He cussed. He took God's name in vain. It had become a habit for him. When something went wrong, he often muttered words he knew displeased God.

As the game continued, Zak grinned at him. "Hey, Erik, I thought you were a Christian."

Erik stared at him, surprised. "Well, I am."

"Then how come you cussed like that? I thought that was one of the Ten Commandments."

Erik turned red and pretended he didn't hear. But when they were all taking a breather, Zak commented, "It's OK, Erik. I won't tell anyone. Most Christians don't act like they should anyway."

Erik was deeply embarrassed. That night, he went home and went to the passage in the Bible about taking God's name in vain. Finally, he knelt by his bed. "I'm sorry, God. I shouldn't do that. Please help me to act like a real Christian."

Things improved after that. Erik wasn't perfect, but he was trying.

John the Baptist saw the hypocrisy of the Pharisees when they came to him for baptism. They didn't want to change their lives or conduct. But that was wrong.

Prayer: Jesus, let me be ready for you to work in me. I trust that you will make me like yourself.

Words from a Loving Father

Matthew 3:16, 17: After his baptism, as Jesus came up out of the water, the heavens were opened and he saw the Spirit of God descending like a dove and settling on him. And a voice from heaven said, "This is my dearly loved Son, who brings me great joy."

The Extra Mile: Matthew 3:13–17

As Jose stood at the plate, he heard the parents in the stands yelling out cheers and encouragements. But when he glanced to them, he saw his father hunkered down and not paying attention. Why didn't that man ever say anything nice to him?

He steeled himself for the pitch. Listrom wound up and hurled a fastball. Jose waited, zeroing in. Then he swung.

Connection. The ball line-drived over the third baseman. It could be extra bases. Jose tore down to first. He looked at the field and saw that the left fielder still hadn't retrieved the ball. The first-base coach yelled, "Go to second. Run!"

Jose pushed himself into it. He sprinted for second and made it without a hitch. Then he saw the third-base coach waving him on. He glanced at the left fielder who was picking up the ball in the far corner. Could he throw to third and catch him?

The coach yelled, "Come on!" Jose dug in and dashed for third.

Looking to his right, the left fielder cocked to throw. The ball was in the air. The bag was less than twenty feet away.

"Slide! Slide!" the coach yelled.

And then he saw something else: his father at the fence, yelling too. "Go, Jose. You can do it."

He slammed into the slide and made it.

We all like to hear compliments and praise. Imagine how Jesus felt when he heard his Father's voice from Heaven at his baptism.

Prayer: God, may my praise always be honest, even when I'm scared or down.

WEEK 1

Tempted to the Max

SUNDAY

Matthew 4:4: But Jesus told him, "No! The Scriptures say, 'People do not live by bread alone, but by every word that comes from the mouth of God.'"

The Extra Mile: Matthew 4:1–11

Do you ever get those little whispers in your heart that say . . .

"Go ahead, hit your sister. She deserves it."

"It's just a little thing. Just put it in your pocket and walk out of the store. No one will stop you."

"Don't tell the truth. If you do that, you'll really get punished."

Where do those whispers come from? The Bible shows us over and over that the devil has the power to "plant thoughts" in our minds. He can whisper an idea, a plan, a temptation into our minds faster than the strike of a rattlesnake. Have you heard the devil's words come into your mind at important moments?

What should you do?

The Bible tells us several ways to fight our spiritual enemies: Flee from them. Resist them. Draw near to God. One of the most effective ways, though, is what Jesus did with Satan in the wilderness. To every one of Satan's temptations, Jesus quoted a verse of the Bible. He then obeyed what the Bible said.

That's how to defeat Satan every time. Recite the Bible to him and he'll get out of there fast!

You can't quote the Bible, though, if you don't know it. That's why memorizing verses is so important. What are you memorizing today? How can you use that verse against the devil?

Prayer: Lord, teach me to set the devil on the run by using your Word today.

365 New Testament Devotions for Kids

Testing the Lord

Matthew 4:7: Jesus responded, "The Scriptures also say, 'You must not test the Lord your God.'"

The Extra Mile: Matthew 4:12–17

Have you ever wondered if this faith thing is real? Have you ever thought that maybe Christianity is just a big hoax? How can you test it to be sure? How can a person like you get God to prove himself?

God warns us in the Bible about testing him. No one is ever to throw himself in front of an oncoming train to make God save him at the last second to prove he really loves that person. We're never to do something crazy or stupid—challenge some tough guy to a fight, jump off the top of a building, pick up a rattlesnake, drink poison—just to see if God will step in at the last moment and rescue us.

But there is one way God says we can test him: through obeying his Word and doing as it says. God promises to bless us when we obey. If you really want to see God work, if you want him to "prove" himself to you, try it. Obey the Word. Live it out. Listen to God, and keep on doing it.

God promises to bless you in a way only he could.

Prayer: Lord, I will obey you, even if I'm not always sure why. Let me trust you to come through.

What Jesus Intends to Do with You

TUESDAY

Matthew 4:19: Jesus called out to them, "Come, follow me, and I will show you how to fish for people!"

The Extra Mile: Matthew 4:18–25

Have you ever gone fishing? You sit in the boat, or on the shore. You cast. And cast. And cast. And then there's a strike. You've got one! The fish fights. He goes back and forth. He tries to shake the hook. But it holds firm. Soon, you're holding a live fish—slimy, wiggly, and beautiful.

When Jesus invited the disciples to follow him, some of them were fishermen. They didn't fish like we do today. Mostly they used nets. But when Jesus told them he'd show them how to fish for people, they understood. They knew he meant that their mission would be to tell other people about him.

How does someone like you do that?

By speaking up: "I liked your comment in class today. It's like something I know from the Bible."

By asking a question: "Hey, have you ever thought much about who Jesus was and what he came to do?"

Just being a friend sitting around: "I was wondering what you believe about God. Do you have any beliefs?"

These are all ways to get a conversation started.

Prayer: God, lead me and help me to speak your truth to my friends and everyone else.

Become a Peacemaker

Matthew 5:9: God blesses those who work for peace, for they will be called the children of God.

The Extra Mile: Matthew 5:1–9

Ally and Nicole fired hot words at each other.

"I heard you say that to Angie!" Ally yelled.

"I didn't say anything to Angie," Nicole shouted back.

"Don't lie. I heard you."

"Then what did I say?"

"That I'm an ugly little toad."

"You're nuts!"

They were about to come to fists, when Paula stepped in. "All right, just hold it," she said to both of them, ducking between them.

Both girls stared at Paula with fury, but said nothing. Paula said, "Look, let's get the facts straight. I heard you say something to Angie, Nicole. And you've been after Nicole for a month, Ally. Why not just apologize and decide to either be friends, or at least not say nasty things about each other?"

Ally's eyes met Nicole's. Suddenly, she held out her hand. "I'll work on it."

Nicole took it and nodded. "So will I."

Many times peacemaking isn't this simple. But you get the idea. To be a peacemaker is a blessed thing in the eyes of God. The peacemakers will inherit God's kingdom.

What are you—a peace maker, or a peace taker?

Prayer: Help me bring others together, Lord, even when it looks tough.

365 New Testament Devotions for Kids

WEDNESDAY

Enemies Everywhere!

Matthew 5:10: God blesses those who are persecuted for doing right, for the Kingdom of Heaven is theirs.

The Extra Mile: Matthew 5:10–13

Tyler was known in his sixth-grade class as one of the smartest kids. Plenty of kids went to him for advice. In time, he was elected president of his class because of the friends he made along the way.

But there were some people who didn't like Tyler. They came up with a plot. They'd accuse him of a crime in school.

When Tyler was sent to the principal's office, the principal questioned him. "Where were you when this happened? What did you do then? What happened next?" The principal decided to investigate further. When he did, he caught the real culprits. Tyler was glad the principal proved the truth.

Do you have enemies? Are there people who try to make you look bad, or kids who tell lies or spread rumors about you?

Don't worry about them. You know what? God will take care of them. God is great at dealing with our enemies.

God will never let your enemies get away with the bad things they do to you. What matters, though, is that you please God. Forget those enemies. God will take care of them. Trust him.

Prayer: Jesus, I will serve you always because I know you will never let me down.

Directions

Matthew 5:18: *I tell you the truth, until heaven and earth disappear, not even the smallest detail of God's law will disappear until its purpose is achieved.*

The Extra Mile: Matthew 5:14-26

Billy's dad called him into his office at home. "Your little brother has a new bike," he said. "I want you to follow the directions and put the bike together for me, OK?"

Billy liked putting things together, so he walked out to the garage and started. He laid out the directions for how to put the bike together and began reading them. But halfway into the first picture, Billy noticed something. "That washer shouldn't go there," he told himself. "It should go over here."

As he looked over things, Billy thought these were the stupidest directions he'd ever seen. "I should put the back wheels on first, then the front wheel, not the other way around," he said as he set the bike down.

He began working on the bike, following his own ideas instead of the directions.

You can guess what happened. Soon, everything was a mess. Parts were left off the bike. Things didn't fit together. Billy had a real problem.

Finally, he went to his dad. "It doesn't go together right," he said.

His dad then took everything apart and put the bike together the right way. Then he said, "Directions always have a reason. Follow them, and you succeed."

The Bible is full of directions from God. We can't overlook even the smallest letters of it. So follow God's directions, and you will succeed.

Prayer: Help me to learn to follow your directions, Lord, and not to argue about them, because in obedience is success.

Anger Can Lead Us into Sin

Matthew 5:22: But I say, if you are even angry with someone, you are subject to judgment! If you call someone an idiot, you are in danger of being brought before the court. And if you curse someone, you are in danger of the fires of hell.

The Extra Mile: Matthew 5:27–48

"You're just a big jerk."

"Well, my mom says you're a loser. And your nose is bigger than an elephant's."

"Oh, so that's how you feel. Then I think you're a stupid idiot! You have so many pimples."

Ever been in one of those fights? You say one nasty thing. Your opponent says a nasty thing back and pretty soon you're in a whale of a fight.

Nasty words hurt, though, beyond just the moment. How many times have you turned over and over in your mind some nasty words a friend said to you? Sometimes mean things have truth in them.

Words can hurt. We need to guard our lips, like the verse we read today says. Even when people say nasty things to us, sometimes being silent and taking it is better than saying something back.

Prayer: God, teach me to watch my tongue. When it runs free, it often runs down others.

Don't Hold It Back

Matthew 6:3, 4: But when you give to someone in need, don't let your left hand know what your right hand is doing. Give your gifts in private, and your Father, who sees everything, will reward you.

The Extra Mile: Matthew 6:1–18

You're in the car with your mom or dad and at the corner a man appears. He's dirty. His face is unshaved. If you were close enough, he might smell. He has a sign up: "Vietnam Vet. Please help me out."

What do you do?

Most people just pass these folks by. Why? Because they say if that guy had any sense, he'd get a job. Then he'd be out of the trouble he's in.

Yes, getting a job can be an answer. But in the Bible, God tells us over and over not to forget poor people. They may be poor for many reasons. Maybe they squandered the good things God gave them. Maybe their parents were alcoholic. Maybe they were wounded and have never really recovered.

God wants us to remember such people.

Where do you start? With just one—a kid in school who doesn't have the best clothing, or the boy who never has lunch, or the girl who doesn't talk to anyone. Go to them. Reach out. Help them. Offer a hand, or even some money. Offer your friendship, your heart.

You never know how God might use you in another person's life.

Prayer: Lord, use me in a bad situation, and guide me to look for more ways to serve you.

Admit It Up Front

Matthew 6:12: Forgive us our sins, as we have forgiven those who sin against us.

The Extra Mile: Matthew 6:19–34

Imagine this. Your mom tells you to clean up the dirt and dust and waste paper in your bedroom. So you figure out an easy shortcut. You shovel it all under your bed.

A week goes by. There's another cleanup. You shovel more stuff under your bed.

Still another week passes. More shoveling. More dirt. That pile under your bed is getting pretty big. But you figure no one will notice. It's out of sight, right?

One day, your mom comes up to your room. She smells something strange. She says, "What's that smell?"

"I don't know," you answer.

She looks in the trash can, the closet, the drawers, and finally, under your bed.

"What on earth is this?" she cries. There's so much dirt she sneezes—six times. "There're old banana peels under there. It's gross. "

Like the dirt under your bed, many Christians pile their sins in a closet in their hearts and forget about them. But God doesn't forget.

When you pile up sin under the bed of your heart, not only is God displeased, but your heart is dirty in his sight. How do you clean it out? By admitting your sins, and asking God to forgive them.

Remember that God will forgive everything. He will never say, "Go away," or "No, I won't."

Prayer: Father, show me anyone I have hurt. With whom can I make something right?

Don't Give Up

Matthew 7:7: Keep on asking, and you will receive what you ask for. Keep on seeking, and you will find. Keep on knocking, and the door will be opened to you.

The Extra Mile: Matthew 7:1–11

Have you ever said something like this to God? "Lord, if you will do this, then I will do that. I promise."

In the story of Hannah in 1 Samuel 1, Hannah went to God and promised to give him her firstborn son as God's servant all the days of his life, if God would just give her a baby. The Bible teaches that it's God who gives children and who makes it possible to have children. So Hannah went to the right one to ask. God heard her prayer, and gave her that son. He turned out to be Samuel, one of the great leaders of the Old Testament. Then Hannah had other children too.

Do you want God's blessing? What are you willing to give up in order to get it? Are you willing to keep asking, even if God doesn't give it right away?

Prayer: Lord, help me to pray in faith, even if the answer takes a long time.

The Golden Rule

Matthew 7:12: Do to others whatever you would like them to do to you. This is the essence of all that is taught in the law and the prophets.

The Extra Mile: Matthew 7:12–29

Don't spit into the wind.

Two wrongs don't make a right.

Whatever doesn't kill you only makes you stronger.

Ever heard one of these old sayings? They make sense in life.

Jesus' rules for living make sense too. One of the best rules is this one, often called "The Golden Rule."

Do for others what you would like them to do for you. Don't worry about what others do to you, though. Do good to them because that's how you'd like to be treated. Do good to them before they do anything for you. Do good to them even if they've done something bad to you. And do good to them even if they keep doing wrong things to you.

Is that awesome? What if everyone acted that way?

The truth is that everyone won't. But you can be one of them. Just choose today that you will always treat others the way you'd like to be treated, even if the other person doesn't.

God promises that he will bless you, even if that person doesn't.

Prayer: Lord, may I go out and do good to everyone. Some of them will not only thank you, but become your friend, too.

Hoping to Be Healed

Matthew 8:2: Suddenly, a man with leprosy approached him and knelt before him. "Lord," the man said, "if you are willing, you can heal me and make me clean."

The Extra Mile: Matthew 8

Have you ever prayed for someone to be healed, such as a grandparent with cancer, a friend with a broken bone, or a teacher who was hurt in an auto accident?

Undoubtedly, the most common prayer we all pray is for healing of some sort. Sometimes it's for us. Many times it's for others.

What does God do for us when we ask for healing? Most of the time, God allows doctors, our bodies, and time to heal most wounds. Most of the time God uses normal body processes to help us get better.

But sometimes a real miracle is necessary. Like the leper in this Bible passage in Matthew. No doctor could heal this man. His own body had betrayed him. And time would only make things worse.

He came to Jesus, asked for healing, and Jesus answered, "I will."

Jesus still answers that way today. Most of the time he uses normal and sometimes supernatural means to heal us. And sometimes he doesn't.

Healing is up to God. We can't force him to do what we want. But we can trust that his love and care for us are so great that he will always do what's right.

Prayer: Lord, thank you for all the processes you use for healing.

Heart of Stone, Heart of Flesh

Matthew 9:4: Jesus knew what they were thinking, so he asked them, "Why do you have such evil thoughts in your hearts?"

The Extra Mile: Matthew 9:1–10

Do you ever wonder why some hateful, angry, or nasty thoughts flit through your mind? You are not alone. All people experience them.

We have "hearts of stone" in our chests. That means our most basic person, who we really are inside, is stony, hard, and tough. We don't easily like people. We don't easily do the right thing. Bad thoughts and feelings come over us all the time.

But God can do something about that.

When we accept Jesus, God does something important inside each of us. He gives us "hearts of flesh:" new hearts, new thoughts and feelings. This heart is kind, merciful, and friendly, and loving to God and others. This heart is the one God wanted us to have all along.

This new heart helps us overcome the bad thoughts and feelings from the old heart. It strengthens us to do what's right. It encourages us that God loves us and is with us.

Prayer: Jesus, help my new heart lead me, and don't let me listen to the old one.

Lowlifes

Matthew 9:11: But when the Pharisees saw this, they asked his disciples, "Why does your teacher eat with such scum?"

The Extra Mile: Matthew 9:11–26

SATURDAY

Who is the most hated kid in your school?

If you're like most of us, you know. You can easily name the kids no one likes, or at least pick them out at lunch. They're the ones who eat alone. They're the ones who often can't look you in the eye. They're the people who are always in trouble with everyone else.

Did you know that Jesus has a special love for such people? One such person—Matthew, a tax collector—became one of his disciples. As a tax collector, Matthew was considered a traitor by most Jews. He probably paid a high price to the Romans to get the right to tax his people. And when he taxed them, he made his people pay every cent. If they didn't, he had the power to cast them into prison.

People hated Matthew. His only friends were other tax collectors and "sinners," people whom everyone regarded as lowlifes.

Why does God care about tax collectors and lowlifes?

Because they're people made in his image like the rest of us. They're sinners like the rest of us.

God loves them because he knows his love can turn them into good people.

Prayer: Jesus, I know no matter how bad I am, you can change me from the inside out.

Listen to Your Mentors

Matthew 9:37, 38: He said to his disciples, "The harvest is great, but the workers are few. So pray to the Lord who is in charge of the harvest; ask him to send more workers into his fields."

The Extra Mile: Matthew 9:27–38

Have you ever heard of a "mentor"? It's a person like a coach or teacher who works with you personally, listens to you, and helps you figure out solutions to problems.

There are many people in the Bible who mentored others. Moses mentored Joshua. Samuel advised King David. Elijah instructed Elisha. Paul led Timothy. And Jesus taught and prepared his 12 disciples.

What is the great goal of a mentor? To help the other person become as capable and effective as the mentor. Jesus wanted his disciples to become "little Jesuses" and get out there and work when he went back to Heaven.

While every mentor can't insure that you will succeed in everything you do, mentors can help you do your best and excel. A mentor is God's way of giving you someone who will stand in your corner. They're usually older people who can guide you because of their life experience.

Prayer: Lord, thank you for my first mentors, my parents and teachers. Will you please lead me to another mentor, so I can begin learning from someone else?

A Traitor

Matthew 10:2–4: Here are the names of the twelve apostles: first, Simon (also called Peter), . . . [and] Judas Iscariot (who later betrayed him).

The Extra Mile: Matthew 10:1–23

Jill was caught. She had cheated on the exam. But she couldn't turn in Betsy, who helped her. Betsy would beat the tar out of her. So Jill told the teacher it was Gwen. "Gwen gave me the answers," she told the teacher.

When Gwen heard it, she whipped around and stared at Jill. She was Jill's best friend. Why had Jill done this to her?

When someone betrays you, it often hurts more than anything else they could ever do to you.

Betrayal is even worse when the one who betrays you is someone you love.

Jesus had a traitor in the midst of his 12 disciples. The traitor was the one the others trusted, for he took care of the money. He often had an opinion and spoke up when necessary, even though some of those opinions weren't very nice. Jesus tried to teach him. But Judas Iscariot was determined. He sold out. And he would pay for his sins.

Has anyone ever betrayed you? It hurts more than anything else. But it can be fixed by taking the right actions.

Prayer: Father, help me work to heal any bad relationships now, before they become worse, because I know you will bless my efforts.

Imprisoned

Matthew 10:23: When you are persecuted in one town, flee to the next. I tell you the truth, the Son of Man will return before you have reached all the towns of Israel.

The Extra Mile: Matthew 10:24-42

O'Brien and several boys from the seventh grade advanced on Artie after school. "Let's see what God does for the little Christian now!" O'Brien yelled.

A second later, he ran at Artie and knocked him down.

O'Brien stood over Artie, seething. "I'm sick of hearing your goody-goody gospel junk," he yelled. "It's over. Don't say anything anymore."

"Jesus forgive you," Artie cried.

"What?"

"Jesus forgive you!"

O'Brien lifted Artie up by the lapels. Then he landed the hardest punch Artie had ever felt in his short life, right in the stomach.

The wind was knocked out of him and he fell to the ground groaning.

Artie had come to this new school with high hopes. He wanted to tell people about how great Jesus was. But it had all backfired. Most of these kids believed nothing, and those that did said nothing about it. Artie found himself all alone.

Have you ever been treated like Artie for your faith? Maybe you weren't beat up. But sneers, slurs, and hatred can be almost as bad.

Sometimes we as Christians are persecuted by unbelievers. But stand firm. God will be there with you, even if it hurts.

Prayer: I know it's OK to be afraid, Lord, but let me always look to you; you've got my back.

I Have Doubts Now

Matthew 11:2, 3: John the Baptist, who was in prison, heard about all the things the Messiah was doing. So he sent his disciples to ask Jesus, "Are you the Messiah we've been expecting, or should we keep looking for someone else?"

The Extra Mile: Matthew 11:1–19

Jimi lay in bed feeling scared. What if all he believed about Jesus was untrue? What if the whole Jesus idea was just a story?

He pondered this question for a while and finally asked his friend Tomas about it. Tomas knew the Bible fairly well. He asked, "OK, if it's not true, then how did all the stuff about Jesus get started?"

Jimi answered, "People made it up."

"What people?"

"The disciples, I guess."

"But if there was no Jesus, or he was just a regular person, who were those disciples? And why would they make up lies about him if they knew they were lies when all he ever taught was to tell the truth and everything like that?"

It made sense to Jimi. He began to ask more questions when something bothered him, and that helped build his faith.

John the Baptist believed in Jesus but had doubts when things went wrong for him. Jesus gave him the answers John needed to build his faith.

Prayer: Lord, when I have doubts, may I always come to you or someone I trust to get answers.

Tradition or Truth?

Matthew 12:11: And he answered, "If you had a sheep that fell into a well on the Sabbath, wouldn't you work to pull it out? Of course you would."

The Extra Mile: Matthew 12

"Grandma," Jenny said, "why do you always use the best china for Christmas dinner?"

"Oh, it's just a tradition, honey," Grandma Stevens said. "I like to have the best for Christmas."

"Why do we always go to church on Christmas Eve?" Jenny said. "Most of my friends don't."

"Oh, that's another tradition," Grandma said. "My parents did it when I was little. We just passed it on."

Jenny asked more questions that day, about the mistletoe and the hanging stockings and other things. She learned everything was a tradition.

Most traditions are good, if they symbolize meaningful events and remind us of truths in our lives.

But sometimes traditions can become bad. The Jews in Jesus' day had taken God's commandment about honoring the Sabbath and turned it into a crazy thing. Their endless rules had become their tradition, and kept people from doing many good and decent things on the day of worship. When Jesus came and healed people on the Sabbath, many of the Jews were angry. Ultimately, they put him to death because of such things.

Love is always more important than any tradition. So is being kind, helping, giving, sharing. No tradition should ever take away your right to do good.

Prayer: Father, let me do good, even if it defies a tradition. I know you will never punish me for it.

Throw Out Some Bread

Matthew 13:23: The seed that fell on good soil represents those who truly hear and understand God's word and produce a harvest of thirty, sixty, or even a hundred times as much as had been planted!

The Extra Mile: Matthew 13:1–23

Imagine one day, you're down at the beach and you notice a bottle with a note in it washed up on shore. It's from someone far away who reveals a mystery, gives you a map to some treasure, or just writes a nice letter.

Wouldn't that be cool?

Most of us will never find such a bottle. But Jesus gives a good picture about how a message in a bottle is like a farmer throwing seed onto the ground. He casts the seed all over the dirt. In Jesus' story, there were good places for the seed, and bad places. But the last one, the good soil, took that seed, made it grow, and soon it produced a huge crop.

That's what God wants us to do: cast out his seed—the good news of Jesus—to everyone we meet. Like that message in a bottle, some people will pick up the Word, become Christians, and go out and plant more seeds.

Who could you plant a seed that may draw someone to Jesus? Share a baseball glove with a kid who doesn't have one, and tell him about Jesus. Give some of your lunch to the girl who looks hungry, and share a verse from the Bible that may encourage her. Give a drink to someone who looks thirsty, and tell him that God loves him.

Prayer: Father, there are a million ways to spread your Word. Help me make sure that I spread it in a good and helpful way.

Treasure!

Matthew 13:44: The Kingdom of Heaven is like a treasure that a man discovered hidden in a field. In his excitement, he hid it again and sold everything he owned to get enough money to buy the field.

The Extra Mile: Matthew 13:24–58

Have you wondered what it might be like to find buried treasure? Gold, diamonds, rubies, crowns, and scepters? What would you do with it? Spend it on a great vacation, a new mini bike, a huge new house for your parents? Would you give it to the church?

Jesus told this parable and compared finding God's kingdom to discovering hidden treasure in a field. God's kingdom will make us rich. We will inherit all of God's wealth when we get to Heaven. God's kingdom also provides us with riches on earth: the feeling of being loved, understood, and cared for. We know peace, joy, goodness, and self-control, to name only a few.

God's kingdom is a treasure you can find anytime, anywhere. All you have to do is ask for it. Tell God you want to be a member of his kingdom. And then watch as God's glories unfold in your life.

Prayer: Lord, the hidden treasure is no longer hidden. It's right in front of me, so let me take it.

Oh, the Pressure!

Matthew 14:9: Then the king regretted what he had said; but because of the vow he had made in front of his guests, he issued the necessary orders.

The Extra Mile: Matthew 14

Here we have a great example of how pressure from your peers can lead to sin. King Herod was so delighted by his wife's daughter's dancing that he foolishly offered her anything. When she asked for John the Baptist to be killed, Herod was sorry he had made such a rash promise.

Herod actually liked John and enjoyed hearing him preach. But now he was caught. Should he do what he knew was wrong because he made this stupid vow?

With everyone looking on, Herod was trapped. Finally he gave the order. Soon John was beheaded and his head brought on a disgusting platter.

Peer pressure often causes us to sin. A kid challenges us with a "double dog dare." Or someone taunts us that we're "chicken." Or when we won't do the sin they want us to do, they call us "sissy" or worse.

Have you been there? What's the remedy? Obey God and walk away. It's really that simple. In fact, you might do a little preaching to that crowd right there.

Prayer: Lord, don't let me back down when I know that you and the truth are on my side.

Meeting Needs

Matthew 15:37: They all ate as much as they wanted. Afterward, the disciples picked up seven large baskets of leftover food.

The Extra Mile: Matthew 15

Jimmie and his family were hungry. They'd driven all day for his dad to find a new job, but Dad hadn't been hired. Now the family sat in a rest area thinking.

"Dad, I'm hungry," Jimmie said.

"What do you want me to do?" his dad retorted. "I have to save the money for gas."

Jimmie looked at his sister. The previous Sunday they'd been in Sunday school, and the teacher told them that God knows about our needs before we even ask.

"Maybe we could pray," Jimmie finally said, feeling a little embarrassed. Their father didn't believe in God, but their mom did.

"Go ahead," Dad said grimly. "See what God does."

Jimmie prayed, and a few minutes later, a man knocked on their car door. "We have all this food left over, and no place to refrigerate it. Would you like it?"

Everyone was amazed, even Dad. God had come through.

Prayer: God, I know you meet needs, and when I have one, I will tell you about it.

"Give Me a Sign"

Matthew 16:1: One day the Pharisees and Sadducees came to test Jesus, demanding that he show them a miraculous sign from heaven to prove his authority.

The Extra Mile: Matthew 16

Katara walked up the street with her friend, Bondie. They were talking about Jesus and suddenly Bondie said, "Why doesn't God just give us a big sign? Why doesn't he write it in the sky, or do some big miracle? That would convince my friends about him."

Katara thought about it. She said, "Remember last Christmas when you wanted that tennis racket, and your dad said it cost too much? We prayed about it, remember? And then Gregory from the youth group offered you his."

"Yeah."

"Well, wasn't that kind of a sign?"

Bondie stomped her foot. "I mean something big."

"But it you didn't believe the little sign of the tennis racket, why should God give you a bigger one?"

It may be human nature to want to see a miracle from God. But belief comes from seeing what God has already done, not asking for more.

Prayer: Lord, let me not demand signs and miracles from you, because if I'm honest, all I have to do is look around.

Predicting Your Death

Matthew 17:22, 23: After they gathered again in Galilee, Jesus told them, "The Son of Man is going to be betrayed into the hands of his enemies. He will be killed, but on the third day he will be raised from the dead."

The Extra Mile: Matthew 17

Do you think you could predict the day and moment you, or anyone else, will die? Unless the person is in prison and sentenced to death at a certain time, it's nearly impossible to tell precisely when a person will die, even if they're very sick.

But Jesus was different. He often predicted things about himself. Jesus told his disciples the circumstances of his death. Later, as the time came closer, he would predict more exact elements of his death. Why? Because it was one more way for Jesus to show his disciples, and us today, that he was God's Son, the Savior and Lord of the earth.

What kinds of things did God do to prove Jesus was his Son? Here are some. Think of more:

Jesus did miracles no one else could ever do.

Jesus spoke words that would be quoted and remembered forever.

Jesus fulfilled prophecies of the Messiah recorded in the Old Testament (such as being born in Bethlehem to a virgin mother).

Jesus rose from the dead.

So what do you think of Jesus? Your beliefs will determine your destiny.

Prayer: Lord, if I haven't told you already, I believe in you.

Bad Things

Matthew 18:7: "What sorrow awaits the world, because it tempts people to sin. Temptations are inevitable, but what sorrow awaits the person who does the tempting."

The Extra Mile: Matthew 18:1–14

Sometimes, no matter how good or nice we are, bad things happen:
You have a fight with a kid at school.
You flunk a grade.
You're in a car accident and lose a limb.
Your parents divorce.
Someone you love dies.
Bad things happen to good people. Matthew 18 records what Jesus said about how sometimes trouble comes because people tempt others to sin. But why does God let it happen?

There are many reasons evil happens to us. Sometimes it's because we sin. Sometimes it's because we're in the wrong place at the wrong time.

But does it really matter? If you're a Christian, how you die, or what bad things happen to you in this life do not change the fact that you will live forever with God in Heaven. And he will never allow evil to touch you there. No matter how bad things get in this world, God is with us. His promise is to get us safely to Heaven, not to make it easy in this world.

Prayer: Lord, I know you deliver, but sometimes not the very first minute.

THURSDAY

When God Has to Stop Something

Matthew 18:15: *If another believer sins against you, go privately and point out the offense. If the other person listens and confesses it, you have won that person back.*

FRIDAY

The Extra Mile: Matthew 18:15–35

Have you ever done something wrong and wished someone had stopped you before you did it?

A boy took a friend's bike without asking the friend ahead of time. He parked it at a shopping center, and when he returned for it, the bike had been stolen.

He said to another friend who had come with him, "Why didn't you stop me from doing this? Now I'll have to pay for the bike."

The friend said, "Don't blame me. You shouldn't have taken it in the first place."

What would it be like to have a great friend who kept you from making mistakes in the first place? We have such a friend in Jesus. Listen to him and he will help you not make mistakes. He'll show you the right way. And even when you do make mistakes, he forgives you when you ask.

Prayer: Jesus, let me listen for you every day. I will listen for you in my heart.

Let the Children Come

Matthew 19:14: But Jesus said, "Let the children come to me. Don't stop them! For the Kingdom of Heaven belongs to those who are like these children."

The Extra Mile: Matthew 19:1–15

What did Jesus look like? What was it like to be near him, to listen to him, to walk with him over the dusty roads of Israel?

Artists have tried to picture Jesus in great portraits of a handsome man with long hair and a beard. But we don't really know what he looked like. We don't know how he told a joke or what his voice sounded like.

The one thing we know about Jesus is how he responded to people. Sick, broken, scared, and poor people flocked to Jesus for help and healing. He must have been very friendly and kind to get that kind of response.

In the verse above we see another side of Jesus. He loved little children. Did he play with them? Did he get down in the dirt and make mud pies with them? Perhaps.

Whatever he did, we know he loved them. He liked to have them around. He told his disciples that they should never prevent little ones from coming to him.

Prayer: Lord, I know your heart is like a great harbor. Big, little, and tiny ships can feel safe there, so I know you will hear me.

Rewards!

Matthew 19:29: *"And everyone who has given up houses or brothers or sisters or father or mother or children or property, for my sake, will receive a hundred times as much in return and will inherit eternal life."*

The Extra Mile: Matthew 19:16–30

Do you ever feel as if you always lose; that being "on God's side" often leads to disaster instead of triumph? Do you think that things just "don't work out" in your life?

Many Christians feel that way at times in their lives. There's nothing wrong with those feelings except one thing: they just aren't true! The feelings are real, but they don't tell the whole story.

Did you know that God intends for all Christians to win in the end? Maybe we won't win in every situation in this life. But when we get to Heaven, we will stand before Jesus and he will reward us for all we did in this life. That reward will be eternal. It will never fade, never be forgotten, never grow old, and never die.

Sometimes, God rewards us in this world and time. But many times, he waits for eternity. But even if it is postponed, you can be sure that reward will be far greater than anything he could give us in the here and now.

Do you hope for God's reward? Don't give up. He will give it in the right time and place. God is always faithful, even when we are not.

Prayer: Lord, may I never forget your faithfulness. I trust you to do right in my life every day.

Sheer Pride

Matthew 20:21: She replied, "In your kingdom, please let my two sons sit in places of honor next to you, one on your right and the other on your left."

The Extra Mile: Matthew 20

Slim grabbed Jose and pushed him into the corner. "How would you like to be my right-hand man?" Slim asked.

"What do you mean?" Jose stammered.

"You know. Be there with me. Work with me. Give the orders to others."

Jose had wanted to be important like this for a long time. But Slim was head of a gang in school. They didn't commit crimes or anything, but they sometimes did bad things and caused trouble. Jose wasn't sure he wanted to be part of that.

"What's the problem?" Slim yelled. "You some Christian idiot?"

Jose bit his tongue. "I'll think about it." Then he walked away.

In the verse above, James and John's mother asked Jesus to give her sons important places in his kingdom. Jesus had to rebuke her, and then them because of their arrogance.

Beware of wanting to be "big man on campus" or "head of the gang," or "top dog." Why? Because sometimes being there is worse than just living your life like you should.

Prayer: Lord, let me never want to have an important position. I will ask you if you want me to go there.

The King on the Donkey

Matthew 21:1, 2: Jesus sent two of them on ahead. "Go into the village over there," he said. "As soon as you enter it, you will see a donkey tied there, with its colt beside it. Untie them and bring them to me."

The Extra Mile: Matthew 21:1-17

Have you ever watched a parade? Have you watched the bands, floats, beautiful girls waving, riders on horses, and kids on motorbikes? Parades can be a lot of fun.

But did you know there was one parade in all of history that was spoken about over 400 years before it happened?

Israel awaited their Messiah. God had told them through his prophets that this person would be a son of Abraham, David, and Solomon. God informed them where this person would be born: in Bethlehem. He predicted that this man would be born of a virgin, and that he would be crucified.

How would Israel know when this Messiah came to them? In Zechariah 9:9, the prophet told Israel he would come on the colt of a donkey.

Here in Matthew we see this event happen. It's a grand parade. Jesus arrives in Jerusalem on a donkey. People throw down their coats and palm leaves in his path to honor him. They shout, "Hosanna," which means, "Save now!"

Prayer: Lord, I love you and praise you! You are the Son of God.

365 New Testament Devotions for Kids

No Excuse Will
Work with God

Matthew 21:28, 29: A man with two sons told the older boy, "Son, go out and work in the vineyard today." The son answered, "No, I won't go," but later he changed his mind and went anyway.

The Extra Mile: Matthew 21:18–46

"I can't do it, Daddy, I'm too little."

"I don't have the time right now, Mom. Get someone else."

"I'm doing something. Don't bother me."

Excuses. They're so easy to sling out there when we don't want to do something. What happens when God asks us to do something for him? The excuses are even more ridiculous.

"I can't witness to him, God. He's bigger than me."

"I can't take on that class, Lord. Those kids are animals."

"I've never spoken in front of the group before, Lord. Can't you use Bill?"

The son in Jesus' story made the same kind of excuse. Christians today offer all kinds of reasons they can't do what God requests: "Witness to your friend." "Go to church and give some money." "Help the teacher today."

Are you making excuses? What are they? Why not stop making excuses and do what God asks? You can be sure he will bless you if you do.

Prayer: I will obey, Lord, because you promise to bless me that way.

Trap!

Matthew 22:18: But Jesus knew their evil motives. "You hypocrites!" he said. "Why are you trying to trap me?"

The Extra Mile: Matthew 22

Have you ever been really afraid?

. . . when you're alone in the house, and it's dark, and there's a noise . . .

. . . you're up to bat against the fireballer of the league . . .

. . . you have to take a test in school and you don't know the answers . . .

Jesus knows what it's like to be afraid. He had many enemies trying to trap him. But he also knew his Father was with him. Jesus wasn't really afraid of these men. He knew just what to do to put them in their places. But at times, Jesus must have wondered what might happen. Although he was God and in perfect touch with the Father, there were times when even he didn't know what the Father would do. Those times could have made him wonder. But Jesus knew where to turn. He trusted his Father to help him deal with any and all situations.

Jesus knows how you feel when you face a tough situation. He invites you to come to him and trust him to help you through it. He assures you that he'll be with you every step of the fearful way.

Prayer: Lord, the next time the house is dark and there's a noise, I will talk to you!

It's All a Big Show

Matthew 23:5: "Everything they do is for show. On their arms they wear extra wide prayer boxes with Scripture verses inside, and they wear robes with extra long tassels."

The Extra Mile: Matthew 23

Claretta watched as Zeta raised her hand. "I'll pray," Zeta said. And of course she did.

But to Claretta, Zeta's prayers just didn't seem right. She always went on and on and used such overly fancy language: "Oh, Lord, the Great Creator and Power of the world, who rules in everything and sees all and knows all, who is our greatest friend and companion, bless those in Zimbabwe. Diseases are rife. People are being killed. And the president just doesn't know what he's doing!"

How did she know all that? Claretta wondered. *And all those words? Words, words, words.*

She talked to her mom on the way home from church. "I can't be sure, but I think she does it all for show. She wants everyone to think she's this great, dynamite Christian because she pretends to butter God up. But it's all pretense."

Claretta stumbled in prayer. She wasn't nearly as eloquent as Zeta. But now she realized she should forget Zeta and just tell God what she felt and leave it at that.

Prayer: Lord, when I pray, I will not put on a show. I'll simply love you and speak the truth to you.

When Is the End?

Matthew 24:7, 8: "Nation will go to war against nation, and kingdom against kingdom. There will be famines and earthquakes in many parts of the world. But all this is only the first of the birth pains, with more to come."

The Extra Mile: Matthew 24

People all over the world want to know when the end of time will come. When will Jesus come back? When is the new Heaven and earth? When will God right every wrong and make life perfect again? Many study the Bible to find answers to such questions.

Jesus answered them, though, in Matthew 24, 25. He told his disciples to look for signs like these: imposters will pretend to be Jesus; wars will start, and there will be rumors of other wars; there will be famines and earth-quakes; Christians will be persecuted; false prophets, teachers, and preach-ers will rise up and many will follow them; and people will feel nothing but hatred.

Take a look at our world. Do you see these things happening? What does the news report?

The signs of the end are as plain as the Bible says. It's up to us to listen to them and prepare for Jesus' coming.

Prayer: Lord, let me keep my eyes on Jesus. Then nothing in the world, no matter how horrible, will destroy me.

You Were There for Me

Matthew 25:35: *"I was hungry, and you fed me. I was thirsty, and you gave me a drink. I was a stranger, and you invited me into your home."*

The Extra Mile: Matthew 25

The old man was picking up things from trash cans and putting some of them in his mouth. Stefan watched and winced. In his Sunday school class, the teacher had talked about helping others, how at the end of time, one of the ways Jesus would be able to tell a real believer was how he treated unfortunate people.

As the old man fished in a trash can outside a fast-food restaurant, Stefan saw him pull out a crust and devour it.

"That's enough," Stefan said. He walked over to the old man. "Sir," he said, "would you like a hot meal, a burger and some fries?"

The man turned to look at Stefan. His eyes were milky, he was stooped over, and the bag around his shoulder looked heavy.

"What you got in mind, son?" he asked.

Stefan pointed to the restaurant. "I'll be glad to take you in and buy you a decent meal. I can't do much for you, but I can do that."

They went in, and as the old man ate, relishing every bite, he said, "Why did you do that? No one cares about me anymore."

"God does," Stefan said. "That's why I helped you."

The old man nodded and they talked more.

Prayer: Jesus, when I see someone who hurts, I will lend a hand.

The Perfume

Matthew 26:7: While he was eating, a woman came in with a beautiful alabaster jar of expensive perfume and poured it over his head.

The Extra Mile: Matthew 26

MONDAY

Alanda sat looking at her latest doll, an expensive one her grandmother sent her for her birthday. It was beautiful, perfect for her collection.

But something had happened a few days before. Alanda's class had a new girl, Ronita, who came in wearing shabby clothing and looking very poor. Alanda befriended her at recess and they talked. At one point, Alanda said, "What would you like more than anything else in the whole world, Ronita?"

The girl thought about it and said, "Once I saw in a store a wonderful doll. It had a porcelain face, beautiful eyes, and an incredible dress. I've always wished for one of them. I'd take good care of it. But my parents—" She looked away. "It'll never happen."

The next day the doll had come in the mail. Alanda stared at it for a long time. It was just what Ronita had described.

"OK, let's do it," she said, grabbed the doll in the nice case, and walked to Ronita's apartment in a tough part of town. When Ronita came to the door, Alanda said, "Here. It's a present for you."

Her eyes went wide, and then she took it. "But why?" Ronita asked. "What did I do?"

"You needed it," Alanda said. "And I wanted to honor you."

Prayer: Lord, I know when I honor others, I honor you too, like the lady with her perfume.

When God and Jesus Parted Ways

Matthew 27:46: At about three o'clock, Jesus called out with a loud voice, *"Eli, Eli, lema sabachthani?"* which means *"My God, my God, why have you abandoned me?"*

The Extra Mile: Matthew 27:1-66

Do you ever think about what Jesus went through on the cross?

When the nails were driven through his wrists and ankles he experienced excruciating pain. Jesus was also whipped mercilessly till the flesh on his back peeled off. He wore on his head a crown made of a thorny bush that cut his forehead and skull. That's all to say nothing of the emotional pain of seeing his disciples desert him and the crowd roar for his death. The thieves crucified on either side of him even taunted him, though one repented in the end.

The real climax of Jesus' agony on the cross, though, was not the physical or emotional pain. It was the spiritual anguish he faced when his Father in Heaven leveled all his wrath at Jesus for the sins of the world. At that moment, Jesus felt the heat of the Father's anger and he and his Father were separated spiritually.

That means Jesus experienced all the terrors of Hell at that moment. It was utter destruction. The Father cut himself off from Jesus. And in that moment, Jesus knew all the pain of eternal loneliness, brokenness, and hellish terror.

Prayer: Lord Jesus, I know you took the pain on yourself for me. Therefore, I will trust in you.

Marching Orders

Matthew 28:18, 19: Jesus came and told his disciples, "I have been given all authority in heaven and on earth. Therefore, go and make disciples of all the nations, baptizing them in the name of the Father and the Son and the Holy Spirit."

The Extra Mile: Matthew 28

You've seen them in the movies: military people scurrying around in a compound, shooting down attacking jets. Officers are giving orders, and the soldiers obey them immediately.

Did you know that Jesus, like a captain or general, also gave us marching orders? They're found in Matthew 28. Like the supreme commander of an army, Jesus told us to go into all the world and make disciples of everyone we can. Jesus gave these orders five times in different forms throughout the Bible. You'll find them in the last chapters each of Matthew, Mark, Luke, and John, and in the first chapter of Acts. We call it "the Great Commission."

Jesus' words are really our orders for leading the world to him. The main job is to "make disciples." That means we take a raw recruit, someone who has just accepted Christ, and we teach him everything we know about following Jesus. We work with him day by day to help him learn to obey and love Jesus just like we do.

It's an awesome task. But it's also the most important in the Christian life. So, who is your disciple? Who is discipling you?

Prayer: Lord, let me be a true disciple, so I can serve you wherever I am.

Let's Go Fishing

Mark 1:17: Jesus called out to them, "Come, follow me, and I will show you how to fish for people!"

The Extra Mile: Mark 1:1-20

Jacob walked out to the car looking a bit deflated. "What's the matter, Jake?" his father asked as they all climbed into the car after Sunday worship.

"I'm no good at fishing," he said.

"Why are you concerned about that, honey?" his mom asked. They drove on toward home.

"You know, in church, how we're supposed to be fishers of men," Jake explained. "I'm not good at real fishing. How could I be good at fishing for people? Nobody listens to me."

There was a brief silence. Then his father said, "In what ways do you think real fishing might be like evangelism and witnessing?"

Jake shrugged. "I don't really know."

"Think about it. What do fishermen do? Do they throw their lines into mud puddles?"

Jake laughed. "No, they go to rivers, and lakes, and stuff."

"Right. A fisher of men has to go where the fish are. Where's that?"

Jake nodded. "School. The playground. All of sorts of places."

"Right. So think about it. Maybe you can come up with some ways you can get out there and fish for people."

Prayer: Lord, help me fish for people like the disciples did.

Starting Out Right

Mark 1:35: Before daybreak the next morning, Jesus got up and went out to an isolated place to pray.

The Extra Mile: Mark 1:21-45

Karenna's teacher looked at each member of the small group. "Having a quiet time is one of the essentials of Christian living. Even Jesus had one, as we see from this passage from Mark 1:35."

The teacher really hammered it home, but Karenna complained to her mom, "I always start out well, but then it gets hard. And then I gradually quit."

"Honey, the important thing is just trying to keep consistent. If you miss, you miss. Don't worry about it. God just wants to meet with you personally. That's all."

Karenna started trying to practice a QT (Quiet Time) at different times of day. Sometimes morning was good; other times, evenings, or lunchtime, or during breaks. She soon found that she liked spending a little time reading the Bible, praying, and thinking about how to apply the Bible to her life. One day she came home and told her mom, "I had a QT every day this week."

"Wonderful!" her mom answered.

"You know, when you just try to have one regularly, without getting like some legal-eagle about it, it's kind of fun. I'm learning a lot about God."

"That's what it's all about, honey."

Prayer: Lord, I will spend time with you. Help me every day to find the time.

Disabled!

Mark 2:3: Four men arrived carrying a paralyzed man on a mat.

The Extra Mile: Mark 2:1-9

Do you have a friend who is disabled? in a wheelchair? confined to a bed? in constant need of care?

Our world is full people who are disabled. We even give them special license plates so they can park in spaces close to stores and malls.

Do you ever feel for persons with disabilities? Do you ever wish you could do something for them to make their lives easier?

During Jesus' ministry he healed many people with all sorts of disabilities: paralysis, seizures, blindness, and deafness, to name a few. When news about him got around town, people brought everyone with a problem to him. He even raised the dead.

In Mark 2, we see Jesus healing a paralytic. There, the first thing he did was forgive the paralytic. After that, he healed him physically. Jesus didn't always work this way. But it's a good lesson. People who are disabled are no different from you or me. They need a Savior. They need eternal life. They need to be forgiven.

Prayer: Lord, let me always honor persons with disabilities.

Proof

Mark 2:10, 11: "So I will prove to you that the Son of Man has the authority on earth to forgive sins." Then Jesus turned to the paralyzed man and said, "Stand up, pick up your mat, and go home!"

The Extra Mile: Mark 2:10-28

When Jesus healed this man who was paralyzed, the first thing he did was tell the man his sins were forgiven. Some legal scholars who sat there thought Jesus was acting as if he were God. They became angry. But Jesus knew what they thought. He could have said, "Hey, I'm God. I can do whatever I want."

But Jesus didn't approach it that way. Instead, he posed a situation to them. Which was easier, to say, "You're forgiven," or to say, "Rise and walk"? What mere person has the power to make a paralytic get up and walk just by saying it?

But Jesus proved to his critics he had the authority not only to heal the man, but to forgive his sins. When people saw that, they realized Jesus really was more than an average human being. He gave them real proof.

Prayer: Lord, I'm so glad you have the power to forgive sins. Thank you for forgiving mine.

Jesus Was Angry

Mark 3:5: He looked around at them angrily and was deeply saddened by their hard hearts. Then he said to the man, "Hold out your hand." So the man held out his hand, and it was restored!

The Extra Mile: Mark 3:1–19

Here we have one of the few times in the Bible when Jesus became angry. A man with a useless arm was present. He probably wasn't there for healing, but there were many people who wanted to catch Jesus doing something wrong. To them, healing on the day of worship was forbidden.

So Jesus called the man forward. Immediately, he looked around at all his critics, as if to challenge them to a duel. Why was Jesus angry with them? Because they made their man-made rules more important than God's rules. To smack that idea in the face, Jesus told the man to hold out his hand, something he couldn't do as it was withered and worthless.

But the man miraculously lifted his arm, whole and perfect. He rejoiced, but Jesus' critics became even angrier.

What angers you? Do you get angry when people get harsh and nasty over a broken rule, especially when you feel the rule is unfair or worthless? Do you get angry when you think there are too many rules, or the rules are too hard to follow?

The most important rules to follow are God's.

Prayer: Lord, if it comes to a showdown between man's rules and your rules, I will always let you win.

The Crazy Jesus

Mark 3:21: When his family heard what was happening, they tried to take him away. "He's out of his mind," they said.

The Extra Mile: Mark 3:20-35

Have you ever been accused of being nuts, or crazy, or even stupid?

Did you know Jesus also faced that accusation—and from his own family?

In Mark 3 we see Jesus' family arriving in town to take him away. They thought he was out of his mind. Why? Because of the things he was saying to people. He told them certain Bible passages were fulfilled in him. He did miracles and then forgave people, something Jews believed only God could do.

When you go out into the world and start telling people what Jesus has done for you, some will think you're crazy. Nuts!

"You say you know Jesus personally? What an idiot!"

"You're telling me that God answered your prayer? Come on. God doesn't answer prayers like that!"

"You've been 'saved'? That's an old religious idea. It's not for today. Are you trying to live in the 1800s?"

When you will be considered strange, or even crazy because of the things you believe, you're in good company. Jesus knows just how you feel.

Prayer: Jesus, I will not be too worried when people tell me my faith in you is stupid. You had the same problem!

Every Secret Exposed

Mark 4:22: For everything that is hidden will eventually be brought into the open, and every secret will be brought to light.

The Extra Mile: Mark 4:1–25

Marko noticed Rico's penknife right away. Rico showed it off to everyone. Marko became friends with Rico for one reason: he wanted to steal the penknife. One day he had his chance at a birthday party. He grabbed Rico's knife lying on his dresser, put it in his pocket, and walked away whistling. When he got home, he hid the knife in a bottom drawer and only used it when no one else was around.

Rico asked around if anyone knew about the theft, but Marko told him he hadn't seen it. "But I'll be glad to help you find it," he said, with even more deception.

In time, Rico and Marko got older and Rico forgot about the knife. Marko, though, stole other things: DVDs, CDs, money, and cell phones. Strangely, he got so good at it, he was never caught.

Years passed, and Marko grew to be an old man and died. How do you think he felt when he stood before God and all of his secrets were revealed? He thought he'd gotten away with his crimes. He never considered that God knows everything!

Prayer: Lord, I know one day every secret will come out. So I will confess to my sins now while I'm still here to do it.

WEDNESDAY

Power Over the Storm

Mark 4:39: When Jesus woke up, he rebuked the wind and said to the waves, "Silence! Be still!" Suddenly the wind stopped, and there was a great calm.

The Extra Mile: Mark 4:26–41

Imagine you're in a boat fishing with your grandfather. Grandpa nods off, asleep. The sky gets dark. Raindrops begin falling. The wind picks up. Soon, you're in the middle of huge storm. Water sloshes over the sides of the boat. You're going to sink.

"Grandpa! Grandpa! We're going to sink!"

Grandpa snorts and then looks up. "What's the problem?"

"It's a huge storm!" you yell. "We'll sink."

"Oh, that's nothing," Grandpa says. He motions to the storm. "Stop storming, you silly weather. We're fishing here!"

Immediately, the storm stops. Everything is calm. And you've got a fish on the hook.

What would you think if your grandpa did that? You might think he was God.

Well, that's what the disciples thought when Jesus stilled the storm for them. He just rebuked the waves and the wind and the rain and it stopped. Right in mid-drop!

Jesus is the most powerful person in the universe.

Prayer: Lord, I know you are powerful, and whoever is on your side will get to see that power in his life.

Go Away, Jesus!

Mark 5:17: And the crowd began pleading with Jesus to go away and leave them alone.

The Extra Mile: Mark 5

It wasn't that Sondra didn't believe in Jesus. She believed he lived and was a teacher some people followed. But she refused to follow him. He would interfere too much in her life. If she followed Jesus she couldn't listen to the music she liked, watch the movies she wanted to, and do the things she thought were fun. "Don't bother me, and I won't bother you" was her motto.

There are many people like Sondra. In the passage above, Jesus cast the demons out of some demon-possessed men and sent them into a herd of pigs. When the owners of the pigs learned what Jesus had done, instead of thinking he'd done a great miracle, they begged Jesus just to go away.

Amazing. Here Jesus could have done many more miracles for them, but all they wanted was for him to go away because he wrecked their business.

Prayer: Jesus, I know when I tell others about you, some will just tell me to get lost because they don't want you to interfere with their lives.

The Power of Unbelief

Mark 6:5, 6: *And because of their unbelief, he couldn't do any miracles among them except to place his hands on a few sick people and heal them. And he was amazed at their unbelief.*

The Extra Mile: Mark 6:1–13

Could God be amazed with anything?

People in Jesus' hometown had seen Jesus grow up. They watched him go from baby to child to young man. Undoubtedly, some had come by Joseph's carpenter's shop to buy or order things. Perhaps Jesus had fashioned a yoke for some of the farmers, or a display table for a merchant, or a chest of drawers for a woman decorating her house.

Naturally, when you've grown up with someone, a few might be skeptical when someone does "big" things. Most people would have been proud of Jesus, though. Most would have welcomed him home and asked him to do everything they needed. Most would have been talking about him and his doings for months.

But no, not these folks. Mark says that Jesus "couldn't" do miracles at this place because so many people refused to believe in him. This is not the same as not being sure about Jesus, or not being able to understand. This was flat-out refusal to believe—willful rejection.

Prayer: Lord, let me never refuse to believe your truth.

365 New Testament Devotions for Kids

Rest

WEEK
8

Mark 6:31: Then Jesus said, "Let's go off by ourselves to a quiet place and rest awhile." He said this because there were so many people coming and going that Jesus and his apostles didn't even have time to eat.

The Extra Mile: Mark 6:14–34

Rebekah and her mom volunteered at the local rescue mission serving breakfast. They were so busy the morning passed really fast. Before they knew it, the mission director asked, "It's almost lunchtime and we're short-handed. Can you stay and help with lunch?"

Rebekah played with some of the little kids there, then helped with lunch and cleaning up afterward. She was pretty tired by then, having gotten up early, but then the director came to them again: "I know this is pushing it, but we really need some people to unload this truck out front, and also help us get ready for dinner."

Her mom just looked at Rebekah and smiled. "Come on, honey. We can do it."

By the end, Rebekah was so exhausted she fell asleep during the message after dinner.

Prayer: Dear God, I know even the most committed Christians need to rest. Jesus knew it too. Thank you for the strength to work and the gift of rest.

The Little Boy's Present

MONDAY

Mark 6:41: Jesus took the five loaves and two fish, looked up toward heaven, and blessed them. Then, breaking the loaves into pieces, he kept giving the bread to the disciples so they could distribute it to the people. He also divided the fish for everyone to share.

The Extra Mile: Mark 6:35–56

Imagine you receive a big check—$100—for your birthday from a very rich grandparent. You're excited. You can buy some cool things for $100.

But then you remember: "I should give the first 10 percent to the Lord." And 10 out of 100 isn't much. You still have 90 left.

It's at that moment that you hear God speak: "I want you to give $50 to the church fund for poor people. It's needed."

Now that makes it more difficult, doesn't it?

You see, true giving isn't just a matter of math—a percentage of what you have. No, real giving is from the heart. Real giving costs you something. Sometimes real giving hurts.

The story here involves a little boy who had five little pieces of bread and two fish for his lunch. He offered all he had to Jesus. What a generous giver he was!

Prayer: Jesus, I really want to give to your work, so help me to give from the heart.

What God Looks At

Mark 7:21, 22: For from within, out of a person's heart, come evil thoughts, sexual immorality, theft, murder, adultery, greed, wickedness, deceit, lustful desires, envy, slander, pride, and foolishness.

The Extra Mile: Mark 7:1-23

What does God see when he looks inside you?

Anger? Hatred? Put-downs? Bad words?

Hope? Friendliness? Joy? Love?

When God selects someone to do an important job, he doesn't look at outward things—her clothing, how beautiful she is, how cool he is. He looks at much greater things: what is going on in his or her heart.

Listen to your heart. What do you hear it saying? What thoughts go through it? God knows all of them. He knows what kind of heart you have toward your parents, your brothers and sisters, your classmates, the kids at church. He knows what you think and say about those people in your heart.

If what you hear displeases you, this is what you can do to get a quieter, happier, more loving heart. For one, memorize Scripture. As you immerse your heart in God's Word, it will take root and grow. Second, think about God and his truth. Meditate on it. Let it fill your mind. Third, refuse to let nasty, horrid thoughts take hold. We can't stop some bad thoughts from flitting through our minds, but we can refuse to dwell on them.

Prayer: Lord, I know my heart is my greatest organ. It tells who I really am. By striving to purify my heart, I will please you.

Healing the Natural Way

Mark 7:33: Jesus led him away from the crowd so they could be alone. He put his fingers into the man's ears. Then, spitting on his own fingers, he touched the man's tongue.

The Extra Mile: Mark 7:24–37

Sometimes Jesus healed someone just by speaking. But not in this case.

Notice what Jesus did here. First, he put his fingers into the man's ears. Then he spit on his fingers and touched the man's tongue with the spittle. *Eeewww,* you say, how unsanitary! But what was Jesus doing here? Why didn't he just say, "Speak, dude," and move on?

Because Jesus wants us to know we're all individuals. Each of us is unique, different, and each has special value in God's eyes. Jesus didn't need to do those things. But perhaps he did them to make that man feel special and loved.

Prayer: Lord, I love you and I know you love me. So thanks.

Not Quite Clear

Mark 8:24: The man looked around. "Yes," he said, "I see people, but I can't see them very clearly. They look like trees walking around."

The Extra Mile: Mark 8:1-26

Here's another strange healing. This time it's a blind man. And when Jesus touches his eyes and heals him, he's mostly healed. But his eyes are unfocused. This wasn't 20/20 vision, but something worse.

Jesus could have walked away. But if you read the story, you see that Jesus gave the guy a second jolt of miraculous power. And the second time, the man saw accurately.

Why did this happen? We know Jesus did not suffer from a power outage. His power is always the same. He can do anything.

We also know God does everything in order to teach us and help us learn about him. So perhaps Jesus was just showing that he wasn't the kind of healer who zapped you and walked on. No, he made sure the job was finished.

Prayer: Jesus, I know you never do half-baked jobs, and neither should I.

You Are the Christ!

Mark 8:29: Then he asked them, "But who do you say I am?" Peter replied, "You are the Messiah."

The Extra Mile: Mark 8:27–38

FRIDAY

Kyla sat down with her best friends at lunch. Her friend Abby said, "Do you believe what Mr. Pettigrew said today, that Jesus was a fake?"

Kyla answered, "Mr. Pettigrew thinks anything that's outrageous is what he should say."

"I know," Abby said. "I just don't get why he's so against Jesus."

"Lots of people are," Kyla said.

"I mean, Jesus really was a nice guy, wasn't he?" Abby replied. "He healed people and stuff. He couldn't have been a fake. Who do you think he was, Ky?"

Kyla studied Abby's face for a second. She'd been waiting for an opportunity to tell Abby about her faith, and finally, the time was right.

Taking a deep breath, Kyla said, "I believe Jesus was God in human form. He came to save the world, and he's alive today in Heaven."

Abby stared at her friend. "You believe all that about him?"

"I do," Kyla said.

Abby laughed. "Cool."

Prayer: Jesus, I know sometimes people will ask me point blank what I believe about you. It's then I know I must speak the absolute truth. I won't hedge.

Razzle and Dazzle

Mark 9:2, 3: As the men watched, Jesus' appearance was transformed, and his clothes became dazzling white, far whiter than any earthly bleach could ever make them.

The Extra Mile: Mark 9:1-13

Jesus offered people all kinds of proofs that he was God in human form. He performed miracles no one could do or had ever done. He healed. He stilled the sea. He fed 5,000 people with a little boy's lunch.

God the Father spoke from Heaven, declaring that Jesus was his "loved son" and "listen to him." Jesus also fulfilled many prophecies from the Old Testament, as well as living a perfect life.

The transfiguration was another of those moments when Jesus proved to his disciples he really was God. What happened? He went up on a mountain with three disciples, Peter, James, and John, and there he was "transfigured." It means he looked completely different from an ordinary person. In fact, Jesus probably looked then like what he will look like in Heaven to all of us.

The fact is that you don't have to believe just because of some feeling you have inside. You can rely on hard facts to build your faith.

Prayer: Lord, when I'm having trouble believing, help me get the facts straight.

Faith and Doubt

Mark 9:24: The father instantly cried out, *"I do believe, but help me overcome my unbelief!"*

The Extra Mile: Mark 9:14–29

Isaac lay on his bed worrying. Was God mad at him? Did God think he was just an idiot? Would God ever help him again?

The problem was Isaac's grandfather. He had fallen ill. His parents had called everyone they knew to pray for Pops. But he'd only gotten worse. Isaac had tried praying, and even fasting. But the more he did so, the more doubtful he became. He knew plenty of people and kids who prayed and nothing happened for them. Why should something happen to his grandpa?

He picked up his Bible and read for awhile until he came to this passage about a father and his son who was possessed by a demon. While Jesus was up on a mountain, the disciples tried to help this boy. But they failed. And the boy only seemed to get worse.

When Jesus arrived, the father said, "Please heal my son if you can." He knew the disciples couldn't heal his son; maybe Jesus couldn't either.

"If I can?" Jesus answered. "All things are possible to him who believes." It's then that the man says the above words, indicating his doubt. Amazingly, Jesus didn't chide the man for doubting; he simply healed his son.

Prayer: God, I know it's OK to doubt sometimes. We all need help in our faith. So I will tell you about my doubts.

What to Do in This Life

Mark 10:17: As Jesus was starting out on his way to Jerusalem, a man came running up to him, knelt down, and asked, "Good Teacher, what must I do to inherit eternal life?"

The Extra Mile: Mark 10

What does God really want us to do? Amos tells us: God wants us to do good, not evil (Amos 5:14).

But what is good? Telling the truth, not lying. Giving of your time and money to a good cause, not wasting time on dumb things. Helping a friend, not turning away. When Mom asks, doing the dishes or cleaning your room, and not running off to do something else.

Anything you can think of that helps people, encourages others, builds people up, and shares the truth is good. Having faith in Jesus is the first step of doing good. Without that faith, nothing else matters.

When the young man above came to Jesus, he wanted to know how to gain eternal life. Jesus told him to obey the commandments, and he said he had. So Jesus gave him a personal commandment: sell everything you have and give to the poor, then come and follow me. That man couldn't do it. He was very rich, and he didn't want to give those things up.

Doing good and keeping the commandments is not enough. You must commit yourself to the Lord and obey him. When you have that kind of faith, you are doing precisely what God wants you to do.

Prayer: Father, I know to obey you and follow you is right, and all the rest is gravy.

The Barren Fig Tree

Mark 11:14: Then Jesus said to the tree, "May no one ever eat your fruit again!" And the disciples heard him say it.

The Extra Mile: Mark 11

This is one of the weirdest situations in the New Testament. As Jesus walks into Jerusalem, he spots this fig tree. He walks over and it has no figs. Why? Because figs are out of season. The tree shouldn't have any figs! However, Jesus cursed the tree for not having figs on it for him, and the next day when the disciples passed the tree, they saw it had withered and died.

Was Jesus being vengeful, mean, or unreasonable? We may never know the real reason Jesus did this, but some scholars say that perhaps this tree never had figs and Jesus knew that, so he cursed it for that reason. Or perhaps there was some other deeper reason.

Jesus was making a comparison to the nation of Israel. He had been rebuking Pharisees repeatedly for their hypocrisy and the fact that they never bore any real spiritual fruit in the name of the Living God. Jesus used the fig tree as a picture of the problem with Israel—they never bore fruit, in season or out of season.

Prayer: Lord, I know you want us to bear spiritual fruit—good character, planting seeds of the gospel, and good works. So help me to get with it!

The Main Issue of the Day

Mark 12:17: "Well, then," Jesus said, "give to Caesar what belongs to Caesar, and give to God what belongs to God." His reply completely amazed them.

The Extra Mile: Mark 12:1-17

Today taxes are a big issue. But even in Jesus' day, one of the main things Jews argued about was whether to pay taxes or not. Many Jews thought you should only pay taxes to God. Others said that in order to keep the peace they should obey the laws of the land.

The enemies of Jesus saw an opportunity here. If they could get Jesus to commit to one side or the other, they might trap him. So they came to him with a question about paying taxes. Jesus answered them as above, a very wise and slamming statement. He told the truth, and he didn't fall into their trap.

This raises an interesting question: do you have people around you who think they can outwit God with some weird or entrapping question?

Then trust God to give you the answer that will amaze them.

Prayer: God, I will trust you to give me answers even when no good answer seems possible.

The Dead Will Rise

Mark 12:24, 25: Jesus replied, "Your mistake is that you don't know the Scriptures, and you don't know the power of God. For when the dead rise, they will neither marry nor be given in marriage. In this respect they will be like the angels in heaven."

The Extra Mile: Mark 12:18-25

Death is the great enemy. If you've ever had a relative, friend, or neighbor you were close to die, you know the pain of that separation. Death is the great destroyer. No one can get around it, ahead of it, or by it. It claims every one of us sooner or later.

In the ancient world, death was also a great mystery. The Egyptians buried their kings in great pyramids with all kinds of provisions for life in the afterlife. Other cultures have given us different ideas about death. Indians believed you went to the "Happy Hunting Ground." Buddhists believe you become one with the cosmic lord. Hindus believe you are reincarnated over and over until you reach perfection.

No one knew the answer to death until Jesus. When Jesus rose from the dead, he showed the world that death was conquered.

Do you worry about death? Do you fear it?

For the Christian, Jesus answers all our fears about death. He rose, and he will raise us too. We will live with him forever in a new Heaven and earth.

Prayer: Father, I will not fear death. It's just a doorway to your side.

Something Special for God

Mark 12:43, 44: Jesus called his disciples to him and said, "I tell you the truth, this poor widow has given more than all the others who are making contributions. For they gave a tiny part of their surplus, but she, poor as she is, has given everything she had to live on."

The Extra Mile: Mark 12:26-44

Have you ever wanted to do something special for God?

Eric Liddell was such a person. He wanted to be a missionary to China, like his parents. But he also had a special gift: he could run fast. So fast, in fact, that he'd captured just about every prize for running in Scotland in the early 1920s.

It came time for the 1924 Olympics. Eric was selected to run the 100-meter dash for Great Britain. Everything looked great until a problem cropped up: the early trial races for the final race were held on a Sunday. Eric Liddell was a Christian. He believed on Sunday no Christian should work or play a sport.

An intense spiritual battle started. In the end, Eric refused to run on a Sunday. That put him out of his best race. But it also put him into another race—the 400 meters.

Eric ran that one and won. It was called the greatest race of that Olympic Games.

Like Eric Liddell, you can do something special for God. What? You can serve him, love him, and worship him all your days. That will make you one in a million in today's world. So few pay God any respect today. If you do, God will take special notice and bless your life, like he did with Eric Liddell.

Prayer: Father, I will serve you in everything I do as you grant me your blessing and support.

In the Last Days

Mark 13:11: But when you are arrested and stand trial, don't worry in advance about what to say. Just say what God tells you at that time, for it is not you who will be speaking, but the Holy Spirit.

The Extra Mile: Mark 13

Jani was worried. She had to stand up in front of her class and give a special message. Her topic was Sacagawea, who helped lead Lewis and Clark across America to the Pacific Ocean. She knew everything about the Indian woman and her arduous journey. But the butterflies in her stomach only seemed to flutter more as the day arrived.

The night before, Jani read Mark 13 for her quiet time with God and she found this verse. She wondered if it would apply to her speech in front of the class. She went to her mom.

After reading the verse, she asked, "Do you think the Spirit will help me speak in front of the class too?"

Her mother thought about it. "Why not?" she finally said. "Certainly God promises to be with us in everything. Why not that?"

That morning, Jani prayed before going to school, then on the school bus, and finally in the class where she had to speak. As she waited, the butterflies seem to go into a hurricane. But then suddenly, when the teacher called her name, she calmed down, walked up, and launched into an excellent speech. God had been with her.

Prayer: Lord, I won't worry when I have to speak up for you. You will always be with me, and when necessary, give me the words to say.

The Hands of Men

Mark 14:41: When he returned to them the third time, he said, "Go ahead and sleep. Have your rest. But no—the time has come. The Son of Man is betrayed into the hands of sinners."

The Extra Mile: Mark 14

Consider this situation. You're walking down the street with a friend of yours. This friend is a very important powerful person. He's the President of the United States.

Secret Service men are all around you. Police cars are parked along the way. People have lined up to wave at the President and possibly meet him.

You're right there, next to him, walking along.

But suddenly, something happens. All the secret service men scatter, and the local biker gang takes control of the situation.

They grab the President. They tie him to a tree. They strip him. They begin beating on him with chains and sticks.

Do you think that could ever happen? No way! The President is too well-protected. Those bikers would be shot the first time they uttered a word.

But something like that did happen once. Jesus, the President of the Universe, was beaten, left hanging naked on a cross for all to see, and murdered. Why?

Prayer: Lord Jesus, I know you could have called a billion angels to wipe out your attackers. But you didn't. Thank you for paying the price so that I can live forever with you in Heaven.

SUNDAY

The One Who Was Set Free

Mark 15:15: So to pacify the crowd, Pilate released Barabbas to them. He ordered Jesus flogged with a lead-tipped whip, then turned him over to the Roman soldiers to be crucified.

MONDAY

The Extra Mile: Mark 15

Today was the day. Lanny's dad would stand trial for preaching on what the Bible said about homosexuality. His dad was a preacher and he believed he had to speak the whole truth and nothing but. But the government had passed laws recently that said no one could say homosexuality was wrong or evil. A man had come to church and heard his father speak out. Then he had charged Lanny's father with "hate speech."

In the trial many harsh things were said about Lanny's dad. It even came out that the man who accused his father was a gay man who went around from church to church trying to send pastors and others to prison for speaking the truth.

It was rigged in Lanny's mind. Why did people do this? The only consolation for him was that he knew God would deal with this person in his timing and place. The accuser didn't know what he was getting into. At the same time, Lanny prayed for him. But it was hard.

Lanny's dad did spend six months in prison. And that accuser went free. It just didn't seem fair.

Prayer: Lord, I know many bad things happen in this world to believers. I take heart, though, that you are with me through everything, even when I hurt.

365 New Testament Devotions for Kids

The Angel in the Tomb

Mark 16:5, 6: When they entered the tomb, they saw a young man clothed in a white robe sitting on the right side. The women were shocked, but the angel said, "Don't be alarmed. You are looking for Jesus of Nazareth, who was crucified. He isn't here! He is risen from the dead! Look, this is where they laid his body."

The Extra Mile: Mark 16

Imagine if you had been there for that moment. After seeing Jesus die on the cross brutally and horribly, you see him laid in a tomb. You're despondent, broken-hearted because Jesus had given you such great hope and joy in life. Now he is gone. Even though Jesus spoke to you about rising from the dead, somehow you didn't get it. It didn't make sense at the time.

Now you're at the tomb and the stone is rolled out of the way. You stare. Has someone stolen the body? You look inside, and there are the wrappings from Jesus' burial. It looks like he just lifted through them supernaturally. And then you see someone bright and powerful-looking sitting at the end of the stone bed.

What would you have said or thought under such conditions? The truth is, when these women, who first came to the tomb, and then hundreds of his disciples, found out about Jesus' resurrection, greater joy and hope filled them. The world had not come to an end; it had just begun.

Prayer: Lord, I know when someone needs something impossible to be done, you are always ready.

Chosen by God

Luke 1:26, 27: *In the sixth month of Elizabeth's pregnancy, God sent the angel Gabriel to Nazareth, a village in Galilee, to a virgin named Mary. She was engaged to be married to a man named Joseph, a descendant of King David.*

The Extra Mile: Luke 1

You're sitting in your room just about to fall asleep. There's a rustling at the window. You sit up and peer into the dark. Something bright and shiny comes through the window and stands in front of you.

You're just about to scream, but the figure speaks. "Hello! Don't be afraid. You are greatly blessed by God."

What would you do? Rub your eyes and see if the "person" went away? Pinch yourself to see if you're really awake?

It happened to Mary, a young woman living in Nazareth. Gabriel, one of God's greatest angels, brought her the message that she would be the mother of Jesus, the Messiah. Mary asked a question about how she could have a child since she was a virgin, and Gabriel told her the Holy Spirit would make it possible. Then Mary bowed and said, "Let it happen to me as you have said."

What if you were chosen by God for a mission like that? How would you answer?

Guess what? You are chosen. God has a mission for you too. You may not be visited by Gabriel, but in his own time God will show you what he wants you to do.

Prayer: God, I know I need to get ready for when you have a job for me to do. I will never be the same again.

Angels, Angels Everywhere

Luke 2:10, 11: The angel reassured them. "Don't be afraid!" he said. "I bring you good news that will bring great joy to all people. The Savior—yes, the Messiah, the Lord—has been born today in Bethlehem, the city of David!"

The Extra Mile: Luke 2

Imagine you're a shepherd out in the hills above Bethlehem in Israel. Wicked King Herod rules your world. All your life you have hoped for something many of your countrymen have also hoped for: the coming of God's Messiah. But people have had this hope for centuries. Why do you believe it could happen to you?

Someone passes around a small bowl of bread and you take a bite. The men around you talk about home, work, what the rabbi said last Sabbath. You nestle down in your cloak and wonder. Could the Messiah come in your lifetime? Would you believe in him? Would you follow him?

You tell yourself, "Yes, I would, without question."

A moment later, the starry night is split open. Bright beings appear in the sky. They're angels, each one shining like the sun.

You cower. You're afraid, but the angels speak. "Do not be afraid." Then they tell you and others with you that the Messiah has been born that night in a stable in Bethlehem.

Moments later, they disappear. You stand, your mouth open with wonder. Then suddenly you're running. "I've got to see him! I have to worship him!"

Prayer: I know from the Bible that through the Holy Spirit, I can worship and know you now, Jesus. You came for me.

365 New Testament Devotions for Kids

Vipers!

Luke 3:7, 8: When the crowds came to John for baptism, he said, "You brood of snakes! Who warned you to flee God's coming wrath? Prove by the way you live that you have repented of your sins and turned to God."

The Extra Mile: Luke 3

A viper was a little snake that lived in the wilderness. If you were walking along through that sandy, rocky area, a viper would look like a stick. If you happened to be collecting firewood, you might even pick it up and be bitten. Its poison was deadly. You wouldn't live more than 10 minutes from such a bite.

In Acts 28, Paul had just such an experience. He picked up some sticks and a viper lay in among them. He was bitten. Everyone thought he'd die in a few minutes. When he didn't, the local people thought he must be a god.

Vipers looked harmless enough, but they were deadly. That's why John the Baptist called the Pharisees vipers. They seemed nice enough, but they were full of deadly poison.

Do you know what a Pharisee is? In Jesus' day, they were respected holy people who wanted more than anything to please God in every way. But they made a major mistake. They thought keeping a list of rules saved them. When they kept the rules, they became proud and cocky and put down everyone else.

That's why John called them vipers. They deceived people into thinking their way was the right way.

Prayer: Father, I will never think that obeying rules is what makes me a Christian. Faith in you and your Son is the beginning and end of salvation.

At the End of Himself

Luke 4:1, 2: Then Jesus, full of the Holy Spirit, returned from the Jordan River. He was led by the Spirit in the wilderness, where he was tempted by the devil for forty days. Jesus ate nothing all that time and became very hungry.

The Extra Mile: Luke 4:1–30

Ever come to the "end of yourself"? You're in the desert with the Scouts. You've all lost your way. The water has run out. Everyone is sick with thirst. Have you ever felt what that is like?

Or your dad tells the family you're out of money and he just lost his job. Your mother makes Ramen Noodles every day for lunch and dinner. That's all you can afford. Soon you're wondering if it will ever end and if you can stand it another minute.

Or take this: you're playing a game, maybe football. The opposing team has ground your team down. Several kids are injured. You're going both ways, offense and defense. Every play you stagger to the huddle breathing hard. How much longer can you go?

The Bible tells us Jesus had not eaten for 40 days. After that long without eating, the human body begins breaking down and using itself for energy. When that happens, a person will die soon if he does not eat.

That's when Satan came to Jesus and started tempting him.

Prayer: Lord Jesus, you were tempted mercilessly so that I can know you are able to help me anytime I face temptation.

No One Turned Away

Luke 4:40: As the sun went down that evening, people throughout the village brought sick family members to Jesus. No matter what their diseases were, the touch of his hand healed every one.

The Extra Mile: Luke 4:31–44

Things can get tough in the real world. Economic problems have put everyone on edge. Perhaps you and your father go down together to the employment center. There are long lines. Finally, one of the people in authority walks out to the line: "Sorry, folks," he says. "There are no more jobs."

You and Dad walk home discouraged.

Later, your sister falls sick. The family goes to the Emergency Room. But when you get there, you find another long line. Everyone's sick. A doctor comes out and tells everyone to try another hospital because they're full.

Maybe you've never been in such a position. But many have. How does it feel to be turned away because there's no help? Nothing is more discouraging or fear-inducing than finding out there's no help anywhere.

Jesus was different. Whoever came to him, he healed. No one was ever turned away. The only thing that ever stopped Jesus from healing someone was when they had no faith.

It's the same today. Jesus turns no one away.

Prayer: Lord, I come to you, and I know your line is never busy.

Scumballs

Luke 5:29, 30: Later, Levi held a banquet in his home with Jesus as the guest of honor. Many of Levi's fellow tax collectors and other guests also ate with them. But the Pharisees and their teachers of religious law complained bitterly to Jesus' disciples, "Why do you eat and drink with such scum?"

The Extra Mile: Luke 5

Have you ever been called "scum"?

Many people have, like Sara. She and her family lived a mobile home park. "Trailer Trash," some people called them. Sara didn't understand when she was young. She thought it was mean, but what could she do about it?

When Sara was in third grade, one of the girls in her class invited everyone in the class to her birthday party—except Sara. And it was because she was "trailer trash."

Later in sixth grade, when Sara went out collecting donations to give to a local mission project, some people said mean things to her, and some even slammed the door in her face.

Prayer: Lord Jesus, you came for all people, from the lowest of society to the top.

Where Do You Get Satisfaction?

Luke 6:21: God blesses you who are hungry now, for you will be satisfied. God blesses you who weep now, for in due time you will laugh.

The Extra Mile: Luke 6:1–21

For some kids it's a ball game. For others it's scoring several million in the latest video game. For still others, it's a hot meal from Mom with beans, hot dogs and ketchup.

What is it for you? Where do you get your satisfaction? What makes life worth living? What turns you on?

We all can admit that there are many good things in life: food, sports, entertainment, a job well done, getting an A in math, making the honor roll.

But the only way to have true satisfaction in life is to have a relationship with God. There's an emptiness in life that only faith can fill.

When you know and love God you can find satisfaction in everything, from your bus ride to school, lunchtime in the cafeteria, study, play, and friends. It's OK to feel good about those things. It's OK to like and enjoy them.

Prayer: Lord, I will never let anyone tell me you are against the good things in life. You just don't want those things to lure me away from you.

Insults and Rip-offs

Luke 6:29, 30: *If someone slaps you on one cheek, offer the other cheek also. If someone demands your coat, offer your shirt also. Give to anyone who asks; and when things are taken away from you, don't try to get them back.*

The Extra Mile: Luke 6:22–36

How does a Christian handle an insult or being ripped-off?

Jesus spoke of this in Luke 6 and also in Matthew 6 in the Sermon on the Mount. Here we find him telling his listeners that if someone slaps you on the cheek to turn and let him slap you on the other cheek. This is not referring to a deadly attack or a punishing beating. Nowhere in the Bible does it say we shouldn't defend ourselves against evil people.

But here Jesus is speaking of an insult. You could apply this to any kind of put-down: being called names, being gossiped about, having rumors spread about you. What should you do when someone puts you down like that? Jesus says to simply turn aside and invite them to do it again.

That's amazing. But it's also very wise. Why? Because if you start returning insult for insult a worse fight might result.

Jesus also speaks of being ripped-off in this verse. Your coat was a source of warmth on cold nights. Your "tunic" was like a shirt and pants. It covered your body from exposure.

What should you do when you're ripped off? Jesus says to offer them more than they want. Why? Because this will take the heat out of the situation. Suddenly, your attacker doesn't know what to say or do.

Prayer: Lord, I know being a Christian will often be difficult, so help me to stand strong always.

The Wrong Thing to Lean On

THURSDAY

Luke 6:38: Give, and you will receive. Your gift will return to you in full—pressed down, shaken together to make room for more, running over, and poured into your lap. The amount you give will determine the amount you get back.

The Extra Mile: Luke 6:37–49

Gabrielle came to church that day with a loaded pocketbook. She had worked all week for Mrs. Langer shampooing the lady's carpets. Mrs. Langer paid her $175. Gabrielle was proud of her hard work, and the first thing she wanted to do was give 10 percent of it to the Lord. She brought the money, carefully counted out in an envelope.

What she didn't count on was the message that morning. Pastor Jefferson introduced a young couple who planned to be missionaries to Colombia, South America. The couple spoke of the people there, how they faced serious hardships from a difficult government. They talked about how criminals waged a huge drug war against everyone, and how poor people were caught in the middle. And finally they spoke of the needs of the orphans, children whose parents were kidnapped and killed by the cocaine cartels. The couple concluded, "They need help and we want to give it to them. But we need to raise $10,000 in the next month to go and bring supplies to them. Any help you can give will be wonderful."

As Gabrielle sat there in church, she felt like crying. These people had so little. It was then the Spirit of God spoke to her heart. Why not give the whole $175 for this mission? It was a worthy cause and God would be pleased.

Gabrielle sat there stunned.

What would you do in this situation?

Prayer: God, I will listen for your voice and leading in my heart. You will never lead me astray.

A Great Sacrifice

Luke 7:37: When a certain immoral woman from that city heard he was eating there, she brought a beautiful alabaster jar filled with expensive perfume.

The Extra Mile: Luke 7

This unknown woman possessed a great treasure. Maybe she inherited it from a family member. It was a very expensive vial of perfume that may have been a family's life savings. It had never been opened, it was so precious.

Maybe this woman had saved it from her youth. All her life she had thought about the different opportunities to use it for something good.

She may have thought of selling it for thousands of dollars and then giving the money to a good cause. She may have thought of taking it to the temple and giving it to the priests. They could use it to perfume the outer area of the temple. She may even have thought of opening it and wearing some of the perfume to a special event like her wedding.

But nothing else seemed quite right until she met Jesus. He became her greatest friend. One day she realized he planned to die for the sins of the world. She understood what he'd come for, and she loved him for that.

It was then she knew what to do with her perfume. She took it to a feast where Jesus was, broke open the vial, and poured the perfume on Jesus.

What a lovely scent! What a tremendous act of faith!

Prayer: Lord, what can I give that would show the same kind of love and devotion as this woman?

Who Is Jesus' Family?

Luke 8:21: Jesus replied, "My mother and my brothers are all those who hear God's word and obey it."

The Extra Mile: Luke 8

Jesus was teaching and one day his mother, Mary, and his brothers and sisters came to hear him. A large crowd had gathered, and they stood out on the rim. They asked for a message to be taken to him and for him to come out to them. Jesus replied with the verse above. Was that callous, unfeeling, or unloving?

Jesus was sinless. He was perfect. So we know that what he said could not have been uncaring. But what was the point? Why does God have this passage in the Bible? Doesn't it make Jesus look kind of harsh?

Actually, from other passages, we know that some of Jesus' family didn't really believe he was the Messiah. In fact, at one point, they considered him a madman. But Jesus had a mission, and he could not be deterred by coddling his family or acting as if they were more important than others.

So here he declared who his real family members were: those who obeyed God's Word. Jesus' brothers and sisters weren't doing this, and maybe that was the message he wanted to tell them: you need to repent.

The point is that while our actual families are important, if they reject us, our beliefs, and our commitments, we have to continue to obey God first.

Prayer: Lord, when it comes to a choice between family and you, I must always choose you. You will help me work through problems with my family.

Ashamed of Jesus

Luke 9:26: If anyone is ashamed of me and my message, the Son of Man will be ashamed of that person when he returns in his glory and in the glory of the Father and the holy angels.

The Extra Mile: Luke 9

There will be many times in your life when you may be challenged about your faith. It happened to Salvatore one day at school. Several kids found out he went to church and was an ardent Christian. Out on the blacktop, several of them challenged him, pushing him around and egging him to fight.

"Is Jesus gonna protect you from us?" one bully roared into his face.

Another said, "Tell me one prayer that was ever answered by your sacred Jesus!"

Salvatore tried to answer, but the words seemed stuck in his throat. Then one of the boys said, "Jesus was a jerk. That's what my dad says: an idiot, a moron. No one should believe in him."

Salvatore remembered the verse above. Somehow he said, "You can call him what you want. I call him Lord and Savior."

They all laughed, but then walked away.

Prayer: Father, I know there will be times when I must stand up for my beliefs. Help me not to be ashamed, no matter what happens.

SUNDAY

Take the Opportunity

Luke 10:34: Going over to him, the Samaritan soothed his wounds with olive oil and wine and bandaged them. Then he put the man on his own donkey and took him to an inn, where he took care of him.

The Extra Mile: Luke 10

God wants you to do great things with your life. Every day, he will put in your path moments, situations, and opportunities that he intends for you to act on.

When a lawyer asked Jesus who his neighbor was, Jesus answered with the Parable of the Good Samaritan. The Good Samaritan saw an opportunity to do good when he came on the man who had been beaten and robbed. He bandaged the man up; then paid for him to stay at an inn until he recovered.

Jesus was saying more than simply who our neighbor is in this parable. He was also pointing out the truth of the opportunity. Every day presents opportunities for us to do good. God has planned it that way.

What opportunities might you have today?
• a friend needs encouraging
• a teacher needs help after school carrying things to her car
• your sister or brother needs someone to explain homework

These are small things, but they're important. Don't miss your opportunities to please God.

Prayer: Lord, sometimes big opportunities may come only once in a lifetime. But the little ones happen every day. Help me be ready to jump in the next time one comes my way.

The Way God Answers Prayers

Luke 11:11, 12: "You fathers—if your children ask for a fish, do you give them a snake instead? Or if they ask for an egg, do you give them a scorpion? Of course not!"

The Extra Mile: Luke 11

Some people expect little from God. Georgina was such a believer. When she prayed, she never seemed to get the answer she wanted. In fact, sometimes it seemed worse things happened, like when she asked for a new bike for her birthday and her parents gave her a Barbie doll! Didn't they know she was too old for those?

Finally, one day she found this verse in her Bible. "OK," she said, "show me, God. I want to see."

After thinking about a prayer, she bowed her head. "God, please bless me with something surprising and fun tomorrow."

The next day Mrs. Morris asked Georgina to come in and move a big box that was too heavy for her. It was hard, but Georgina managed to move it downstairs. Then they had a little chat over cookies and milk, and Mrs. Morris gave Georgina a five-dollar bill.

Prayer: Lord, I'm ready for a surprise!

That Rich Fool

Luke 12:20, 21: "But God said to him, 'You fool! You will die this very night. Then who will get everything you worked for?' Yes, a person is a fool to store up earthly wealth but not have a rich relationship with God."

The Extra Mile: Luke 12

Rich people seem to have it good. They can buy whatever they want. They can go on great trips to fantastic resorts. They have the best cars. And sometimes they have several houses, all over the world.

But do their riches gain them happiness? Many of the truly rich are very unhappy. They go to psychiatrists, asking them to help them find joy in life. They go through terrible divorces, and their families break up. They may fight over money and possessions more than people who have less.

The Bible tells us that loving money is a danger, a root of all kinds of evil. We should never lust after it, like the rich fool above. Instead, we should express our faith in God. He will meet our basic needs. One day in Heaven we will more riches than the richest in this world today.

Prayer: Father, I value the fact that no matter what I have in this world, you are going to give me the things that last.

Unless You Repent

Luke 13:2, 3: *"Do you think those Galileans were worse sinners than all the other people from Galilee?" Jesus asked. "Is that why they suffered? Not at all! And you will perish, too, unless you repent of your sins and turn to God."*

The Extra Mile: Luke 13

Tragedy strikes. A young girl is hit by a car. A mother contracts cancer. An uncle loses his job. When such things happen, people are always ready to offer a reason for the tragedy.

"Well, if Uncle Mack was living like he should, this wouldn't have happened." "She was talking back to her mom last night." "He cheated in school and that's why things went so badly for him."

Our explanations for tragedy often involve some sin. "They did this, so God repaid them with that."

It's sometimes even applied on a national level: "The World Trade Center was attacked because America has so much evil in it." "The war started because Hollywood produces so much smut."

Jesus offered a different view in Luke 13. "You will perish too, unless you repent." In other words, we're all sinners and we need to get right with God by admitting it.

Prayer: Lord, I need to repent. Show me what mistakes I've made so I can make them right with you.

I Want the Best
Seat in the House

FRIDAY

Luke 14:8: "When you are invited to a wedding feast, don't sit in the seat of honor."

The Extra Mile: Luke 14

For many people, the best seat in the house is the only one they'll take. Josh was a little like that. He was cute, smart, and he played on all the sports teams. All the girls thought he was great. When he came to party, everyone *oohed* and *ahhed* over what he wore. The host always invited him to the best spot in the room.

When someone didn't offer Josh those things, he often got snippy, making cutting remarks, and leaving early. A lot of kids didn't get it. But Carlie did. She had watched Josh for years, since kindergarten. She always liked him, but as she got older she realized how stuck he was on himself.

One day in church, the teacher brought up this verse and Carlie mentioned Josh. The teacher said to her, "The more important thing is you. What do you do when you go to a party, or a celebration? Do you demand the choice places?"

Carlie nodded. "I'm learning not to."

"Then you're with Jesus on that one," the teacher said.

Prayer: Jesus, I won't worry about any honors in this world. They don't mean anything in the long run.

Coming Back to God

Luke 15:20: So he returned home to his father. And while he was still a long way off, his father saw him coming. Filled with love and compassion, he ran to his son, embraced him, and kissed him.

The Extra Mile: Luke 15

Are you ever dismayed when you see a new Christian who's bubbling over with joy? New Christians often want to tell everyone what God did for them. Sometimes older Christians get jealous.

But how does God feel about such believers? The Parable of the Prodigal Son is all about God and the way he treats a person who repents and comes back to him. The father's son here demanded his half of the estate and then went out and squandered it. He ended up feeding pigs, the lowest of the low for a Jew. But he realized his father might at least treat him decently, so he went home, full of worry. When his father saw him, he ran up the road, greeted the son happily, threw his personal robe over him, put the family ring on his finger, and threw a feast.

Jesus gave that story as a picture of how God feels about lost people who come back to him, repentant. If you're wondering if your sins have become too great, or that God is against you, stop. Go to him and talk. You may be surprised about how he treats you.

Prayer: Lord, I know you are not into condemnation or putting down people who come to you in faith.

They Would Listen If . . .

Luke 16:31: "But Abraham said, 'If they won't listen to Moses and the prophets, they won't listen even if someone rises from the dead.'"

The Extra Mile: Luke 16

Shanna had become a Christian at camp one summer. She really wanted her sister Lonnie to know the joy and blessings she had since she accepted Christ. But Lonnie was a rebel, bad to the bone, and she wanted nothing to do with Jesus.

Shanna asked for help from her youth minister and other strong Christians whom she thought might have some influence on her sister. But even they struck out. Lonnie refused to believe.

Some people are like Lonnie, and like the brothers in the Parable of the Rich Man and Lazarus. The rich man, in Hell, thought if only someone went to his brothers from the dead, they would believe. But Abraham told him if they didn't believe with the evidence they already had, they'd refuse to believe even if someone came back from the dead.

Prayer: Father, I see that with some people, I have to be patient and keep loving them and praying. One day maybe they will open their eyes. So I won't give up.

Watch Out!

Luke 17:1, 2: One day Jesus said to his disciples, "There will always be temptations to sin, but what sorrow awaits the person who does the tempting! It would be better to be thrown into the sea with a millstone hung around your neck than to cause one of these little ones to fall into sin."

The Extra Mile: Luke 17

Simmie snuck into the kitchen with her friend Maddie.

"What are you doing?" Maddie asked.

"It's really cool."

She walked to the refrigerator, listened, and then opened it. She quickly pulled out a can of her father's beer.

Maddie's eyes were wide open. "We can't do that," she whispered.

"Why not?" Simmie led her out the door. She had put the beer in her purse. When they reached a wooded area, Simmie took out the can and popped the top. She quickly took a swig, and then held it out to Maddie.

"I can't drink that," Maddie said. "I'm not old enough. And neither are you."

"Then all for me." Simmie flashed her eyes and drank more. She held it out each time, and Maddie really wanted to taste it. But something in her head said, "Do not do it."

When the beer was gone, Simmie said, "It feels so good. I'm getting another one."

On the way back, Maddie said she had to go home.

Prayer: Lord, do not let me be led into temptation. Let me run away when it gets too difficult.

Gifts of Children

Luke 18:16: Then Jesus called for the children and said to the disciples, "Let the children come to me. Don't stop them! For the Kingdom of God belongs to those who are like these children."

The Extra Mile: Luke 18:1–17

You are a gift of God.

Oh, you knew that already? Well, most of you probably didn't.

Think about that—a gift of God. God gives children to parents, foster parents, grandparents, and everyone else as gifts. You're not a burden. You're not a pain. You're not just another mouth to feed. Those you live with may get mad at you and discipline you. They may not like you very much at times. They may even say things like, "What am I going to do with you?"

But in God's eyes, you're a gift.

You see, God does not give children to people lightly. He doesn't just wing them out there like they didn't matter. God thought about you and who he would send you to live with for a long time. He planned your birth. He went into great detail about what you would look like. And in the end, he finally gave you to your friends and family as a tremendous gift.

You know, it really doesn't matter if the folks you live with don't see you that way. That's the way God sees you.

Prayer: Lord, I am a gift from you to the world, to my family, to my church. But let me not expect everyone to treat me that way.

365 New Testament Devotions for Kids

The Tale of a Rich Man

WEEK 14

WEDNESDAY

Luke 18:24, 25: When Jesus saw this, he said, "How hard it is for the rich to enter the Kingdom of God! In fact, it is easier for a camel to go through the eye of a needle than for a rich person to enter the Kingdom of God!"

The Extra Mile: Luke 18:18-43

What if Jesus said this to you? "If you really want to be saved, go give away everything you own. Then follow me, and you will have eternal life."

It sounds pretty tough, don't you think? You'd have to give away your bike, your bed, your video games—everything. Wow! That would be hard!

We find Jesus saying this to someone we call "the rich young ruler." He was young, rich, and a leader in his hometown. One day, he asked Jesus what he needed to do to get eternal life. Jesus told him to keep the Ten Commandments. The ruler, somewhat proudly, said that he'd kept them all from his earliest days. That was impossible, but Jesus decided not to argue with him. Instead, he gave the man his own commandment to see if he would obey. That commandment was to sell everything and give to the poor.

The rich young ruler turned away at that moment. He couldn't give up his great wealth to follow Jesus.

What was Jesus really doing here? He was trying to show the ruler that he needed to have faith in Jesus. Faith in Jesus leads to obedience to Jesus.

Prayer: Lord, I know you may never ask me to give away everything. But if I need to give up some things, help me to sacrifice out of love for you.

A Transformed Tax Collector

Luke 19:8: Meanwhile, Zacchaeus stood before the Lord and said, "I will give half my wealth to the poor, Lord, and if I have cheated people on their taxes, I will give them back four times as much!"

The Extra Mile: Luke 19

It isn't every day that a tax collector offers to pay people back. But it happened.

Zacchaeus was a little man with a big job. Tax collectors like him took as much money in taxes from the people as they could. The whole Roman Empire backed up Zacchaeus's decisions. If you fought back, you might end up in prison for life.

But Zacchaeus's life changed one afternoon. Jesus came to town. He spotted Zacchaeus watching from the branches of a sycamore tree and told Zacchaeus he was planning to dine at his house.

Zacchaeus jumped down, and on the way he and Jesus talked. In a matter of minutes, Zacchaeus decided to pay back everyone he cheated, and also give half his possessions to the poor.

Why did he do this? Because of Jesus. The Lord said something to Zacchaeus that transformed him on the spot. Zacchaeus didn't just believe in Jesus. He believed enough to change his life.

When Jesus comes into our lives, his purpose is not just to save us. He also wants to shake up our world, to change us into the kind of people who reflect the character of God.

Prayer: Lord, let me reflect your character in all I do.

True Hypocrisy

Luke 20:47: "Yet they shamelessly cheat widows out of their property and then pretend to be pious by making long prayers in public. Because of this, they will be severely punished."

The Extra Mile: Luke 20

The pastor preached on and on about all kinds of rules in the Bible. He thundered, "If you steal, if you cheat, if you lie, you are in danger of Hell fire."

Bobby listened and cringed. He knew he had to make some things right in his life. He resolved that after this message, he would go home, call his friend Jonah, and tell him what he'd done. That afternoon, he did exactly that, and he felt better.

But that week, something awful happened. It was revealed that the minister who had preached that convicting sermon had stolen money from the church, cheated on his taxes, lied to everyone, and even had an affair with a woman in the church. It was a real scandal, and a lot of people in town were talking about what hypocrites Christians were.

Bobby didn't like what he saw, and he said to his dad, "Why did this happen? Everything is ruined."

"That's what happens when we let sin go on in our lives," his father said. "It happens. Even in the Bible it happened with some of the greats of the faith. Some did horrible things. It's a warning for us to obey God and do what's right, even when no one notices."

Prayer: Father, let me never be a hypocrite. Let me be honest, even if it hurts.

Get This and You Have Everything

Luke 21:14, 15: So don't worry in advance about how to answer the charges against you, for I will give you the right words and such wisdom that none of your opponents will be able to reply or refute you!

The Extra Mile: Luke 21

When Solomon had a chance to get anything he wanted from God, he asked for one thing: wisdom (1 Kings 3:9). It's a powerful resource. What exactly is it, though? Wisdom really means a "skill for living." It's a mental skill that helps you deal with problems effectively.

Consider this: You have two friends who don't like each other. Each invites you to his birthday party on the same day. What do you do? Wisdom would help you decide.

Or think of this: At school, one of your friends comes to you and says he forgot to do his homework last night. Could he copy yours? This is a good friend. But he's asking you to cheat. If you don't help him, he could fail. What do you do? Having wisdom could answer the problem for you.

Here's one more: It's your birthday and your grandmother sends you a check for $150. It's a lot of money. You can think of all kinds of things you might buy with it. But your mom says you should save some of it. And your dad reminds you that you need to give some to the church. Only one problem: that gadget you've been wanting costs $149.95. What should you do? Again, getting God's wisdom, like the verse above talks about, will help.

Prayer: I need wisdom, God. Please help me to grow into the person you want me to be.

Attack!

Luke 22:31, 32: "Simon, Simon, Satan has asked to sift each of you like wheat. But I have pleaded in prayer for you, Simon, that your faith should not fail. So when you have repented and turned to me again, strengthen your brothers."

The Extra Mile: Luke 22

Satan is like a roaring lion. He prowls about looking for some unsuspecting victim. Then he pounces.

Here in Luke 22 we see Jesus and Peter talking about something that would soon happen. Jesus tells Peter that Satan has "asked to sift you like wheat." Note that Satan had to get permission from God to do this. Satan can't touch anyone unless God lets him.

As if this wasn't enough bad news for one day, Jesus tells Peter that he's praying that Peter's faith not fail. Again, that's powerful encouragement. When Jesus prays, you can be sure God answers. And the Bible assures us that Jesus is right now at God's right hand praying for us Christians.

In the end, Peter learned that he would deny three times that he even knew Jesus.

This was scary information. But it points out a solemn truth: even the greatest and strongest among us is not immune from attack and falling.

Prayer: Forgive me, Lord, for all the terrible mistakes I have done, and give me the power to do right everywhere.

Father, Forgive Them

Luke 23:34: Jesus said, "Father, forgive them, for they don't know what they are doing."

The Extra Mile: Luke 23:1-35

Kerry stared down the four girls who surrounded her in the parking lot.

"We hear you been talking about us," one said.

"Yeah, saying we cheated on the paper," a second added.

"Well, no one turns us in," the first said again.

"I didn't turn anyone in," Kerry said.

"We heard different," the second girl said.

Kerry knew these girls weren't going to let her go free. For a second, she didn't know what to do. They were alone, so there was no one nearby who could help her.

As the first girl advanced on her, she suddenly fell to her knees, closed her eyes and prayed, "Father, forgive them."

For a second, it seemed all was deadly still. Then Kerry heard the scrape of Nikes on macadam.

She opened her eyes. The four girls were gone.

Standing, Kerry looked around, sure it had to be a trick. But her attackers were gone.

Prayer: Father, when people attack me, I will forgive. Period.

The End of Everything

Luke 23:48: And when all the crowd that came to see the crucifixion saw what had happened, they went home in deep sorrow.

The Extra Mile: Luke 23:39–56

TUESDAY

Do you ever feel as if everything has gone wrong, and you'll never really be happy again?

Maybe your parents have divorced. Maybe one of them died. Maybe you're about to flunk a grade, or someone is threatening to hurt you.

At such times, doubts strike. Does God really care about me? Can he do anything about my situation? Can he change things for the better?

In these verses we see the followers of Jesus in deep sorrow. Their Lord and leader had been crucified. It looked like everything was over, and hope was gone. Have you ever been at that point in your life?

Stop worrying. Go God's way and God will be on your side. No matter how bad you think your life is, the person who stands up for God will have God stand up for him.

Prayer: Lord, I know I can't see the future, but you can. You know where you're leading me. Help me to keep trusting you, even when things seem hopeless.

He Is Near

Luke 24:36: And just as they were telling about it, Jesus himself was suddenly standing there among them. "Peace be with you," he said.

The Extra Mile: Luke 24

Imagine that you walk into your bedroom, and Jesus is sitting on your bed. Or that he's in your classroom standing by your desk to offer help with an assignment. When you walk into church he's sitting in the second pew. How would you feel?

One of the reasons Jesus' appearances after his death were so sudden and spontaneous is because he was trying to get the disciples used to something new. What was it? That even though he was returning to Heaven he was there with them all the time. That no matter where they were or how dark it was, he was with them.

When Jesus rose from the dead, it became possible for him to be anywhere and everywhere. While he was on earth, he could only be in one place at a time. But when he rose, he became "omnipresent." That means "present everywhere." So wherever you are, he is there too.

Prayer: Jesus, I'm counting on you. Lead me to the place that is higher than me.

Jesus Created Everything

John 1:3: God created everything through him, and nothing was created except through him.

The Extra Mile: John 1:1–8

Imagine it! God began everything with a sentence: "Let there be light!" But according to John 1:3, Jesus actually did the creating. Think about that. As Jesus spoke, light shined out everywhere! When God was done, he said it was good—and not just in an OK sense. It meant, "Fantastic!" "Amazing!" "Awesome!"

Did you know Jesus feels the same way about you? When he created you in your mother's womb, he made you just the way he wanted. Some people might not think you're big enough, or smart enough, or good enough. But Jesus made you exactly the way he wanted to.

You—with braces, or a less-than-perfect body, with all your quirks. You, with your smile, and your way of telling a joke, and your ability to draw, or play Scrabble, or skateboard. He made you just right. He didn't make a mistake.

How can this be? It's because Jesus has a purpose for your life. If he made you a different way, you'd have a different purpose. So the way he made you is because of the purpose he has for you.

Prayer: Jesus, show me my purpose. I will start simply by asking you to reveal it to me.

The Word Became Flesh

FRIDAY

John 1:14: So the Word became human and made his home among us. He was full of unfailing love and faithfulness. And we have seen his glory, the glory of the Father's one and only Son.

The Extra Mile: John 1:10–51

Kelly watched the bird fly into her picture window. "No!" Kelly yelled at the bird. "Don't do that. You'll hurt yourself."

She pulled on her coat and ran outside, just as the bird crashed headlong into the window one more time.

Dazed only a moment, it soon flew up into the air again. "Please don't do that, bird," Kelly called, signaling to the bird. She stood in front of the picture window and waved her arms.

The bird dived right at the window again. The moment it struck, it fell to the ground, unconscious.

Kelly stooped down and stared at the poor creature. "If only I could tell you in bird language so you would understand," she said to the silent bird. A few minutes later, it shook itself and flew away.

Kelly had learned a valuable lesson that day. If you want to communicate with someone—from another country, or even from another species—the best way is to become like them. Speak their language. Walk in their shoes.

Prayer: Lord, I know you were "made flesh" so you could be one of us and save us. I thank you for your love and goodness.

What God Asks of You

John 2:16: Then, going over to the people who sold doves, he told them, "Get these things out of here. Stop turning my Father's house into a marketplace!"

The Extra Mile: John 2

Have you ever asked, "What does God want of me? I try to do everything he says, but it seems he always wants more. What does he want?"

It can be frustrating. But after we finally trust Christ, God's requirements are very simple. These aren't things you do to get into Heaven. These are things you do because you know you're going to Heaven. They're like thankyous to God for saving you.

What are they?

- To obey God and Christ. To live out his Word.
- To worship God as he desires with integrity.
- To love mercy. This is what you do in response when someone hurts you. Be merciful. Don't take revenge. Forgive them.
- And to walk humbly with God. This means you don't make demands of God. You don't start thinking you're real important and someone big. You don't do something cool and think the world should bow down before you. No, you see yourself as a little person with a great God.

Prayer: Lord, let not my church be turned into a market, but always a place of worship.

WEEK
15

How God Feels About You

SUNDAY

John 3:16: "For God loved the world so much that he gave his one and only Son, so that everyone who believes in him will not perish but have eternal life."

The Extra Mile: John 3

How would you like to get a letter like this from a person you really love?
"Dear _____,
You are my delight.
I love just sitting with you and talking.
Let me sing you a song about how much I love you."
OK, maybe you're not ready for that stuff yet. But believe it or not, one day you'll love getting a mushy note like that from some guy or girl you like.

But guess what? You did get a note like that, from God. Look at what he says here in John: "I love you so much that I allowed my son to die in your place. If you believe in him, I'll give you eternal life. Is that a deal or what?"

God feels like that about you. He's given you a Bible full of such thoughts and feelings. Do you ever wonder if God really loves you? You don't have to wonder any longer. Read John 3:16. Read all of John 3. Read the whole book of John. You'll soon get the feeling that this God John is talking about is crazy about you and will do anything for you if you believe in him.

Prayer: Lord, sometimes it's hard to believe you really love me. Help me to believe it even more strongly than I do now.

Getting Them to Talk

John 4:7: Soon a Samaritan woman came to draw water, and Jesus said to her, "Please give me a drink."

The Extra Mile: John 4:1–22

Christians know that "witnessing," sharing your faith with others, is important. No one can learn the truth about God and Heaven without someone telling them. Jesus' last command to us was to go into the world and make disciples.

But sharing your faith can be difficult. Will the person I'm talking to get angry with me? Will they put me down? Will they yell? Could they become violent?

These are all things we need to consider. But they shouldn't deter us. In John 4, Jesus gives us a powerful example of how to start a conversation about the gospel.

Jesus asked a woman at a well to give him a drink. It's a simple request, nothing out of the ordinary. Except for two things: Jews didn't normally talk to Samaritans. And men rarely talked to women, especially a woman with a bad reputation like this one.

The woman was startled, so she fired a question back at Jesus. Soon, the conversation moved to spiritual things. And in the end, Jesus led her to faith.

Witnessing becomes easier when we realize we're just sharing what has happened to us. If someone's interested, great! If not, it's their loss.

Prayer: Lord, give me some good conversation starters, and help me to be brave enough to talk about spiritual things.

Real Worship

John 4:24: "For God is Spirit, so those who worship him must worship in spirit and in truth."

The Extra Mile: John 4:23–54

Have you ever been in a worship service where the people in church just "partied" with the Lord? They praised God, loud and long. They let God know how much they appreciated him, strongly and robustly. They told God he was number one and always would be.

In the Old Testament we read how David worshiped God "with all his might" in 2 Samuel 6. Why don't you try it? Go to your room or some special place alone. There, with no one else looking on, tell God what you think and how you feel about him. You can shout. You can scream. You can dance. You can run around in circles and raise your arms and just "party."

There is a place for quiet reflection and thanks in worship. There's a place for thought-through prayers and well-reasoned words. But there's also a time for letting go, for letting God know you really love him.

Prayer: Father, could I show you how much I love you—with a shout, a dance, and waving my hands?

God Knows What You Need Before You Ask

John 5:6: When Jesus saw him and knew he had been ill for a long time, he asked him, "Would you like to get well?"

The Extra Mile: John 5

Jason sat down to dinner with his family. He knew afterwards his father would ask if anyone had a request for prayer. He'd thought about that tonight. What did he really need? Not much. He had just about everything he could want. Sure, he wanted to make the baseball team at school, but he just wasn't that good. Jason was sort of embarrassed to even mention it.

Dinner was finished and prayer time arrived. Everyone pitched in a request. Jason just sat there. Finally, his dad turned to him. "Anything on your mind, Jase?"

"Not much," he said.

"Would you like to pray about the ball team?"

"Aw, Dad, I'm not going to make it."

"Is there something else you could do?"

Jason had thought about this. He shrugged. "I guess we could ask God about that."

The next day the coach asked Jason if he would like to be the batting practice catcher.

God knows what we need before we ask. In the Scripture reading for today, the man didn't even ask for what he needed from Jesus. But Jesus gave it to him.

Prayer: Jesus, I know you sometimes give us what we need, without our asking. Why? Because that's how much you care about us. Thanks.

The Boy's Lunch

John 6:8, 9: Then Andrew, Simon Peter's brother, spoke up. "There's a young boy here with five barley loaves and two fish. But what good is that with this huge crowd?"

The Extra Mile: John 6:1-44

He might have been the same age as you. He'd heard about Jesus from many people. This was his first chance to see him.

Setting off for the day, his mom gave him a pouch with a little lunch in it. "Just in case you get hungry," she said. Five little bread slices and two pieces of fish.

It wasn't much.

Jesus spoke all that morning. The boy was enthralled. Jesus was the best teacher he'd ever heard. People sat all around him. One man, whose name was Andrew, sat down next to the boy. "What's your name?" he asked.

"Hezekiah," the boy said.

They talked. He offered Andrew some of his lunch, but Andrew told him to save it for later when he was really hungry. Then it happened. Jesus wanted to feed everyone—over 5,000 people—and they didn't have any supplies.

Andrew turned to Hezekiah. "Can I borrow your lunch for a moment?"

"Borrow?" thought Hezekiah. "How do you 'borrow' a lunch? If I give it, it's gone," he decided, but he handed it over. And the next thing he knew Jesus was feeding everyone—and it was the best-tasting fish and bread Hezekiah had ever eaten.

Prayer: Lord, I know little things can go a long way. Show me a thing I can do today.

Where Would We Go?

John 6:68: Simon Peter replied, "Lord, to whom would we go? You have the words that give eternal life. We believe, and we know you are the Holy One of God."

The Extra Mile: John 6:45-71

Hillary sat on her bed crying. Her mother caressed her hair and said, "I'm sorry, honey. I'm so sorry."

Hillary had just learned that her best friend had cancer. Ally might die, and Hillary was both scared and angry. How could God let this happen?

She looked up at her mother and said, "Mom, why did God do this to Ally?"

Her mom shook her head. "Honey, God didn't do this to Ally. We live in a world where bad things happen to people, even good people like Ally. God won't choose to do a miracle every time something bad happens to someone. I'm sorry about Ally. But I know God loves her and will help her. In the end, she will be with him forever."

Hillary struggled with something probably every Christian will face some day. We will all lose friends and relatives to death for various reasons. In the Bible story above, Peter is asked if he wants to leave Jesus with some others who were angry about some of Jesus' teachings. Peter replied wisely, "Where else would we go?" He saw that his only real hope in this world was in God.

So it was for Hillary. Her best hope was God, and turning to him was the wisest choice she could make.

Prayer: I will trust you, God, even when I don't understand what you're doing.

The Living Stream

John 7:37, 38: On the last day, the climax of the festival, Jesus stood and shouted to the crowds, "Anyone who is thirsty may come to me! Anyone who believes in me may come and drink! For the Scriptures declare, 'Rivers of living water will flow from his heart.'"

The Extra Mile: John 7

Living water . . . sounds marvelous, doesn't it?

You may know that salt water cannot be used to grow crops. It cannot be used by animals or people as drinking water. Salt depletes fluids, so if a person drinks salt water, the salt water uses up more fluid than it can replace. The person dies of dehydration.

Fresh water, on the other hand, gives life. It waters plants. It quenches thirst. It is absolutely necessary for living.

John 7:37, 38 is considered one of Jesus' great promises. God will fill us with a kind of spiritual "living" water that will refresh our lives like no other kind of water, real or imagined.

For the Jew living in Jesus' day, such a vision brought great joy. Water was scarce in Israel and the surrounding region. Water was precious. But the living water he promised is abundant, free, and lifegiving. Imagine drinking that—water that refreshes and gives life to all who will drink of it.

Prayer: When I am thirsty for physical water, Lord, please remind me of the living water you promised.

Shine On

John 8:12: Jesus spoke to the people once more and said, *"I am the light of the world. If you follow me, you won't have to walk in darkness, because you will have the light that leads to life."*

The Extra Mile: John 8:1–33

"This little light of mine, I'm gonna let it shine." Did you sing that song when you were little?

We need to let the spiritual light of our relationship with God shine in the world. We don't light up literally. But we can give off joy and love that does shine like clicking on a flashlight.

Did you know that there actually was one person in history who was lit up? It was Moses. (OK, it wasn't his hairdo). When he met with the Lord, God's glory was so powerful that it turned a little sun on in Moses' soul. It shone out through his face.

The same thing happened to Jesus when he was transfigured on the mountain. He lit up!

You can get that light by meeting with and worshiping God. When we worship and love him, he gives us that "shine" that won't fade away.

Prayer: Lord, let me shine for you in all I do.

The Lying Organ

John 8:44: "For you are the children of your father the devil, and you love to do the evil things he does. He was a murderer from the beginning. He has always hated the truth, because there is no truth in him. When he lies, it is consistent with his character; for he is a liar and the father of lies."

The Extra Mile: John 8:34–59

Pretend there's such a thing as a lying machine. You put in a dollar and it tells you a lie to use for any occasion.

You were late getting home because you wanted to finish playing video games at your friend's house. Put your dollar into the machine, and it says this: "An old woman had a carload of groceries, so I helped her bring them into her house."

Wow! Suddenly, you're a hero.

Here's another one: You and your brother were throwing a ball around in the house and you knocked over Mom's favorite lamp. What to do? Put in your dollar: "The dog accidentally knocked into it while retrieving a ball."

Hey, that's almost true!

Have you ever put a dollar into the lying machine? It's simple. Just listen to your heart. Without Jesus, your heart can be a lying machine! It'll give you a lie for every occasion.

The devil is the original lying machine. We don't even have to put in a dollar. He'll give us his lies for free.

Prayer: Jesus, help me not to sin by lying when I get in trouble. Help me to depend on you and admit the truth.

Who Sinned?

John 9:2: "Rabbi," his disciples asked him, "why was this man born blind? Was it because of his own sins or his parents' sins?"

The Extra Mile: John 9

Some people believe that a child with spina bifida, cerebral palsy, or blindness is born as a result of sin—their parents' or their own. Two religions, Buddhism and Hinduism, believe in the Law of Karma, which says you pay in this life for sins in a previous life. This kind of attitude is unfair to people with disabilities.

Jesus rejected this belief. We read in John 9 what he said: neither the man's sin nor his parents' was the cause of his blindness. The purpose was that God's love and power be displayed in him.

You ask, "How is God's love and power displayed in a child who is handicapped?" By the positive attitude of the parents who raise the child; by the love and commitment of the family; by the care of the church; by the child's joy in life, and his love for others.

Prayer: God, I know you don't give babies problems because of past sins. Help me to help others understand that.

Real Life That Satisfies

John 10:10: The thief's purpose is to steal and kill and destroy. My purpose is to give them a rich and satisfying life.

The Extra Mile: John 10:1–26

Charla lay on the beach with her friend Debra. The sun turned their skin a deep tan. The water was cool and the swimming was a delight. And over there, two boys kept looking over their way. Would they come over?

Charla suddenly said, "You know, Deb, ever since I became a Christian in February, I feel better all the time. Every day there are cool surprises. I just feel like I'm living an adventure. Know what I mean?"

The two boys began throwing a flying disc around.

Debra, who had been a Christian for several years, said, "That's what the Bible says Jesus came to do—to give us a rich and satisfying life."

"Where is that? I have to memorize that one."

At that very moment the flying disc hit Charla's feet. She smiled and gave Debra a thumbs-up. Another adventure had begun.

Prayer: Lord, I know not everything in life can be fun and fulfilling, but I do know you will bless me daily if I look to you.

Help! I'm a Sheep

John 10:27, 28: "My sheep listen to my voice; I know them, and they follow me. I give them eternal life, and they will never perish. No one can snatch them away from me."

The Extra Mile: John 10:27–42

Have you ever seen sheep up close? If you have, you know they are
- tangly, dirty, slow-moving creatures
- quite stupid
- totally dependent on their owner for everything—food, water, shelter
- easy marks for predators like wolves and lions
- stubborn and uncooperative

In the Bible, people are compared to sheep. Jesus was even called "the lamb of God" because he was the sacrifice for all people's sin. But Jesus described himself as the "good shepherd, who lays down his life for the sheep."

You and I are sheep. We're utterly dependent. We can't do anything in this world without God. We're easy marks for the temptations of the devil, and we're stupid enough to fall into sin.

A lot of young people don't know that. They think they can do whatever they want and not answer to God for anything. But they do. We are all in God's hands. If he chooses to discipline us, make us fail, or allow us to get sick, we can't do a thing about it.

Prayer: Lord, teach me to depend on you about everything.

Jesus Is the Resurrection

John 11:25, 26: Jesus told her, "I am the resurrection and the life. Anyone who believes in me will live, even after dying. Everyone who lives in me and believes in me will never ever die. Do you believe this, Martha?"

The Extra Mile: John 11

"I am great."

"I'm cool."

"I'm smart."

"I'm the king of the mountain."

Young people like to exaggerate. They're king of the mountain until someone comes along and throws them off. They're cool till someone cooler happens by. They're smart until the straight-A student steps to the front of the room.

Jesus often used the phrase "I am" when he taught his disciples. Remember some of those? "I am the bread of life." "I am the vine." "I am the way, the truth and the life."

Here in John 11 we see another "I am." This time Jesus says, "I am the resurrection and the life." What exactly does he mean?

Jesus is the source of life after death. He literally IS the resurrection. He's the beginning, end, source, power for, and physical embodiment of the resurrection. He's the one who invented it, in fact. No other person ever has or will raise himself from the dead.

Prayer: Father, keep me remembering that I have eternal life, and one day I'll be with you.

One Woman Sold Out for God

John 12:3: Then Mary took a twelve-ounce jar of expensive perfume made from essence of nard, and she anointed Jesus' feet with it, wiping his feet with her hair. The house was filled with the fragrance.

The Extra Mile: John 12:1-12

Carrie slapped her hands on her thighs. "I hate being a girl."

"How come?" the teacher asked.

"Boys get everything. Girls have to watch and clap."

Everyone laughed, but a lot of women and girls feel that way. The truth is women play important roles in the Bible. From the beginning in Genesis, women were recognized, responsible, and loved.

Many other cultures in our world downgrade women. They can't vote. They must wear certain clothing. In some cases, they can't even go to school or walk outside.

God gives women an equal place with men in the Bible. Both have God-given roles in life. If you're a girl, you are just as important as any boy. You have a special place in God's plan, and you are precious in God's eyes.

If you're a boy, remember that God loves and honors girls as much as you. God wants you to respect and love the girls and women you know (yes, this includes your sister!). Their love and care for you will make your life better.

Prayer: Lord, let me give everyone honor, so you will honor me.

Give God a Holy Shout

John 12:13: They shouted, "Praise God! Blessings on the one who comes in the name of the Lord! Hail to the King of Israel!"

The Extra Mile: John 12:13–50

Do you ever feel so good you want to shout? How about in church? What would grown-ups in your church think if you let out a good old, belly-whumping, ear-tingling yell?

Joy is like a huge geyser inside of us that simply has to burst free sometimes. Ever seen Old Faithful, that geyser in Yellowstone Park? It's magnificent. At regular intervals it simply spews up in the air. It can't help itself.

In worship, there are times to celebrate and times to be silent. And some people worship best with action, while others worship best quietly.

When you're alone, worship God as you worship best. Whoop it up, let loose, and shout: "Yippee yi-yay!" "Hallelujah!" "Praise the Lord!" "I feel blessed!" Or kneel quietly, thinking of God, and listening in silence for him to speak in your heart.

Prayer: God, I want to tell you how much I love you in every way I can.

An Ugly Job

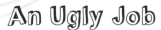

John 13:4, 5: So he got up from the table, took off his robe, wrapped a towel around his waist, and poured water into a basin. Then he began to wash the disciples' feet, drying them with the towel he had around him.

The Extra Mile: John 13

"I refuse to do that," Dave said. "Let Carl do it. He likes that kind of thing."

"I do not," Carl answered.

Dave glared at his little brother; then turned to his mom. "Why should I have to do that? Can't you hire someone?"

Dave's mom needed her car cleaned out. It was a mess: fast-food fries on the floor from their last visit, trash, dirt, spilled drinks. It was an ugly job. No wonder Dave didn't want to do it.

But ugly jobs have to get done, even if they are ugly.

Jesus knows about doing ugly jobs. One night with all his disciples gathered around him for dinner, a very important job had been overlooked. In those days, foot washing was important because people wore sandals. Their feet got dirty and smelly. Normally, a slave or servant washed the feet of guests. But Jesus was the host here. And he had no servants.

No one said a word. But Jesus stood, took off his cloak, and began washing his disciples' feet.

Prayer: Lord, I know some jobs are not fun, but let me do them for you, and you alone.

When Bad Things Happen to Good Kids

TUESDAY

John 14:1, 2: *"Don't let your hearts be troubled. Trust in God, and trust also in me. There is more than enough room in my Father's home. If this were not so, would I have told you that I am going to prepare a place for you?"*

The Extra Mile: John 14:1–22

Josh sat in the principal's office. He knew he was innocent. But one of the kids in his sixth-grade class had accused him of bullying. Josh prayed as he waited, but he felt discouraged. Why had God let this happen to him?

When bad things happen to Christians, we often feel conflicting emotions. Doesn't God care? Couldn't God stop it? If he could, why didn't he? Maybe God isn't really like the Bible says he is. Maybe he isn't that powerful. Maybe the enemies of God really are stronger.

Questions and hard thoughts always shoot through our minds when we get hurt, especially when we're innocent. Think of the people who died in the terrorist bombing on September 11, 2001. Think of the Christians who are persecuted all over the world today. We ask, "Where is God? Why doesn't he do something?"

Well, here's the good news: Jesus is with us, always with us, and he'll come back to get us and take us to a new place where no sin will ever be allowed again.

Does this encourage you?

Prayer: Lord, no matter how bad it looks, I know you're in charge.

The Spirit Right Inside of You

John 14:23: Jesus replied, "All who love me will do what I say. My Father will love them, and we will come and make our home with each of them."

The Extra Mile: John 14:23-26

Did you know that God lives inside you?

If you're a Christian, Jesus has moved into your heart. His Spirit, the Holy Spirit, lives inside you.

That means wherever you are, wherever you go, God is with you. He's close by, ready to help, listen, speak, encourage.

How do you know the Spirit is in you? One very special way: the Spirit will tell you deep in your heart that you belong to God. It's called the "witness" of the Spirit. God speaks in a quiet voice deep inside you. You may not always hear him. But sometimes you will hear him if you are listening.

When the Spirit works in you, you will have spiritual power to please God. Think of it this way: imagine you're a glove. A glove lying on the table can do nothing. But if there's a hand in the glove, it can do anything the hand wants to do.

That's the Spirit. Like the hand, he lives in you (the glove), and gives you power to please God.

Prayer: God, please work through me today, like that glove!

God Right in Our Midst

THURSDAY

John 14:28: *"Remember what I told you: I am going away, but I will come back to you again."*

The Extra Mile: John 14:27-31

You've just gotten home. You've had a bad day. You're tired. You don't want to do anything but sit on your bed and play on your PlayStation. You just want to be left alone.

But your mom says, "There's someone here who will be living with us for awhile."

Now you're really worried. "I'm not going to have to share my room with him, am I?"

"No, he will have his own room," Mom says. "But I'd like you to meet him."

"Is he old?"

"Very."

Oh man, now you're really upset. What is this—some old guy coming to live in your house? Why couldn't he go to the shelter or something?

You finally climb off your bed. You go downstairs. Your mom leads you into the guest room. There he is sitting on the bed, leafing through a book.

He looks up. Your eyes meet. And your eyes pop.

Why? It's Jesus. He's right there in your guest room!

"Hey," you say. "That's impossible!"

Prayer: Father, I can't wait for Jesus to come back. Hurry, Lord Jesus.

The Branch That Covers the Earth

John 15:5: "Yes, I am the vine; you are the branches. Those who remain in me, and I in them, will produce much fruit. For apart from me you can do nothing."

The Extra Mile: John 15:1–12

The tree in Bob's yard had the coolest branch. It stuck out sideways. It was thick as a fencepost. And when you sat on it, it swayed.

Bob spent a lot of time on that branch, thinking, talking to God, and enjoying the breeze. At times he hung a swing from it. Another time, he climbed all the way out to the tip and sank down to the earth as if he had a parachute. He even stood on it once jumping like a maniac.

Bob loved that tree and that branch. He grew up with it, and it seemed like it was always there—hanging like a big sure thing he knew would always be.

In today's Scripture Jesus speaks of himself as the vine, and his followers as the branches. The branches are connected to the vine and depend on it. You and I are connected to Jesus. He provides us with the spiritual power to help us live, speak, work, help others, and serve. Without him, we can't do anything. But with him, we can do the impossible.

Prayer: Lord, let me operate as a real branch, letting you work through me.

The Friend That Sticks

John 15:13: "There is no greater love than to lay down one's life for one's friends."

The Extra Mile: John 15:13–27

There's no one like a true friend. Who is yours?

The kid down the street?

The girl in the desk across from you?

That guy on the swim team?

There are times in life when the days are tough. You may want to give up. It's then that a friend will help you hang in there.

David had a great friend in Jonathan. When King Saul wanted to kill David, Jonathan stood by his friend and warned him of the trouble.

Moses enjoyed a great friendship with Joshua. They were both great leaders, but you can be sure they shared many stories around the campfire.

Paul had Barnabas and Timothy.

Jesus had the three closest disciples—James, John, and Peter. Do you have a friend who sticks closer than a brother? That's a guy or girl you can depend on. That's a person you know will be there when everyone else is gone.

Prayer: Help me, Jesus, to be a true friend to my friends, and most of all, a friend to you.

How We Know It's the Truth

John 16:12, 13: "There is so much more I want to tell you, but you can't bear it now. When the Spirit of truth comes, he will guide you into all truth. He will not speak on his own but will tell you what he has heard. He will tell you about the future."

The Extra Mile: John 16

Stefan listened as his teacher talked about the Bible, saying it was full of errors and no one should believe it. "How on earth can we believe that these men who followed Jesus could have remembered all those details about him without a mistake? It's foolish."

Stefan had been reading in his Bible lately, and he remembered something about this. He went home that day and found the passage above. He wrote it down, and the next day he went into class prepared. He raised his hand after Mr. Senns started the class. "Yesterday, you said it was impossible to believe all the things in the Bible were without mistakes. But let me read you this."

He read the passage. Mr. Senns looked dismayed. "It's just more propaganda. I wouldn't believe it. No more questions on that."

Stefan sighed and listened to the rest of the lesson. But afterwards a boy he didn't know well came up to him and said, "You gave a good answer. It's too bad Mr. Senns refuses to believe."

Prayer: Teach me, O Lord, to find the answers in the Bible so I can speak the truth when necessary.

Who Jesus Prays For

John 17:9: "My prayer is not for the world, but for those you have given me, because they belong to you."

The Extra Mile: John 17

"What good is he?" Salom asked his father one day as they cut the grass in the yard.

"You mean Jesus?" his father asked.

"He never does anything. I pray sometimes, but nothing ever happens. Why should I believe in him?"

His father stopped the mower. "Let's sit down."

They walked to the deck and took a seat under an overhang. "Jesus did a lot of things for you, Salom. He died for you. He gave you your life, your personality, your looks. Everything in life comes from him."

"But what's he doing now? It doesn't seem like anything."

His father pulled out a little pocket Bible. He showed him the verse above. "What was Jesus doing, according to this verse?" he asked.

"Praying?"

"Exactly—he was praying for me and you. Jesus prayed for those who would believe in him in the future. And elsewhere in the Bible it says that in Heaven Jesus continues to talk to God on our behalf."

"He's really praying for me, right now?" Salom asked. "That's awesome!"

Prayer: Lord, I know you're praying for me right now. So show me what to ask.

Traitor!

John 18:3: The leading priests and Pharisees had given Judas a contingent of Roman soldiers and Temple guards to accompany him. Now with blazing torches, lanterns, and weapons, they arrived at the olive grove.

The Extra Mile: John 18

You're in a group of friends. Everyone has a great time. But later you find out that two of them have been talking about you and cutting you down.

You and your best friend have been buds since kindergarten. Then you discover he likes the same girl you do and he's been telling her what a jerk you are.

A friend steals something from school. When she's caught, she passes the blame onto you. And you didn't know anything about it.

Have you ever been betrayed by a friend? Betrayal can sting. Movies, books, and music have all been written about betrayals.

Perhaps the worst betrayer of all time was Judas Iscariot. He walked with Jesus for three years. He saw all the miracles. He sat in on all the special teaching sessions. He knew Jesus' heart. But in the end, 30 pieces of silver was enough to turn him.

Why do people betray one another? Money, jealousy, and any number of reasons, but they all hurt the one betrayed like nothing else.

Prayer: Father, help me to forgive anyone who has betrayed me.

The Son of God

John 19:7, 8: The Jewish leaders replied, "By our law he ought to die because he called himself the Son of God." When Pilate heard this, he was more frightened than ever.

The Extra Mile: John 19

You may hear from some people who reject Jesus that he never really claimed to be God incarnate, the Son of God. Teachers, skeptics, friends, and even religious people make that claim. "Jesus never really said he was God."

It's an old argument. But it gets dashed to pieces when you look at a verse like John 19:7. Jesus was on trial before Pontius Pilate. Pilate realized that in spite of the Jews' accusations, Jesus had done nothing wrong.

Pilate's own wife was frightened because she had a nightmare about Jesus. She wanted her husband to let Jesus go, and Pilate tried to release him. But the crowd called out, "Crucify him!"

The clincher came when the Jews told Pilate what Jesus had done. They said he'd committed blasphemy because he claimed to be the "Son of God." To the Jews, that meant he was the Messiah, God come to earth among people. Even the Jews who hated Jesus clearly understood his claims. They knew what he meant when he said he was the Son of God.

Prayer: Jesus, I believe that you are the Messiah, the Son of God.

Seeing Is Believing

John 20:18: Mary Magdalene found the disciples and told them, "I have seen the Lord!" Then she gave them his message.

The Extra Mile: John 20:1-24

Christi walked around with her hands in the air. "I don't see anyone. No one's here. So where is he?"

Webber was trying hard to convert her friend Christi. But it always seemed to come to this: Christi said since she couldn't see God, or feel him, or hear him, or taste him, or touch him, she would not believe.

Webber knew some of the answers: when you became a Christian, by faith you saw and tasted and touched and felt God. But that happened after you believed, not before.

She chewed her lip. Then she said, "Maybe you have to see through the eyes of those who did see."

"What do you mean?" Christi asked.

Webber took her to the above passage. "The disciples saw him, touched him, and ate with him. So we put our faith in those facts, and doors open up."

Prayer: Let me always be faithful, Lord, even if it's difficult.

When You Have Doubts

John 20:25: They told him, "We have seen the Lord!" But he replied, "I won't believe it unless I see the nail wounds in his hands, put my fingers into them, and place my hand into the wound in his side."

The Extra Mile: John 20:25-31

Thomas is the classic case of the doubter. Why did he doubt? If you study Thomas in the Bible, you find several interesting facts. For one, he was willing to die as long as he was with Jesus (see John 11:16). For another, when Jesus told the disciples he was going to Heaven to build a new kingdom for them, Thomas immediately wanted to know the way to get there, so he could be with Jesus (John 14:5).

Thomas was the one disciple who was probably a loner too. When Jesus was crucified, Thomas of all the disciples was devastated. His whole life was wrapped up in being with Jesus. So, when the disciples saw Jesus resurrected, Thomas was skeptical. If this was real, he had to know for himself, for sure. He couldn't stake his life again on a ghost.

When Jesus appeared again, what did he do? Did he yell at Thomas for his doubts? put him down? reject him?

No. Jesus opened his arms and told him to feel the nailprints in his hands.

Prayer: I may have doubts, Lord, but I know you'll help me find the answers in time.

Don't Play Games

John 21:3: Simon Peter said, "I'm going fishing." "We'll come, too," they all said. So they went out in the boat, but they caught nothing all night.

The Extra Mile: John 21:1-19

Jesus had risen from the dead. He appeared to numerous disciples numerous times. To Peter he went first, perhaps because Peter had denied him. Maybe Jesus wanted to make sure Peter knew he was still loved.

If the disciples needed evidence or motivation to go out and tell the world what they'd seen, what more did they need?

Peter went and did what he knew, which was fishing. Maybe he thought that out on the sea, rocking, casting the net, he could think about all that had happened. It would take his mind off things. But he caught nothing.

. . . Until Jesus appeared on the beach. He cooked breakfast and performed a miracle by providing a net-breaking catch of fish.

Even though Peter was confused and upset, Jesus stood by him. When you struggle or ask hard questions, Jesus will stand by you.

Prayer: Lord, I know there's nothing wrong with stepping back sometimes, taking a breather, and thinking about all that's happening. You don't hold it against me.

How Great Jesus Was

John 21:25: Jesus also did many other things. If they were all written down, I suppose the whole world could not contain the books that would be written.

The Extra Mile: John 21:20-25

Mattie sat down at the table and began writing. "What are you doing?" his mother asked.

"About Grandpa. He's the greatest person ever, and I want everyone to know. So I'm writing a book about him."

His mother smiled. "Good luck. Writing a book takes a long time."

"Not for me."

Mattie ran out of steam two days later. "It's too hard," he said.

His mother patted him on the back. "Don't worry, honey. Take it one step at a time."

The Bible contains four Gospels: Matthew, Mark, Luke, and John. They are the accounts of Jesus' life from four different points of view. When John finished his Gospel, he added the last verse, the one you read above. Who could write everything about Jesus, all he said, all he did, and everything that happened?

It couldn't be done. But aren't you glad those men wrote what they did? Through them, we know the greatest person of all time.

Prayer: Help me to spend time in your Word, Jesus. Every day.

Taken Up

Acts 1:9: After saying this, he was taken up into a cloud while they were watching, and they could no longer see him.

The Extra Mile: Acts 1

MONDAY

For 40 days after his resurrection Jesus appeared often to his disciples. He encouraged them, and used the time to prepare them for going on without him. He repeated the instructions for their most important job: to go to everyone everywhere and tell people about Jesus.

When Jesus finished saying that, he began to rise up into the air before them. He wasn't flapping his arms or trying to fly. He just rose out of sight. That was the last time on earth the disciples saw Jesus.

Why did Jesus do this? Why didn't he simply stick around? Wouldn't it have been great if Jesus were on earth today, telling the same message? How many more people might be converted!

No. Jesus had to go to Heaven, not only to fulfill the Scriptures, but because only then would the Holy Spirit come (see John 14:15-30).

Prayer: I'm glad you rose from the dead, Lord, and sent the Holy Spirit to be with me every day.

The Coming of the Spirit

Acts 2:2: Suddenly, there was a sound from Heaven like the roaring of a mighty windstorm, and it filled the house where they were sitting.

The Extra Mile: Acts 2:1-21

The disciples gathered in the upper room. This was the same place that Jesus ate the last supper with his disciples. They were being obedient to Jesus' instruction to wait for something, but they didn't know exactly what.

The scene was dramatic. They heard the sound of a mighty wind. They saw flames of fire appear on them. They felt a tremendous power in the room and began to speak in languages they'd never spoken or studied before.

They rushed out into the street to tell the people what was happening. "The Spirit has come." "Jesus is risen." "The whole world is about to be changed!"

People from different countries heard the message in their own language. It was incredible. And more important, 3,000 people believed the message of Jesus and received the gift of the Holy Spirit that day.

Did you know the Spirit lives inside of you? Have you ever heard him speak? He will. In a "still small voice" at times, and maybe with a megaphone at other times, he will tell you the truth of God. He will teach you. He will comfort you in hard times. He will help you when you're weak.

Prayer: I'm excited, Holy Spirit. You're going to change my life every day, for the rest of my life.

How Did Jesus Become Lord and Messiah?

Acts 2:36: "So let everyone in Israel know for certain that God has made this Jesus, whom you crucified, to be both Lord and Messiah!"

The Extra Mile: Acts 2:22–40

Pamela stood out on the grass outside school. She and the other cheerleaders needed to practice. They needed to show they each could do the cheers, and then Mrs. Mathews, their coach, would choose the 12 girls who would make the squad.

Pamela felt especially nervous. But Mrs. Mathews arrived, blew her whistle, and Pamela cheered her heart out.

At the end of the day, after the girls showered and dressed, they walked out to the hallway where Mrs. Mathews posted the list. Pamela quickly scanned it and saw her name. She wanted to yell and do a little dance, but she felt for the ones who hadn't made it.

What made Pamela a cheerleader? She had learned the cheers. She had performed well. And she was chosen by the leader.

Similarly, Jesus had done all his Father had asked of him—he led a perfect life, taught the people, performed miracles, and then died on the cross. Most important of all, he rose from the dead. God made Jesus Messiah when he'd completely fulfilled his ministry.

Prayer: Lord, I know study, good grades, and a great record don't make me a junior high school graduate. Graduating does. So let me do well and complete the job.

You Need to Fellowship

THURSDAY

Acts 2:46, 47: They worshiped together at the Temple each day, met in homes for the Lord's Supper, and shared their meals with great joy and generosity—all the while praising God and enjoying the goodwill of all the people.

The Extra Mile: Acts 2:41-47

Josh's dad woke him early on Saturday. "Come on, Son," he said. "We've got a lot to do."

"What?" Josh asked sleepily. "I was planning on working on my fort with my friends."

"Hey, we need to be in God's house, don't you remember?" Dad said. "There are people who need our help."

Grumbling, Josh followed him out of the house. But when they arrived at church, they found people working, counseling, studying the Bible, eating together. It was amazing. Everyone seemed happy and full of joy.

"This is what all of life should be like," Josh said.

"You're right," his father said. "God wants us to spend time with his people every day if possible, doing good and praising God and having an impact."

Josh felt differently after that. Maybe fellowshiping at the church was the right thing to do after all.

No one can make fellowship his everyday activity, 24/7. But when we keep our own hearts active, sharing, and giving, God is pleased.

Prayer: Jesus, help me to give you my best, and to encourage others to do the same.

When Healing Doesn't Come

Acts 3:7, 8: Then Peter took the lame man by the right hand and helped him up. And as he did, the man's feet and ankles were instantly healed and strengthened. He jumped up, stood on his feet, and began to walk! Then, walking, leaping, and praising God, he went into the Temple with them.

The Extra Mile: Acts 3

What do Christians pray for the most? In a word, healing. Someone's sick. Someone has cancer. Someone has broken a leg. So we pray for them, that God would heal them, fix the problem, and make everything right again.

How often does healing come? Frequently. The natural process of healing that God gave us in creation fixes the problem in most cases.

But then there are other people who are not healed. God chooses not to perform a miracle for these people. Sometimes the people must suffer for years because of their illness, and sometimes people die.

In this story, we see a man who was healed. He begged at the temple, and Peter and John used their supernatural power from God to heal him.

Why did God heal this man and not others who have had similar faith and commitment? God does not tell us why in most cases. Many Christians pray and weep and do not get healing. God usually does not say why. He reserves that explanation for Heaven.

Prayer: Does someone I know need healing? I will go to you, God, and accept your answer.

FRIDAY

Whom Do You Obey?

Acts 4:19, 20: But Peter and John replied, "Do you think God wants us to obey you rather than him? We cannot stop telling about everything we have seen and heard."

The Extra Mile: Acts 4

Before the bell rang his science teacher overheard Cal talking, contrasting Intelligent Design with evolution. After class, the teacher asked Cal to stay for a minute to talk.

"I heard you talking about your faith, Cal, and I want you to know I will not put up with you talking about such things in my class. There's no place for Christian myths in a science class."

Cal felt punished and defeated. The next day in science class, though, one of the guys asked Cal another question about evolution. Cal took a deep breath and thought about what to do. He decided it was more important to do what God wanted than to obey his teacher. He explained his belief to his friend and the teacher walked over. "I thought I told you to stop talking about this."

Cal just said, "I know, sir. But I have to obey God."

For that, Cal was sent to the principal's office.

Prayer: Protect me, Lord, from school rules that may prevent me from talking about you. May I always stand up for the truth.

Suffering for Jesus

Acts 5:41: The apostles left the high council rejoicing that God had counted them worthy to suffer disgrace for the name of Jesus.

The Extra Mile: Acts 5

Bad people will hurt Christians.

In many places of the world today, Christians are attacked, beaten, and killed for only one reason: they believe in Jesus. Paul warned us that living a godly life will invite persecution (see 2 Timothy 3:12). All through the book of Acts we see Christians punished, ridiculed, thrown into prison, and even murdered. To be a Christian doesn't mean you will always be safe or secure or on top of the world.

What is the proper response to such things? Should we run and hide? If we can we should protect ourselves.

Should we fight back? Nowhere does Scripture say we shouldn't defend ourselves.

But should we take up arms? Should we start a revolution? Should we try to kill those who hate us?

The first Christians did not fight a holy war. Ten of the remaining 11 disciples (after Judas Iscariot committed suicide) were killed by people who rejected their message. In Acts 5:41 we read the disciples' response to such hatred and attacks: they rejoiced that they had been counted worthy of suffering for Jesus.

Prayer: Let me be considered worthy, Lord, to take whatever life dishes out.

Rumblings of Discontent

Acts 6:1: But as the believers rapidly multiplied, there were rumblings of discontent. The Greek-speaking believers complained about the Hebrew-speaking believers, saying that their widows were being discriminated against in the daily distribution of food.

The Extra Mile: Acts 6

Alston and Jeremy sat on the edge of the group as they ate and partied. "We're always left out," Alston said to his friend.

"The cool people are the ones who get everything," Jeremy responded.

The cool kids ate supreme pizzas and got lots of attention from the adult leaders. Alston and Jeremy ate plain cheese and felt invisible.

It happens, even in churches. Some people are overlooked, or worse, treated differently. That's what happened in the early church. Some of the people weren't given the same love and attention as others. Their leaders complained about it to the apostles.

So the apostles decided to appoint a group of men to solve the problem. The qualifications they looked for in the men weren't diplomacy, conflict resolution skills, or a college degree in social work. The apostles wanted men who had a reputation for honesty and were full of the Holy Spirit and wisdom. Soon things were straightened out.

Prayer: Lord, is there a problem in my group or church? Help me to stand up, speak out, and ask for some leaders full of the Holy Spirit to help deal with it.

A True Man of God

Acts 7:59, 60: As they stoned him, Stephen prayed, "Lord Jesus, receive my spirit." He fell to his knees, shouting, "Lord, don't charge them with this sin!" And with that, he died.

The Extra Mile: Acts 7

"I'm going to beat him to a pulp," Bradley told his friend Finnegan. "He deserves it."

The two of them sat watching the sidewalk for their enemy to appear. He usually went home that way, and they knew they could get him alone if they were careful enough.

As they sat waiting, Archer, another of their friends who also happened to be a Christian, came by. He saw them and asked what was up. When the two explained and then asked him to help, Archer shook his head. "It's not right, no matter what he did," he said. "Last week in church our minister talked about this guy named Stephen. The Jews hated him so much that they stoned him. At the last second, as he died, he said, 'Don't hold this against them, Lord.' Maybe you just need to let it go. Or forgive him."

The boys listened, then told Archer to leave.

Prayer: Dear God, I know some people will do anything to get revenge or hurt someone who has hurt them. But you say to forgive, so I will.

Give Me the Words!

Acts 8:4: But the believers who were scattered preached the Good News about Jesus wherever they went.

The Extra Mile: Acts 8

Carla and her new friend Paige sat together on the bus. Carla met Paige the week before at lunch and now they were fast friends.

On Carla's mind, though, was how she could get a chance to share the gospel with her friend. As a committed Christian, Carla always wanted to tell the greatest news anyone could ever receive to everyone she met.

But much of the time, she just didn't know how to begin. She worried that she might not be able to answer any objections, or simply explain how to be a Christian.

As Paige chattered on, Carla prayed. "Please, Lord, show me what to say. I don't know how to tell Paige."

Have you ever felt like that?

Sharing the gospel is important, but many Christians don't know where to begin. As some say, "When it comes to sharing the gospel, Christians are like the Arctic River—frozen over at the mouth."

No Christian likes being frozen. But there is help.

Prayer: Jesus, help me to study, prepare, and learn answers to questions about faith. But most of all, teach me to trust you.

The Kindness of a Gentile

Acts 9:26, 27: When Saul arrived in Jerusalem, he tried to meet with the believers, but they were all afraid of him. They did not believe he had truly become a believer! Then Barnabas brought him to the apostles and told them how Saul had seen the Lord on the way to Damascus and how the Lord had spoken to Saul.

The Extra Mile: Acts 9

Have you ever been helped by someone of a different faith, like a Muslim, Buddhist, or Hindu?

God often uses people of other faiths to help us. It does not mean their faith is better than ours, or that it is even correct. As Christians, we believe the one true faith is the one revealed in the Bible.

But that doesn't mean God won't work through others to help us. Kindness comes in many forms.

Barnabas, whose name means "encouragement," was a real encourager. He was from Cyprus, a good man, whom people trusted. When Saul, who was later called Paul, was first a Christian, he came out of a situation where he had been persecuting Christians for a long time. Nobody trusted him. Some thought he might have gone undercover to sneak into the church and expose more people.

But Barnabas came along, introduced Saul to others, and showed them he was the real thing.

Prayer: Let me be an encourager, Lord, to everyone I meet.

Peter the Failure

Acts 10:14: "No, Lord," Peter declared. "I have never eaten anything that our Jewish laws have declared impure and unclean."

The Extra Mile: Acts 10

Peter really blew it. Three times he lied and denied he even knew Jesus, and refused to stand up for him. And in this case he blew it again. He argued with the heavenly voice that instructed him to eat unclean foods. It was as though Peter thought he knew more than God.

Finally, however, he obeyed, and because of his obedience he was able to have the joy of preaching the gospel to a whole new group of people—Gentiles.

God used Peter to lead many people to himself. Peter's failure didn't stop him from serving Christ in the end.

Prayer: Lord, I failed. I will repent, admit my guilt, and then get on with the job. That's what I know you want more than anything.

Included

Acts 11:18: When the others heard this, they stopped objecting and began praising God. They said, "We can see that God has also given the Gentiles the privilege of repenting of their sins and receiving eternal life."

The Extra Mile: Acts 11

Sometimes people, even Christians, exclude some people from their groups because they think negative things about those people. This is what happened in the early church. Peter had a dream where God told him to include Gentiles in the church worship and fellowship. Although prior to that Peter would not eat with Gentles or associate with them, he saw clearly that God wanted them to be part of the church. Peter then led Cornelius, a Gentile, and his household to Christ.

Many of the Jews who had become Christians didn't get it. They thought Gentiles were still excluded, so they argued about it. But Peter told them his story, and they accepted it. Soon, all the Jews praised God because he had given them "the privilege of repenting of their sins and receiving eternal life."

Do you ever think certain people should be kept from coming into your church because of national, ethnic, or other differences? What if a Muslim terrorist repented, became a Christian, and asked to join your fellowship. Would you let him in? How about the bully from your school, or someone who committed a crime?

Prayer: Father, I realize all are welcome in God's church. No one should ever be turned away.

God Answers Even When We Don't Believe!

Acts 12:14: When she recognized Peter's voice, she was so overjoyed that, instead of opening the door, she ran back inside and told everyone, "Peter is standing at the door!"

SUNDAY

The Extra Mile: Acts 12

Have you ever prayed something that you honestly didn't believe God would do? Maybe you asked God to heal a person who was dying, or you asked him to get your parents back together when they were getting a divorce.

Many times we pray prayers that we really don't believe God can or will answer. We think it's impossible. We pray because it's a "last ditch effort" or something like that. But in reality, we just don't think God can come through.

You're in good company. In Acts 12, Peter was in prison. The Christians prayed at the house of Mary, the mother of John the disciple. They were earnest. They believed. But when Peter appeared at the door and a servant named Rhoda answered, she was astounded. When she told the rest of the Christians, they thought she was out of her mind, or had seen a ghost.

They had prayed, but they really didn't expect God to answer.

Certainly, when we pray, we should believe God can and will answer yes. But sometimes when we pray, we're full of doubts.

It doesn't matter.

Prayer: Father, let me pray and keep praying because you can do the amazing whether I believe it or not.

To Be a Missionary

Acts 13:4, 5: So Barnabas and Saul were sent out by the Holy Spirit. They went down to the seaport of Seleucia and then sailed for the island of Cyprus. There, in the town of Salamis, they went to the Jewish synagogues and preached the word of God. John Mark went with them as their assistant.

The Extra Mile: Acts 13

Have you ever thought about being a missionary? Angela had thought about it many times. Each time, though, that she heard God talking in her heart about it, she pushed him away.

"I don't want to be a missionary," she told her friend Bobbie. "They have to live with bugs, and no electricity, and make all sorts of sacrifices."

When her teacher asked, Angela said, "No, I don't think I want to be one. I don't think I could live without air conditioning."

The teacher laughed and said, "Many missionaries work in places where there is air conditioning."

Angela was astounded.

Then one day she read in the book of Acts about how Saul and Barnabas were the first missionaries. She saw how they traveled all around and led many people to Christ. She decided, "OK, God, if you want me to be one, I'll do it."

Prayer: Jesus, I know you may call me to be a missionary. If so, I'll listen. There is no sadder person than one who has refused your call.

You Are a God

Acts 14:11, 12: When the crowd saw what Paul had done, they shouted in their local dialect, "These men are gods in human form!" They decided that Barnabas was the Greek god Zeus and that Paul was Hermes, since he was the chief speaker.

The Extra Mile: Acts 14

As Marcie and Davida walked to the door of the run-down house, they both felt nervous. This was the first time they'd ever gone witnessing door-to-door and it felt weird. But they knew some kids from school lived in that house, so they knocked anyway.

When the door opened, a horrible smell almost knocked them over. The little girl who answered had a dirty face and no pants on. The girls heard noises and voices further in, so Marcie said, "Can we talk to your mom or dad?"

A big man came to the door and asked what they wanted. The girls told them about a program their church had to give free supplies of food, clothing, and other things to needy families. They soon made friends with these people, and Marcie got several of the young men from church to come and make some needed repairs on the house. They also brought several bags of food and clothing for the four children who lived there.

One day, the little girl who had answered the door that day, now dressed neatly and cleaned up, said to Marcie, "Are you Jesus?"

Marcie was amazed and explained that, no, she only served him.

It might seem funny to you, but such things occur. People who are helped sometimes think the person who helped is God.

Prayer: No one will ever think I'm you, Lord. But if they do, like what happened to Paul and Barnabas, I'll just set them straight and love them anyway.

False Teaching

WEEK 22

Acts 15:1: While Paul and Barnabas were at Antioch of Syria, some men from Judea arrived and began to teach the believers: "Unless you are circumcised as required by the law of Moses, you cannot be saved."

The Extra Mile: Acts 15:1–21

Sad but true, many people go about in the world teaching false things. There are many false religions that are against God, or distort what the Bible says. There are also some people who say they're Christians but really aren't. You can tell them by what they teach.

When Paul and Barnabas were going about teaching the church, they ran into some false teachers who were leading the Christians astray. They opposed these men and taught the people the truth. But of course, some people hung onto these characters and joined with them. It's so sad to see people you thought were strong Christians get sucked into something like that.

Beware of false teachers and teaching. It's all over the world.

Prayer: Lord, help me to know the Bible so well that I recognize false teaching and will not be ensnared.

WEDNESDAY

The Church Takes Action

THURSDAY

Acts 15:30, 31: The messengers went at once to Antioch, where they called a general meeting of the believers and delivered the letter. And there was great joy throughout the church that day as they read this encouraging message.

The Extra Mile: Acts 15:22-41

You can always spot false teaching because it is contrary to the truth of the Bible. If a teacher or leader tries to tell you that sex outside of marriage is a "lifestyle," that all gods and all religions are the same, or that the Bible was for people in the past and doesn't apply to us today, you can be absolutely sure the teacher is wrong. If some leader denies important truths about Jesus—that he was born of a virgin, died on the cross for our sins, and rose from the dead—don't listen to that leader.

Sometimes false teachers are just mistaken. Many times, however, they are trying to lead people astray for selfish reasons. Be on guard.

Prayer: Jesus, if I hear false teaching, I will point it out. Even if I don't know how to argue with those people, I will not let them infect me.

Where to Go When
You Need to Know

Acts 16:4: Then they went from town to town, instructing the believers to follow the decisions made by the apostles and elders in Jerusalem.

The Extra Mile: Acts 16:1-12

Decisions come in many forms. "What clothes should I wear today?" "What will I have for breakfast?" "Should I go to school, or cut it?" "Which is better—to try smoking marijuana, or to avoid it?"

Many decisions, like the first two above, are completely up to each of us. Of the clothes Mom and Dad approve of, we can wear whatever we want. For breakfast we can try cereal, scrambled eggs, or just a glass of juice. It's up to us.

But many decisions in life are so important that we shouldn't decide on the basis of the feelings of the moment. Taking drugs, drinking alcohol, cutting school, stealing from a store—these are decisions with lifelong consequences.

If we take the advice of the wrong people, we may become convinced that doing such things are OK. But God wants all of our lives. That means letting him in on our decisions and inviting him to guide us in making them.

In this Bible passage, Paul and others decided to go to all kinds of places and teach about Jesus and how to avoid evil. Be glad those men decided to head out. Because of them, the gospel has come to us today.

Prayer: I will ask you, God, to help me make decisions. I will find out what the Bible says so I can choose wisely in issues like using drugs, drinking alcohol, and cutting school.

Doing Stupid Things for God

Acts 16:18: This went on day after day until Paul got so exasperated that he turned and said to the demon within her, "I command you in the name of Jesus Christ to come out of her." And instantly it left her.

The Extra Mile: Acts 16:14-24

Has God ever asked you to do something you thought was stupid? Like, "Get up right now and go to that person over by the soda machine and tell him the gospel." Or, "Stop what you're doing right now and pray for everyone here that I will work in them."

If you ever have had a situation like that, you may have questioned whether it was from God, or from your imagination. "How can I do that?" you might ask. "They'll all think I'm an idiot."

That's what almost happened to Paul when a demon-possessed slave girl kept shouting out things about him and his message. Paul put up with it for awhile, but finally—maybe because he decided it was stupid to let this go on—he rebuked the evil spirit.

Most of us have never seen something like this. It even sounds a little weird today. But look in Scripture to see how many times God told people to do things they thought were weird: Moses going to free Israel from Egypt, Matthew leaving his tax business to follow Jesus.

Prayer: Lord, if you ask me to do something I think sounds dumb, help me to know for sure that it's you asking, and help me to obey.

You Just Never Know

Acts 16:25: Around midnight Paul and Silas were praying and singing hymns to God, and the other prisoners were listening.

The Extra Mile: Acts 16:25–40

It was the classic dark and gloomy night. Paul and Silas sat shackled to a wall in a prison in Philippi. They decided to make the most of their time, so they began singing hymns of praise to God.

Maybe they weren't great singers. But the other prisoners listened to them quietly, perhaps moved by Paul and Silas's faith in the face of trouble. The jailer himself had probably listened for a while before he went to bed.

It was then a violent earthquake struck. Paul and Silas and everyone else were freed. The whole prison rocked open.

When the jailer heard it, he ran to the prison. When he saw the damage, he drew his sword to kill himself. The Romans would have executed him if his prisoners escaped, so he tried to do it before they got to him.

Paul stopped him though, telling him everyone was still there.

It was then the jailer said something very surprising: "What must I do to be saved?"

Where did this come from? Undoubtedly sometime in the past day the jailer had learned Paul and Silas were believers. In the end, he was convinced they truly believed. That conviction led to his salvation.

Prayer: Father, I can never know who's watching me! So I will always do what's right.

Look for the Opening

Acts 17:23: *"As I was walking along I saw your many shrines. And one of your altars had this inscription on it: 'To an Unknown God.' This God, whom you worship without knowing, is the one I'm telling you about."*

The Extra Mile: Acts 17

We all want to share Jesus with other people. But sometimes it's hard to find just the right opening.

In this passage, Paul was in Athens walking around. He went up on Mars Hill because that was where people were allowed to speak to a crowd about anything. Paul had noticed that the people of Athens had many religious statues around the city. But then he saw one that said, "To an unknown God."

Strange, isn't it? But Paul saw his opening. These people didn't know about Jesus, so he was the unknown God. Paul began preaching about who Jesus was and what he'd come to do, and people were converted.

If you're sensitive to look for them, you'll recognize opportunities to bring Jesus into your conversations. For example, if you notice that someone displays a religious symbol on their house or clothing, you may ask, "I noticed your symbol. What does it mean? Do you know what the cross stands for?" Or you're playing in band and the guy next to you is having a hard time. Maybe you say, "Do you know that the Bible says God will put a song in your heart?"

It can be anything. Just look around.

Prayer: Help me be creative and bold when it comes to talking about you, Lord.

Be Teachable

Acts 18:6: But when they opposed and insulted him, Paul shook the dust from his clothes and said, "Your blood is upon your own heads—I am innocent. From now on I will go preach to the Gentiles."

The Extra Mile: Acts 18

Some people just never learn!

Ever heard someone say that? In Paul's day it was a big problem. Some of the Jews simply didn't want to hear about Jesus. Even though it was the greatest news they would ever hear, many of them rejected it. And not only did they reject Paul's message, but they also beat him up, just because he was trying to tell them good news.

Teachability is an important human trait. It means you can be taught, that you're willing to listen and learn, and that you're open to new ideas and thoughts.

Anyone, from 1 year old to 101 can be teachable. It's a matter of the heart. Are you teachable? Here's a little test:

- Do you often listen attentively in church or school? Or do you shut down and draw on scrap paper?
- Do you ask questions when you don't understand something, or do you think, "Why bother? It's stupid anyway"?
- Do you eagerly tell your parents or friends about something new you learned, or do you forget it the minute you walk out of the classroom?

Prayer: Lord, keep me teachable.

Pushed Away Here, Go There

WEDNESDAY

Acts 19:9: But some became stubborn, rejecting his message and publicly speaking against the Way. So Paul left the synagogue and took the believers with him. Then he held daily discussions at the lecture hall of Tyrannus.

The Extra Mile: Acts 19

Marty was a courageous new believer. At only 12 years old, he had learned well to speak up for Jesus when he could. One day at lunch, he sat down at a table with some guys there he didn't know.

He learned their names and then asked, "Do any of you guys ever think about who Jesus was?"

One guy named Sam said, "Yeah, he was the village idiot."

All of them laughed.

Marty tried several other ways to get a conversation going. But each time, the guys just cut up and refused to listen to him. After finishing his lunch, Marty stood up. "I like you guys," he said, "but you're not willing to listen. So I won't be back. I'll try people at another table. But you're always welcome to join us."

Everyone sat there stunned. "Who does he think he is?" someone asked.

Marty smiled. "If you want to talk, I'm available. But I believe God wants me to go to people who are receptive."

The table went quiet as Marty walked away. Then someone said, "He's an idiot."

And they all went back to their lunches.

Prayer: Lord, let me take action when I hear your voice.

Falling Asleep in Church

Acts 20:8, 9: The upstairs room where we met was lighted with many flickering lamps. As Paul spoke on and on, a young man named Eutychus, sitting on the windowsill, became very drowsy. Finally, he fell sound asleep and dropped three stories to his death below.

THURSDAY

The Extra Mile: Acts 20

Have you ever fallen asleep in church? Some of us can remember being in church when another person started snoring during a sermon. It was always embarrassing for them, and someone usually roused them when it got loud.

Here's a funny story about a guy named Eutychus. He was eager to hear Paul and he took a spot on the windowsill to listen. Maybe he wanted to feel the cool night air. Or perhaps the room was so crowded that was the only seat left. Maybe he had worked hard all day long, and was tired to begin with. The point was that Eutychus listened and listened and listened. But finally he began to nod off. Even the great preacher Paul had gotten a little tiring. No preacher can be enthralling all the time.

Eutychus fell asleep, plummeted off the ledge, and died. Paul went out, stricken with guilt perhaps, and raised him up.

One minister used this Scripture to make a joke: "Don't fall asleep in church," he said, "unless you know your pastor can raise the dead!"

Prayer: Lord, I want to be an eager listener when someone is teaching about you.

Testimony Time

Acts 21:19: After greeting them, Paul gave a detailed account of the things God had accomplished among the Gentiles through his ministry.

The Extra Mile: Acts 21

Jerold loved it when people in the church stood up and told the story of how they were converted, or how some prayer had been answered, or how God had been working in their lives.

The people in his church called it "testimony time," and most people liked it a lot. Why? Because the stories made you laugh, or cry, or just feel good.

One day, Jerold had something he wanted to say. He prepared all night and the next morning he was ready. When he stood up to tell the story, he spoke about how his friend Walter had been asking questions about Jesus. Jerold didn't know how to answer many of them, so finally he invited Walter to church to hear one of the teachers. The teacher answered many questions, and Walter continued to be interested. Jerold turned to his left and concluded, "And here he is right now."

In time, Walter became more interested and kept coming. One day, he decided he was convinced. Jesus was God. He wanted eternal life. So he accepted Jesus and that evening they baptized him in church.

Before Walter went into the water, Jerold repeated his testimony. Everyone clapped and praised God.

Prayer: Lord, I know it's important to tell the stories about how you work in our world. It encourages others, and helps us remember how good and powerful you are.

Using the Law When It's on Your Side

Acts 22:25: When they tied Paul down to lash him, Paul said to the officer standing there, "Is it legal for you to whip a Roman citizen who hasn't even been tried?"

The Extra Mile: Acts 22

Many people are trying to get God out of everything in our society. They want "in God we trust" off our money. They demand that we not say, "under God," when we recite the Pledge of Allegiance. They won't let us sing Christian songs at Christmas, or speak of the Ten Commandments in school. As a result, many kids grow up without any sense of values or morals.

What should you do? In the above passage, we see the apostle Paul about to be whipped. He turned to the Roman centurion and informed him he was a Roman citizen. It was illegal for the centurion to have a Roman citizen punished without a trial.

What was Paul doing? He used the law of the land to defend and protect himself. You can do the same with any injustice or wrong thing you see in your schools too. It is never wrong in God's eyes to use the law when it's on your side.

Prayer: Lord, help me to always obey the law, but I will feel free to use it when it will help me gain an advantage for your sake.

God Speaks Up

Acts 23:11: That night the Lord appeared to Paul and said, "Be encouraged, Paul. Just as you have been a witness to me here in Jerusalem, you must preach the Good News in Rome as well."

The Extra Mile: Acts 23

Many times in life it seems that God is silent. You pray, and nothing happens. You have to make a decision, and you don't feel God is involved. You need some guidance, but God says nothing.

Do we then think God doesn't care about us, or that he has disappeared from our universe?

No, sometimes God takes his time about things. He has his reasons. In the passage above, we learn through several chapters in Acts that Paul has been put in chains and prison, and that he's now on trial. Lots of people are against him. All throughout this ordeal, God remains silent. But Paul did not lose faith. He knew his mission and his purpose, and he didn't waver.

And then God did speak the encouraging words above. God never leaves us helpless. He is always ready to let us know he's on our side, even if we feel as if he's vanished.

Prayer: Lord, I want to hear you speak. Even if you choose not to, I will do what I know to do.

A Clear Conscience

Acts 24:16: *"Because of this, I always try to maintain a clear conscience before God and all people."*

The Extra Mile: Acts 24:1-23

Josie sat down to dinner with a grim look on her face. No one said much. Josie was not known to be overly happy, but finally her mother asked, "What's up, Josie? You look angry."

"Nothing," she said, and stared down at her food. She forced down several bites. Her brother and sister and parents talked quietly as they ate.

In Josie's mind, a problem swirled. She had told a lie to her mother. It wasn't a big one. She'd gone to a party at a friend's house instead of helping her with her homework. But Josie felt bad about it.

Suddenly, she blurted, "I did something wrong."

Everyone turned to her. With a red face, she spilled out the story. When she finished, her mom took her hand. "I'm proud of you, honey. Having a clear conscience is an important thing in life. We certainly forgive you."

Prayer: Help me to listen to my conscience, Lord, and to make things right when I've done wrong.

"I Can't Make Up My Mind"

Act 24:25: As he reasoned with them about righteousness and self-control and the coming day of judgment, Felix became frightened. "Go away for now," he replied. "When it is more convenient, I'll call for you again."

The Extra Mile: Acts 24:24–27

Jenny had a friend named Carla who was a Christian. Carla often talked with Jenny about believing in Jesus. But Jenny had grown up with parents who had no strong beliefs.

The problem for Jenny wasn't Jesus. It was what she knew she'd probably have to stop doing. She liked sleeping in on Sundays. If she became a Christian, she knew she'd probably have to go to church. She also enjoyed watching movies that she knew Carla didn't watch. Sometimes Jenny told lies, too, and cheated in school. She knew all these things would change if she became a Christian. She just didn't see how she could take that step and be happy.

One day she told Carla that she'd visit with her in church. Another time she went with Carla to a Christian concert. Each of those times, Jenny found herself wanting to become a Christian. But when she got home, she would always say, "Whew, I'm glad I didn't do it."

Jenny just couldn't make up her mind.

Is that you? You believe, but you don't want to obey. If you call out to God, he will help you come to a decision.

Prayer: Lord, I know you welcome all people, even doubters and those who can't make up their minds. I will try to encourage such a friend today.

Serious Accusations

Acts 25:7: When Paul arrived, the Jewish leaders from Jerusalem gathered around and made many serious accusations they couldn't prove.

The Extra Mile: Acts 25

"He said he had a secret all of us would like to know, and he would tell it to us if we paid him a dollar," Chevy told the teacher. "Then it was just some weird thing about Jesus."

"Yeah, and he's always trying to get us to pay something for whatever he's selling," Piper added. "It's stupid."

"Then don't pay him for anything," the teacher said.

"He always makes it sound so great," Chevy chipped in.

The teacher turned to Gareth, who was accused of these things. "What do you have to say, young man?"

Gareth hedged and hawed, but finally said, "They got what they paid for."

The teacher nodded. "That settles it for me."

Prayer: Father, if I am falsely accused because of speaking up for you, help me not to be afraid. I depend on you to defend me.

Who Will You Serve?

Acts 26:19, 20: *"And so, King Agrippa, I obeyed that vision from heaven. I preached first to those in Damascus, then in Jerusalem and throughout all Judea, and also to the Gentiles, that all must repent of their sins and turn to God—and prove they have changed by the good things they do."*

The Extra Mile: Acts 26:1-23

Tim knew the showdown would happen today. His friend, Bill, had pushed for Tim to be on his baseball team. But a new friend, D.G., wanted Tim to join his.

Tim didn't know what to do. He liked both guys a lot. It would be a hard choice.

He walked out to the fields that day with a heavy heart. As usual, his friends were playing on the baseball field behind the school. As Tim walked closer, he heard Bill say to the others, "OK, he's here."

Bill and his group ran up to Tim and stood around him. "Did you decide?" Bill asked.

Tim was about to answer, when D.G. ran up with several of his friends.

"Whose team will you be on?" D.G. asked.

Tim knew one would be hurt no matter which choice he made. Inside his heart, he prayed and hoped that God would give him an answer.

But God said nothing. In fact, God was so quiet, Tim's ears tingled.

In life, you have to make decisions. Sometimes, they will be minor and harmless. Sometimes they will be painful, like Tim's choice of teams. And sometimes, your decisions will be a matter of life and death, or life and eternity.

The decision to follow Jesus is one of those eternity questions. Who will you serve—Jesus, or the world? Jesus, or your own desires? Jesus, or the devil? You must decide.

Prayer: I have decided to follow you, Jesus. Give me the strength to never turn back.

Out of His Mind

Acts 26:24: Suddenly, Festus shouted, "Paul, you are insane. Too much study has made you crazy!"

The Extra Mile: Acts 26:24–32

Which is better—
- to cheer for the football team, or to sit quietly and watch?
- to read your Bible eagerly, or act like you've been sentenced to prison?
- to tell a story with punch and passion, or in a monotone?

Probably you'd say that cheering is good, vigorous, and makes the game more fun. Reading the Bible with eagerness is the only way to go. And everyone likes a story told with fire and enthusiasm.

What about telling others the good news of Jesus? Should we ever get excited? Should we ever really get into it and gesture and raise our voices a little? Shouldn't we try to act as if this is important to us?

Of course. That was how Paul spoke when he shared the good news of Jesus. In Acts 26 we see Paul giving his testimony to a king and a governor. Paul stated his case with such passion and excitement that at one point the governor, Festus, shouted, "Paul, you are out of your mind!"

Wouldn't it be great if some Christians got a little excited, a little "out of our minds" about the gospel?

Prayer: I will be enthusiastic about my faith, Lord, knowing some people will be attracted to you because of it.

Reading the Signs

Acts 27:10, 11: "Men," he said, "I believe there is trouble ahead if we go on—shipwreck, loss of cargo, and danger to our lives as well." But the officer in charge of the prisoners listened more to the ship's captain and the owner than to Paul.

The Extra Mile: Acts 27

Paul wasn't a sailor. But he'd been on many ships during many travels. He knew how to read the weather and the signs of trouble brewing. On this trip, he was a prisoner, going to Rome to stand trial before the emperor. The ship and crew had many problems getting to this point. But to Paul it was clear they could soon be in a worse state. He stood up and told them what he thought.

Have you ever been in a situation where you knew there might be trouble, but you kept your mouth shut because you were afraid the others might laugh at you, or just ignore you? There are many situations in life where God will give you some insight into what could happen. To remain silent at such a time is dangerous and wrong. Even if you're the youngest guy there, or you're not one of the leaders, God wants you to speak up.

After Paul gave them his prophecy, they ignored him and continued on. In the end, they would lose the whole ship and its cargo. But because of Paul and his counsel, even after they had rejected his words, everyone on the ship survived.

Speaking up is not hard. Just shoot it out there. Let the others decide whether they believe you or not. You have to obey God, not people.

Prayer: Lord, when I have an insight, even if it's only in a class or in school, I won't hold back. What I say could help someone else who is silent.

365 New Testament Devotions for Kids

Hard Hearts

Acts 28:26, 27: "Go and say to this people: When you hear what I say, you will not understand. When you see what I do, you will not comprehend. For the hearts of these people are hardened, and their ears cannot hear, and they have closed their eyes—so their eyes cannot see, and their ears cannot hear."

The Extra Mile: Acts 28

Why do some people believe in Jesus when they hear a sermon or a message or read a book? And why do others not believe, even though they heard the same message? Sometimes it's in families. Two kids go to the same church and the same classes, but only one believes and the other doesn't. What's up?

The Bible teaches that people "harden" their hearts against the truth. They refuse to accept the truth. They push it away. They close it out of their lives. When you harden your heart like that, you pull yourself far away from God. Eventually, you may get so hardened that you actually oppose and fight against the truth, becoming angry and abusive when it's brought up.

Don't ever let yourself be brought to that condition. A hard heart leads to a hard life, and a really hard eternity.

Prayer: When you speak, Father, help me to listen and accept the truth.

Watch Out!

Romans 1:14: For I have a great sense of obligation to people in both the civilized world and the rest of the world, to the educated and uneducated alike.

The Extra Mile: Romans 1:1–14

Kelly excitedly took the cards to school. She planned to invite all her friends to a special party at her church. The party would feature a magician, prizes, and a presentation of the gospel. Kelly especially wanted to see her friends accept Jesus.

When she got to school, she found some kids in the hall. "Here," she said to the first person she met, a boy named Rod. "It's for a party."

He tore it open. "At a church?" he said after he read it. "I don't go to church."

"That's OK, it's just a party," Kelly said nicely.

"I said I don't go to church," Rod said, ripping up the invitation.

Kids gathered around. "What is it?" someone asked.

Kelly passed out the invitations. Almost immediately kids were grumbling. "We have our own church." "Who do you think you are—Billy Graham?" And, "You're not allowed to do this on school grounds."

Kelly was called into the office and told she couldn't pass out her invitations on school grounds because it was a religious activity.

That afternoon, Kelly went home discouraged and tearful.

Prayer: I know the devil will oppose me in all I do for you, Father, but I will trust you to help me defeat him.

Not Ashamed

Romans 1:16: For I am not ashamed of this Good News about Christ. It is the power of God at work, saving everyone who believes—the Jew first and also the Gentile.

The Extra Mile: Romans 1:15–17

Uncle Gabe was the shame of the Jones family. He talked too loud. He got too "hopped up" when he told a story. Sometimes he cornered people and made them listen to his tales of adventure and horror.

The family didn't much want Uncle Gabe around. He was an embarrassment. You see, Uncle Gabe was a Christian.

No, not just a Christian, Uncle Gabe was a committed, always-happy, determined, got-to-tell-you-the-good-news-right-now kind of Christian.

Sure, most of the members of the family were Christians too. But they didn't like acting so nuts about it.

Do you know others like Uncle Gabe? They're just not ashamed of the gospel. They tell it everywhere they go. Jesus is their greatest friend and they want to tell the world about him.

Paul was that way too. He wasn't ashamed of the good news for one basic reason: because it had the power to convert people on the spot.

Prayer: I must remember, Lord, it's not my stories or testimony, but the gospel that leads a person to Christ.

The Thoughts of a Fool

Romans 1:19, 20: They know the truth about God because he has made it obvious to them. For ever since the world was created, people have seen the earth and sky. Through everything God made, they can clearly see his invisible qualities—his eternal power and divine nature. So they have no excuse for not knowing God.

The Extra Mile: Romans 1:18–32

Carrie and her friend Rinn talked on the playground. Carrie liked Rinn a lot, so she wanted to say something to her about Jesus. When she did, Rinn's answer shocked her.

"Oh, I don't believe in God," Rinn said.

"You don't believe there's a God at all?" Carrie said, amazed.

"Nope."

"Why not?"

"Because too many things go wrong in life. If there was a God, life wouldn't be so hard."

It was a hard answer, but Carrie responded, "But what about all the good things? Where do they come from?"

"Good and bad, it's all the same to me," Rinn said. "Neither is better than the other."

"But what if Billy Tompkins comes and punches you in the nose and breaks it? Would you say good and evil were the same then?"

Rinn thought about it. "Yeah, I guess I'd rather have good than bad. But that doesn't mean there's a God."

"If there really is no God," Carrie said, "then you have nothing to worry about and me believing is just a waste. But if there is a God, then the Bible says he'll reward me greatly if I believe. But he'll punish you."

Rinn laughed. "I don't know. I'll have to think about it."

Prayer: Lord, I know many people don't believe in you today for the same reasons Rinn gave. But I see it's a foolish position to take.

Stubbornness

Romans 2:5: But because you are stubborn and refuse to turn from your sin, you are storing up terrible punishment for yourself. For a day of anger is coming, when God's righteous judgment will be revealed.

The Extra Mile: Romans 2

Davis tried hard to speak the truth to his friend, Arty. But Arty seemed to have a counterjoke for everything Davis said. One day, Davis discovered that Arty was a hard-core shoplifter. It surprised him, because Arty seemed like such a good guy.

"Why do you do that?" Davis asked one day when they'd been in a store and Arty had heisted some collector cards.

"It's the cheapest way to get stuff," he said with a laugh.

"Don't you know one day you'll stand before God? He'll bring up all this stuff."

Arty just laughed. "I don't think God, if he even knows anything about me, cares about this."

"But what if he does? And what if he does judge you, like the Bible says?"

Arty gave Davis a push. "Look, if you're gonna talk like this to me, you can just disappear. I don't want you around."

"All it takes is to admit it's wrong and stop doing it."

Arty glared at him. "I said stop it. I don't care. I'm gonna do what I want, regardless of what you or the Bible or God says. Got it?"

Prayer: Let me never be stubborn about the truth, Lord. Never.

The Fear That Pleases God

Romans 3:16–18: *"Destruction and misery always follow them. They don't know where to find peace. They have no fear of God at all."*

The Extra Mile: Romans 3

Fear the Lord? You mean we're supposed to "fear" him? Aren't we supposed to love, obey, and draw near to him? How can you be close to someone you're afraid of? Won't you run away?

When the Bible speaks about "fearing" the Lord, it means we respect and revere him. We'd never diss him. We always want to obey him.

What is it to fear God?

• You fear displeasing him because you know he'll discipline you.

• You fear disobeying, because you know he'll call you to account.

• You fear for others who disobey or disrespect him, because you know he could move against them any moment.

In a real sense, we are to fear God just like we fear doing something wrong that our parents might find out about. We fear that they'll punish us for wrong-doing. We fear that they'll yell at us if we get poor grades or commit a crime.

While fearing God involves respect and reverence, we should be afraid of crossing God or having him discipline us.

Prayer: Lord, I will love and fear you always, to the very end.

365 New Testament Devotions for Kids

Confidence

Romans 4:20, 21: Abraham never wavered in believing God's promise. In fact, his faith grew stronger, and in this he brought glory to God. He was fully convinced that God is able to do whatever he promises.

The Extra Mile: Romans 4

Where does confidence come from? Do you know someone who is always confident—such as a parent, a pastor, or a friend on a sports team?

Confidence is a wonderful quality to have. It gives you the determination to try new things. It helps you learn to become better at a sport or subject in school. It drives you to excel and succeed.

Confidence comes from many things: education, experience, encouraging words from others. But one of the main ways is from God. When you believe what God tells you in the Bible, you become more confident that God is with you, that he will lead and help you in difficult situations, and that he hears when you pray to him.

Without confidence no one would ever attempt anything great and brave. But with God, anything is possible.

Prayer: I trust you to lead me, Lord, wherever I have to go.

Peace

Romans 5:1: Therefore, since we have been made right in God's sight by faith, we have peace with God because of what Jesus Christ our Lord has done for us.

The Extra Mile: Romans 5

Katie and her sister Alisha didn't get along. Katie borrowed Alisha's clothes without asking. Alisha played her music too loud.

"When will we have some peace around here?" their mom yelled one day. "Can't you two ever get along?"

Peace is the opposite of turmoil, trouble, pain, and hurt. When you have peace, you feel quiet inside. Your heart isn't always trembling. Your mind stops whizzing with worries.

Jesus came to bring us peace. He came to bring peace with God. Jesus paid for our sins. When we trust Jesus, we have peace with God.

Jesus also came to bring peace with others. He shows us how to get along with difficult people. He wants us to live in harmony with those around us. He makes it possible by showing us how to make peace with others through an apology, a confession of sin, or just a declaration that you want to get along.

Last, Jesus came to give us peace in our hearts. No more guilt. No more fear of death. No more endless tossing and turning on our beds with the fears about tomorrow.

Prayer: Jesus, I know you came to bring us real peace, so I will grab hold of you and gain it.

United with Jesus

Romans 6:5: Since we have been united with him in his death, we will also be raised to life as he was.

The Extra Mile: Romans 6

When Jesus died on the cross, three things happened in the spiritual realm. First, God laid all the sins of the world on Jesus. He paid the penalty for all of them. When we believe in him, we can be forgiven and made new inside.

A second thing that happened was that our old nature or our sin nature was killed with Jesus when he died. Your old self had lots of problems. You didn't much like rules, God, or anything God wanted you to do. So when Jesus hung on the cross, God nailed your old self up there with him. When he died, your old self died, and you became a "new creation."

A third thing that occurred through Jesus' sacrifice was he got rid of eternal death for Christians. Because he paid the price for our sins once and for all, we will never have to experience the "second death" of eternity apart from God.

Do you see the joy of "being united" with Christ? You're set free. You can have real peace. And you can rejoice that you never have to face eternal death.

Prayer: Jesus, I know when I died with you, all the bad old stuff was finished off. I'm new, so help me act like it.

Those Devilish Desires

Romans 7:15: I don't really understand myself, for I want to do what is right, but I don't do it. Instead, I do what I hate.

The Extra Mile: Romans 7:1–20

We all have desires. In the morning, we want to sleep in. At lunchtime, we want to eat junk food. In the afternoon, we want to goof around, not do homework. In the evening, we want to stay up and watch TV, not go to bed.

If you always do whatever you want at that moment, your life is probably a mess. Always following our desires is not a good way to live. They can lead us into trouble, and sometimes sin.

In the Old Testament, Samson was a man with uncontrollable desires. Because he was strong and could kill his enemies easily, he didn't try to control his desires. He fell in love with a foreign woman, Delilah. God had already ruled that Jews should marry people in their own nation of Israel. But Samson desired her, and he didn't care what God said.

Samson's relationship with Delilah led to disaster. An enemy cut Samson's hair. This was a no-no because Samson was a Nazirite. But Samson wanted Delilah, and he didn't care what God said. What happened? God left him; he was blinded by the Philistines and turned into a slave they mocked in public.

Prayer: Help me, Jesus, to control any desires that are wrong: overeating, anger, oversleeping, overspending, impure thoughts, and rebellion.

The Answer to Everything

Romans 7:25: Thank God! The answer is in Jesus Christ our Lord. So you see how it is: In my mind I really want to obey God's law, but because of my sinful nature I am a slave to sin.

The Extra Mile: Romans 7:21-25

It's the answer for global warming, wars, injustice, and suffering. It's the answer for living a good and fulfilling life, conquering bad attitudes and habits, and making a difference for good in the world.

You might say it's reading the Bible, or going to church, living right, or obeying your parents. These are all good things.

But what's the ultimate answer? It's what Paul says in the verse above. Jesus. Jesus is the answer. Without him you can't fix anything, or be anyone.

Jesus is the key to everything in life. With him, you can succeed. With him, you can learn and grow. With him, you can defeat your enemies and triumph in the end in Heaven.

So don't flinch. Get close to him. Be intimate. Follow him even when you're not sure where he's leading. Give him complete power in your life and you will see many good things happen.

Prayer: Father, I know the sky is the limit! So help me always shoot for it.

No Condemnation

Romans 8:1, 2: So now there is no condemnation for those who belong to Christ Jesus. And because you belong to him, the power of the life-giving Spirit has freed you from the power of sin that leads to death.

The Extra Mile: Romans 8:1-15

At one time God was angry with you because of the words you said in your heart about people you didn't like. He was angry about the things you said to kids at school when you were fighting. He was angry with your actions, including the lies, stealing, put-downs, and cheating because you know all those things are wrong.

But God isn't angry anymore. Do you know why? Because of Jesus.

Jesus took all of God's anger onto himself. He felt the fire as he hung on that cross. God the Father spilled all the ferocity and passion of his anger at Jesus.

Now we can know that God will never be angry with us again. If we've trusted Jesus, and if we ask for forgiveness, God doesn't see our sin anymore. He sees us as if we were Jesus.

Do you ever feel condemned? Do you ever feel as if God doesn't like you? Do you ever wonder if God might cast you out, or turn against you, or tell you to get out of his life? God would never do such things. Why? Because he put all the anger on Jesus, and with you he offers forgiveness, joy, and hope.

Prayer: Lord, I know no Christian ever needs to feel condemned, hated, or rejected. Thank you that I can know and love you because of Jesus.

God's Care

Romans 8:16, 17: For his Spirit joins with our spirit to affirm that we are God's children. And since we are his children, we are his heirs. In fact, together with Christ we are heirs of God's glory. But if we are to share his glory, we must also share his suffering.

The Extra Mile: Romans 8:16-25

Israel had done horrible things in the Old Testament. They lied, murdered, stole, committed sexual sin, and in every way disobeyed their God.

Jeremiah spoke against the sins of the people. For his honesty and integrity, the people threw him into prison. They didn't like his message, even if it was true.

When the Babylonians destroyed Jerusalem, their leader found Jeremiah. This man could easily have had Jeremiah killed, but he didn't. He told his officers to take care of Jeremiah and be kind to him.

God was in charge. Even though the people rebelled against God, God had one person he could trust. God wasn't going to let that person go down the tubes. So he made sure Jeremiah survived.

Many times life treats people badly. Bad things happen to good people. But on the other side, good things happen to good people too. God is on the throne. He makes sure good people can do the work he has for them.

Prayer: Lord, I know being good will never make me rich or a star in the NBA. But as long as you are with me, you are enough.

FRIDAY

The Purpose of Pain

Romans 8:28: And we know that God causes everything to work together for the good of those who love God and are called according to his purpose for them.

The Extra Mile: Romans 8:26-28

Mason's dad sat the family down at dinner.

"I've got bad news," he said to everyone. "We can't afford this house anymore since I lost my job. We're going to move into an apartment."

Mason was upset, but said nothing as their house was put on the market. Mason's family moved into a dingy apartment that he hated. He shared a room with his two little brothers. They felt like sardines. Every night Mason prayed, "I know there's something good in this, Jesus. So just show me. I don't want to be a sardine anymore." But he didn't see what good there could possibly be.

Soon, his dad got a new job and things looked better.

Then one morning something happened. "Did you hear about your old house?" one of his friends exclaimed when Mason walked into class.

"No, what?"

"It burned down last night. They said it was a gas leak."

Mason gasped. But later that night, he said at dinner, "It could have happened to us!"

Mason's dad said, "You know, I've been wondering how God would do good in our terrible situation the last few months. And maybe this is it."

Prayer: Father, I may not always know what good you have in mind when something difficult happens to me. But I'm sure of one thing: you know what you're doing, so I will trust you.

365 New Testament Devotions for Kids

Why God Does What He Does

Romans 8:29: For God knew his people in advance, and he chose them to become like his Son, so that his Son would be the firstborn among many brothers and sisters.

The Extra Mile: Romans 8:29–39

Have you ever wondered why God does what he does? Have you ever asked God, "Why are you doing this to me?"

This passage provides a clue to the answer: God does what he does so that he might make you like Jesus.

"Oh," you say, "but I haven't seen any changes." Think again. Has he changed you from a liar to an honest person? Has he changed you from a fighter to a peacemaker? Has he changed you from a selfish to a selfless person? Though you're not perfect, are you better than you used to be? That's God's work in you.

Don't think of God's changes as only miracles, like turning a river into blood like God did in Egypt. Turning bad people into good people and good people into great people is more like the kind of wonder God does today.

Prayer: When bad stuff happens, let me not ask, "Why are you doing this to me?" but, "What are you going to do with me now, Lord?"

God Chooses

Romans 9:14, 15: *Are we saying, then, that God was unfair? Of course not! For God said to Moses, "I will show mercy to anyone I choose, and I will show compassion to anyone I choose."*

The Extra Mile: Romans 9

Many Christians do not understand why one person is blessed and another goes through hard times. Why is one person successful when others have to work hard all their lives and get nowhere?

While we don't know all the reasons for this, we do know that God reserves the right to bless each of us in the way he sees fit. When Josh received his birthday presents, all he got were some collector cards. Meanwhile, his friend Carlo got a big video game that cost almost two hundred dollars. You might say that ultimately God was in charge, and God allowed Josh to get a lesser gift.

While that's tough to swallow because of so many different elements involved, including the money the parents had to spend, it shows the truth: everything you have and are is ultimately from God. That includes your personality, your looks, your abilities, your home, and your place in the world. God gave all these things as gifts because his wisdom and knowledge tells him what to do with each person.

Prayer: Lord, bless me the way you want. That's all I ask.

365 New Testament Devotions for Kids

The Truth Hurts

Romans 10:14, 15: But how can they call on him to save them unless they believe in him? And how can they believe in him if they have never heard about him? And how can they hear about him unless someone tells them? And how will anyone go and tell them without being sent?

The Extra Mile: Romans 10:1-15

The missionary sat with the tribal chieftain and told him the gospel of Jesus. The chief was amazed. He had never heard a story like this. He cried, "When did this happen? How long ago?"

The missionary told him, "Many years ago—over 2,000."

The chief stood there shaking. "Why didn't someone tell my father, or his father before him? Why have we had to wait so long to hear this good news?"

"I'm sorry," the missionary said, a little embarrassed. "We've only had the chance now."

That chief accepted Christ and went on to lead many others to the Lord. But he never forgot that for 2,000 years no one came to his people and told them about the greatest event in human history.

Do you have a burning conviction to tell others the story of Jesus? If not, why not? It's the greatest news you can give anyone.

Prayer: Father, I pray for my friends who don't know you. *(Name them.)* Open their hearts to hearing about you, and give me the right words to say at the right time.

Open Arms

Romans 10:21: But regarding Israel, God said, "All day long I opened my arms to them, but they were disobedient and rebellious."

The Extra Mile: Romans 10:16–21

A group of boys sat around the campfire listening to the speaker. It was time for questions, and Brad raised his hand. "How does God really feel about us?" he asked.

The leader looked around at the group. "You really want to know?"

They all nodded.

"Jesus told a story about a father and his sons. We usually call it the Parable of the Prodigal Son, but the story is really about the father."

He continued: "The younger son took his part of his father's estate and went away. He spent all he had living a rebellious and extravagant life. In time he ran out of money and friends. He went back to his father and hoped only that his father would hire him to work. But how did the father greet him when he came back?"

"Open arms," Bradley said.

"That's how God feels about you."

Prayer: I will never stop from coming to you, Lord, and asking for all I need.

365 New Testament Devotions for Kids

The Greatness of God

Romans 11:33: Oh, how great are God's riches and wisdom and knowledge! How impossible it is for us to understand his decisions and his ways!

The Extra Mile: Romans 11

Lefty and his two friends, Gabe and Robin, lay outdoors looking up at the clouds. "Hey," Lefty said, "sometimes you can look at the cloud formations and see patterns. What do you see, Gabe?"

Gabe was a really smart guy. He said, "See that one right overhead? To me it looks like President Truman. Remember him?"

Everyone looked. Then Gabe said, "And then, up there, that one looks like the outline of the state of New Jersey."

They all agreed he was right. Finally, Gabe said, "And that one over there! It looks like an amoeba going through the process of mitosis!"

Lefty was amazed and nodded. Gabe was a genius. So he turned to Robin. "What do you see, Robin, my man?"

Robin didn't always get very good grades. He wasn't a visionary like Gabe. He said, "Well, I was gonna say I saw a ducky and a horsey, but I changed my mind."

The kids laughed. Do you have friends like that? One real smart? Another not so much?

Think of how smart and great God is. He made the clouds, the stars, and the mountains. And the amoeba. And President Truman.

Prayer: Lord, you are great! It is good for us to honor you every day.

I Present Myself

Romans 12:1: And so, dear brothers and sisters, I plead with you to give your bodies to God because of all he has done for you. Let them be a living and holy sacrifice—the kind he will find acceptable. This is truly the way to worship him.

The Extra Mile: Romans 12:1-10

Every morning Mack did a strange thing. He woke up, looked up toward the heavens and said, "Lord, I am here. My bed is the altar. This room is your temple. I am presenting myself to you on this altar. You can use me however you want today, because I am yours." Then Mack jumped up, took a shower and went off to school, expecting that God would use him that day.

Perhaps Mack is a little different from the average guy, but what he did each morning was an important spiritual reality. God wants our bodies, our minds, and our hearts. He wants us because he longs to employ us in the adventure of bringing his kingdom to the world. He needs to know that you will obey him in the clutch, even when others run.

That's the truth of Romans 12:1: present your body as a living sacrifice.

Prayer: I present my body to you, right now, Lord. Do with me as you please.

Getting Back at the Bad Guys

Romans 12:19: Dear friends, never take revenge. Leave that to the righteous anger of God. For the Scriptures say, "I will take revenge; I will pay them back," says the Lord.

The Extra Mile: Romans 12:11–21

Some people say, "revenge is sweet." But when it comes to revenge in this world, God says no. He tells us he will be the only one to get revenge. The rest of us must trust in his ultimate judgment on evildoers.

In the Old Testament, David knew God's commandments about revenge. Surely, if anyone deserved to get revenge, David did. King Saul stalked him around Israel and into other countries. Jealousy so consumed Saul, he would do anything to kill David.

What did David do about it? While he and his men were hiding in a cave, Saul stepped in not knowing they were there. David crept up on Saul while he was not watching, cut off a piece of his robe, and then stole away.

When David confronted Saul, the king felt real shame. You can read about it in 1 Samuel 24.

Revenge is not sweet for Christians. God wants us to love our enemies and pray for them. He commands us to treat our enemies with respect and try to win them to the truth without attacking them.

Prayer: Let me treat even my enemies with your love, Lord.

God's Top Ten List

Romans 13:9: For the commandments say, "You must not commit adultery. You must not murder. You must not steal. You must not covet."

The Extra Mile: Romans 13:1–9

You've probably heard of things like a "Top Ten List." Often, they're funny.

Did you know that God has a Top Ten List? It's found in Exodus. We call it the Ten Commandments. As you read the list, you'll see these things:

1. The first four commandments are about our relationship with God.
2. The fifth commandment is about our relationship with our parents.
3. The last five are about our relationships with each other.

Probably no better list of basic rules has ever been put together. If people followed these laws, imagine what our world would be like. No stealing. No cursing. No killing. No lying. It would stop just about everything bad in life!

But did you know that we can't keep the Ten Commandments? It's impossible, because we've got a problem. We don't want to obey them. What do we need? You guessed it: God's power. His power is like spiritual electricity. It gives you the strength to do what God wants you to do.

Prayer: Let me live out the Ten Commandments, Lord, wherever I am.

Don't Do It

Romans 13:13, 14: Don't participate in the darkness of wild parties and drunkenness, or in sexual promiscuity and immoral living, or in quarreling and jealousy. Instead, clothe yourself with the presence of the Lord Jesus Christ. And don't let yourself think about ways to indulge your evil desires.

The Extra Mile: Romans 13:10–14

What's the most important thing in life to you: getting straight A's; attending the next party; making the team; being popular?

It's easy to give your heart to the wrong things. While none of the things listed is wrong in itself, if it becomes more important to you than God, it becomes wrong. For some people, money, power, success, and notoriety are what they live for.

How would you feel one day if you stood before God and he revealed to the whole world what took his place in your life—and it turned out to be a video game, or playing on the computer, or kicking a soccer ball well? Don't let your desires rule your life.

Prayer: Help me not to waste my life on junk, Lord. I will look to you, and you will give me a purpose that lasts forever.

We Will Answer to God

Romans 14:12: Yes, each of us will give a personal account to God.

The Extra Mile: Romans 14

Bad guys are everywhere. From drug gangs to crime bosses to terrorists, our world is full of bad guys. It's enough to make a good guy or girl feel like it's not worth trying to be good.

In the book of Esther in the Bible, we meet a classic bad guy, Haman. He was a racist, one of the worst kind of bad guys out there. He hated the Jews because he hated Mordecai, a Jew who would not bow down to him when Haman passed in his chariot.

Haman possessed great power as King Xerxes' right hand man. He used it evilly. He asked the king to make a decree that would kill all Jews because of Mordecai. What was the result? God engineered circumstances so that Haman's evil plot was exposed. He ended up hanged on the very gallows that he intended to use to hang Mordecai.

Do you have any bad guys in your life? Pray that God will change their hearts so they will no longer be bad. But also protect yourself from them. And if necessary, defend yourself.

Prayer: Lord, I see that in the end all the bad guys will stand before you and answer for what they did. I know that you will cause good to win over evil, and that encourages me.

365 New Testament Devotions for Kids

What the Bible Is
Supposed to Do in You

Romans 15:4: Such things were written in the Scriptures long ago to teach us. And the Scriptures give us hope and encouragement as we wait patiently for God's promises to be fulfilled.

The Extra Mile: Romans 15:1-6

How does God get his truth into us? It's not by beating us over the head with the Bible, or reading Scripture to us while we're asleep.

Every time you read or hear God's Word, a little of his truth stays in your heart. You've probably heard some Bible stories over and over. They're like reruns on television or your favorite DVDs. You know what's going to happen, but the stories don't get old.

God knows that we're forgetters. We need to hear the message over and over to get it sometimes. But also, as we grow and change and experience God more, his Word speaks to us in new and different ways. So even when we're old we can still keep learning from God's Word.

Prayer: Help me to keep learning, Lord, every time I read or hear your Word. Don't ever let me think I know it all.

Accept Them

Romans 15:7: Therefore, accept each other just as Christ has accepted you so that God will be given glory.

The Extra Mile: Romans 15:7–33

Sometimes Christians can be a weird bunch, even to other Christians. Some are always praising the Lord, even in public. Some keep themselves separate from the world by the way they live and dress. Some don't seem to fit in with other people, and stick out like sore thumbs in school. Some use words and jargon that only makes sense to Christians like them.

Often kids who are friends at church aren't friends at school. Occasionally, you find Christians who are ashamed of their brothers and sisters in Christ because they're different from the average kids.

Such behavior greatly displeases God. He wants us to accept one another and love one another, no matter how strange we may think others are.

Remember, God didn't always choose the great, smart, and cool people to serve him. Even now, God chooses losers, weirdos, and kids on the fringes. Don't be surprised.

Prayer: Let me accept others, Lord, whether they accept me or not.

Causing Divisions

Romans 16:17: And now I make one more appeal, my dear brothers and sisters. Watch out for people who cause divisions and upset people's faith by teaching things contrary to what you have been taught. Stay away from them.

The Extra Mile: Romans 16

Jolie was one of those kids in church who liked to cause trouble. She purposely raised issues that she knew people disagreed on, just to start an argument. For Jolie, it wasn't about honest discussion and trying to understand how believers can read the same Scripture and interpret it differently. She thought it was funny to see people fight. Sometimes people who heard her got so mad they left the church.

It's not that Christians shouldn't discuss these things. But there are appropriate ways to discuss controversial subjects without causing division in the church.

The important thing is the attitude Christians have toward each other when they disagree. God wants Christians to love and respect each other as brothers and sisters, even if they have different ideas.

One day, Jolie said in class, "My dad thinks the President is an idiot. I can't see how a Christian could approve of him."

If you had been there, what would you have said to Jolie?

Prayer: Lord, please help Christians like Jolie. And help me not to get tangled in arguments over things that aren't essential.

The Burned-Out Area

1 Corinthians 1:18: The message of the cross is foolish to those who are headed for destruction! But we who are being saved know it is the very power of God.

The Extra Mile: 1 Corinthians 1

When the first pioneers traveled west they often faced brush fires. Ahead of them, they would see smoke. A scout would ride out from the wagon train and see what it was. Soon, he'd return. "It's blowing right toward us," the scout would say.

Everyone in the wagon train would fear for their lives. But the leader knew what to do. "Go behind us and set the prairie on fire. The wind will blow it away from us."

"But we'll be surrounded by flames," the people would cry.

"No," the wagon train leader said. "Just watch."

They set the prairie behind them on fire. The smoke billowed high into the sky. The grass and brush burned quickly and out of control. Meanwhile, the fire before them drew closer.

Soon the fire behind them left a burned-out area. All the wagons and people would drive into it. There, when the forward fire reached them, they were safe. With nothing more to burn, the fire died out.

Prayer: Father, thank you for protecting me in this life, and offering me salvation for eternity.

Why They Reject Jesus

I Corinthians 2:14: But people who aren't spiritual can't receive these truths from God's Spirit. It all sounds foolish to them and they can't understand it, for only those who are spiritual can understand what the Spirit means.

The Extra Mile: 1 Corinthians 2

Kent talked to his friend Jon about Jesus many times. For several years, he really tried to win Jon to the faith.

But Jon thought it was all stupid.

Kent invited Jon to retreats, special trips, and even a couple of skiing weekends with his church. Jon went, and enjoyed the fun. But when it came to Christ and listening to the gospel, Jon always ducked out. "I'm glad you believe what you do," Jon told Kent one day, "but I just don't believe like that."

Kent didn't give up. He prayed. He kept inviting Jon to special events. But Jon didn't change.

Do you have a friend or friends like that? They listen, they argue, and at times they even admit you're probably right. But they never sign on the dotted line. They never accept Jesus.

First Corinthians 2:14 offers us two reasons some people never "get it." First, they don't have the Spirit of God, and the things of God seem stupid to them. Second, they don't understand the things of God, because those things are spiritual, not earthly.

It's a tough situation. Don't give up, though.

Prayer: Lord, I realize your Spirit can break through a hard heart at any time. So I'll keep praying and inviting my friends.

Spiritual Babies

1 Corinthians 3:1: *Dear brothers and sisters, when I was with you I couldn't talk to you as I would to spiritual people. I had to talk as though you belonged to this world or as though you were infants in the Christian life.*

The Extra Mile: 1 Corinthians 3

Have you ever tried to communicate with a baby? You say, "Hello, baby." He says, "Goo goo." You tickle him and say, "You're cute." He replies, "Maaa!" You pick him up and ask, "Would you like to go for a walk?" He answers, "Goo Laaa."

It can be frustrating. But of course we all know, he's just a baby. He can't be expected to do much more.

When Christians, though, remain babies like that, it's irritating. They have accepted Christ, but they haven't grown. You mention Jesus' lordship and they're not really sure what you're talking about. You ask them what book of the Bible they've been reading lately and they give you a blank look. You suggest to them that maybe they'd like to come over and spend some time in prayer for the church-supported missionaries. They say, "How long will it take? I have to go out and get some new shoes tonight."

When such a person is your best friend, or at least someone you care about, you might feel like screaming. Paul felt the same way. The Christians at Corinth were all spiritual babies. When you read the book, it's just one big problem after another. Paul had to work to get down on their level.

Prayer: Lord, please help me to grow. I don't want to stay a spiritual baby.

Praise from God

I Corinthians 4:5: So don't make judgments about anyone ahead of time—before the Lord returns. For he will bring our darkest secrets to light and will reveal our private motives. Then God will give to each one whatever praise is due.

The Extra Mile: 1 Corinthians 4:1–10

Do you ever wonder if anyone notices the nice things you do?

Say you take out the trash for Mom without a complaint. But she says nothing to you about it. Was it just a wasted effort?

Perhaps you really study for a test. You work hard. You think you have the material down. You want to do well. But then you get a B, nothing stupendous. Was all that study worth it?

Or maybe you do something in secret. Give an extra couple of dollars to the offering at church. Give a secret gift to your brother or sister. Pray for someone you love.

Does anyone really ever notice these things?

Yes! God does. Look at 1 Corinthians 4:5. That verse tells us God will show the whole world what we've done in secret. If we have good, loving motives about what we do, God will bring that out too.

Nothing is forgotten. No one is missed. Do good. God will praise you for it one day.

Prayer: Jesus, help me to never stop doing good.

A Stiff Neck and a Battered Bottom

WEDNESDAY

I Corinthians 4:21: Which do you choose? Should I come with a rod to punish you, or should I come with love and a gentle spirit?

The Extra Mile: 1 Corinthians 4:11–21

"You better watch that anger, boy," Kerry's dad said to him one day. "It'll get ahold of you and won't let go."

Kerry thought his dad was stupid.

A second time when Kerry "lost it" with his little brother, his dad said, "Hey, you keep acting like that, someone's gonna take your head off one day."

Kerry just ignored him.

The third time, Kerry's dad clipped him on the head when he started spouting off at dinner. "Didn't I tell you to stop yelling at everyone? Now get with it!"

Some people just don't get it even after being told many times. It's called "stiffening your neck" or being "arrogant." Paul spoke of this as something the Corinthian Christians had a problem with.

Kerry never did get control of his anger problem. When he grew up, he was stabbed by some guys he got into a fight with. He almost died. But in the hospital, as his dad and mom sat by his bed, he whispered, "I've got to change, but I don't know how."

His dad said, "We'll help you, son. And Jesus'll help you if you ask him."

That night Kerry prayed to become a Christian.

Prayer: Father, I'm a Christian now, so please start changing me for the better.

Not "In" the World?

1 Corinthians 5:9, 10: When I wrote to you before, I told you not to associate with people who indulge in sexual sin. But I wasn't talking about unbelievers who indulge in sexual sin, or are greedy, or cheat people, or worship idols. You would have to leave this world to avoid people like that.

The Extra Mile: 1 Corinthians 5

Karol told his parents he wanted to go to Christian school. "I don't want to be around those creeps in the public school anymore."

One day after church, he informed them, "I now only have Christian friends from church. I've dumped all the others who don't know Jesus."

His parents were shocked a bit, but they decided it was just a phase.

As Karol grew up, he cut himself more and more off from the people of the world. He worked in a Christian business. He hung around only with Christians. He didn't associate with anyone else.

One night at church, the pastor preached on how the people needed to get out there and win the world to Christ. "Go to your friends and find a way to share the gospel with them. Soon it may be too late."

Karol walked up front to talk to the pastor after that. "I don't know any non-Christians," he explained. "I've made a point not to associate with them."

God wants us to penetrate the world and share the gospel, not run away from it.

Prayer: I know, Lord, that my friends without Jesus are here because you put me in their lives. So let me speak up.

Lying, Cheating, and All That Rot

1 Corinthians 6:9, 10: *Don't you realize that those who do wrong will not inherit the Kingdom of God? Don't fool yourselves. Those who indulge in sexual sin, or . . . are abusive, or cheat people—none of these will inherit the Kingdom of God.*

The Extra Mile: 1 Corinthians 6:1–11

"Everybody does it," Mel complained.

"No one can always tell the truth," Jenny answered.

"Sometimes you just have to lie," Grant said.

"You can't expect people to tell the truth when it will hurt others," Alyssa replied.

Lying. It's so easy to do. Sometimes it's out of your mouth before you've even thought about it.

People lie about all kinds of things: their weight, where they're going, where they've been, what they did, and whether they cheated on a test.

In the above passage, Paul speaks about people who indulge in all kinds of sins that he says Christians should not do. In other passages, he lists lying too. God hates lying and cheating.

What about you? Ever consider lying or cheating? People may never know about it. But God knows.

Prayer: Jesus, help me to speak the truth when I am tempted to lie.

It's All Permissable

1 Corinthians 6:12: You say, "I am allowed to do anything"—but not everything is good for you. And even though "I am allowed to do anything," I must not become a slave to anything.

SATURDAY

The Extra Mile: 1 Corinthians 6:12–20

Some Christians say going to movies is wrong. Others say playing cards is evil. Some demand that no one ever read certain books. Occasionally, you will meet Christians who condemn dancing, listening to rock music, playing sports, and just about everything else. For some Christians, anything that's really fun is bad for you. So you shouldn't do it.

Is that true? Is that how God feels about soccer and movies and music?

In 1 Corinthians 6:12, Paul gives us a powerful principle that can help us sort through this maze. He gives three things that can guide us in making choices about music, movies, and everything else.

First, if something is not obviously against God and his truth—if it's morally neutral, neither good nor bad—it's all right.

Second, is it beneficial? Does it help you grow as a person, as a Christian? Does it contribute something good to your life?

Third, does it master you? Do you become obsessed with this activity? Some kids play video games constantly. The games have mastered the person. That's not good.

Prayer: Lord, I know you don't condemn most fun activities. You just want us to be sure they help us live for you.

Buying Back the Sinful Woman

1 Corinthians 7:23: God paid a high price for you, so don't be enslaved by the world.

The Extra Mile: 1 Corinthians 7

Imagine you're a slave before the Civil War. Your master stands you on the block and announces that he's selling you to the highest bidder.

Now imagine one other thing. Suppose you were also married to someone before you became a slave. Suppose this person loved you with all his heart and treated you well. But you lit out one day and ran away from him, stealing his money and everything else. You thought things would be better somewhere else.

Unfortunately, it didn't work out that way. You ended up a slave, owned by a nasty man who beat you and used you. Finally, he got so sick of you and you got so messed up, he didn't care about you anymore. So he put you up for sale.

So, you're standing there on the auction block, naked, alone, without a friend in the world.

But then someone steps out of the crowd. It's your former husband. He looks at the seller. "I bid everything I have for her!"

Your husband clothes you and takes you home. There he says, "You're free. I free you from your slavery."

What would you do for that man at the point? Run? Cuss him? Or love him?

That's what God did for you. He bought you out of slavery to sin and set you free. Now what will you do?

Prayer: Lord, I know you gave your life to pay the penalty for my sins, so I will hold nothing back from you.

A Clear Conscience

1 Corinthians 8:9: But you must be careful so that your freedom does not cause others with a weaker conscience to stumble.

The Extra Mile: 1 Corinthians 8

Joni and Cara stood outside the theater. "I don't know," Cara said. "It's pretty violent and bloody."

"It's nothing," Joni replied. "I see them all the time."

"But I thought Christians didn't go to these kinds of movies."

"Sure they do." Joni took her friend's hand. "Come on. It's going to start."

Joni led her friend into the horror movie. Cara groaned and curled up in her seat through most of it. When the movie was over and Joni excitedly took Cara outside, Cara looked upset.

"What's the matter now?" Joni said.

"I feel like God's mad at me."

"Why?"

"For seeing that movie."

Joni shook her head. "We can see any movie we want. That's what it means to be a Christian. We're free."

For the next week Cara thought a lot about what she had done. She made a decision: she would choose to spend time with other friends besides Joni; friends whose values were closer to hers.

Prayer: Help me never to make another Christian stumble, Lord, if I am more open to some things than they are.

Should Those Who Minister Be Paid?

1 Corinthians 9:11: Since we have planted spiritual seed among you, aren't we entitled to a harvest of physical food and drink?

The Extra Mile: 1 Corinthians 9:1–23

TUESDAY

Many people believe pastors, ministers, and others shouldn't make much money, or be paid well for their work. They don't like the idea that the money they donate to the church should go to pay for the pastor's gas, or his new shoes, or anything like that.

But the Bible is clear about such things. God says that a minister is worthy of being paid for his work and we, as members of the church, shouldn't hold back in paying him well. Why? This person ministers to us about spiritual things, the most important things in life. If he's not paid well, he might not take the job as seriously, or he might not have the time to devote to give us God's truth every Sunday with accuracy.

Ask your mom or dad how your pastor is paid. You might consider praying that the church could afford to pay him more.

Remember, God is watching. When we treat our leaders poorly, he is not pleased.

Prayer: Lord, I know nothing I give to the church is wasted. You will use a good person's money wisely.

Run All Out

1 Corinthians 9:24: Don't you realize that in a race everyone runs, but only one person gets the prize? So run to win!

The Extra Mile: 1 Corinthians 9:24–27

Jazzie ran fast. No one could beat him on the playground. But Jazzie had a problem. He only ran when he felt like it. As a result, he missed many races because he just didn't feel like running.

Many people treat being a Christian like Jazzie treated running: they only practice it when they feel like it. They read their Bible if they happen to feel like it at the moment. They pray when the urge strikes. They go to church if they feel like it on Sunday morning.

Such Christians often lose in the race of life. You don't stop when you just don't feel like running anymore. It's an everyday thing.

How are you running? In 1 Corinthians 9 Paul talks about the race. He tells us to run in such a way that we might win. Are you running to win? Are you going all out? Is the race the most important part of your life?

If not, you're in danger of being a Jazzie. But if so, you may be on the verge of winning!

Prayer: Lord, let me run swiftly and steadily. I will never give up.

The Danger of Being Important

1 Corinthians 10:12: If you think you are standing strong, be careful not to fall.

The Extra Mile: 1 Corinthians 10

"Don't think you can get away with that with me, young lady," Mrs. Williams said to her daughter Chandra. "I know you're president of the sixth-grade class. But that doesn't entitle you to talk back to me."

Chandra stood in the hallway ready to fight. Who did her mother think she was, after all? Chandra was an important person in school. She should be able to do what she wanted. She shouldn't have to listen to her mother about everything!

Ever find yourself thinking like Chandra? Sometimes because of honors given to us or a position we hold, we begin to think we're very important. We become proud and cocky. We start doing things we know we shouldn't, because we think we're such important people!

Danger zone! Pride always leads to a big fall. No matter where the pride comes from, it can fell you.

Do you think you're important, and others should notice you? Perhaps you should think real hard about who you are in God's eyes.

Prayer: Father, help me to have an honest self-concept, knowing that I am valuable to you, but not more valuable than others.

What Could Anyone Possibly Give to God?

1 Corinthians 11:29, 30: For if you eat the bread or drink the cup without honoring the body of Christ, you are eating and drinking God's judgment upon yourself. That is why many of you are weak and sick and some have even died.

FRIDAY

The Extra Mile: 1 Corinthians 11

Zim didn't appreciate the Lord's Supper. "I just think it's strange," he said. "How can a tiny piece of bread and a cup of juice represent Jesus' bloody, crucified body? And how can remembering such a gross thing be good?"

"It's symbolic," his friend Craddock answered. "When you participate in the Lord's Supper you are remembering the sacrifice Jesus made; but most of all you are expressing your gratitude for his paying the penalty for your sin."

"Why don't they use real wine, then? That's what they did in the Bible." It seemed Zim had a problem with everything these days.

Then one day Zim came down with a horrible sickness. The doctors didn't even know what it was. He writhed in bed, had fevers, and threw up constantly. Craddock visited him frequently. "Maybe you should confess your sins," he said to Zim one day.

Zim just laughed at him. But when he was alone, Zim thought about it. "Is that what I need to do?" he asked God. That afternoon he went down on his knees and confessed everything, and especially his contempt for the Lord's Supper. In time he got better and from then on he respected everything God said in the Bible.

Prayer: Lord, I see now that while not all sickness is because of sin, some of it is. Help me never to let sin get between me and you.

You Count!

I Corinthians 12:15: *If the foot says, "I am not a part of the body because I am not a hand," that does not make it any less a part of the body.*

The Extra Mile: 1 Corinthians 12

Do you ever feel as if you don't matter or you don't really count in the church? After all, you're not the minister, to whom everyone listens. You're not the worship leader, whom everyone thinks is wonderful. You're also not the cool youth pastor, or the Sunday school teacher. You can't even play a musical instrument or sing in the choir.

Do you ever ask, "Where do I fit in?" The only thing you do is set up the chairs for junior worship. Do you sometimes wonder if you're important at all?

Guess what? You are! You're a part of the body of Christ. You may be a finger, an arm, an ear, a tongue. You could be any part of it. But the important thing is that you are a part.

Over time your job will probably change. But in the meantime, ask yourself, "What do I enjoy doing? What do I do well? What would I like to do?"

Answer those questions and you'll be on your way.

Prayer: Lord, help me to figure out something to do in the church, and then go do it.

Can You Give It Up?

I Corinthians 13:3: If I gave everything I have to the poor and even sacrificed my body, I could boast about it; but if I didn't love others, I would have gained nothing.

The Extra Mile: 1 Corinthians 13:1-3

Sooner or later it will happen.

It could be running for student government. Maybe it'll be choosing wrong over right with one of your friends. Maybe it will involve something you've always wanted, like a video game or a NASCAR ticket.

Could you give it all up for God? Could you say, "Not my will, but your will, Lord?" Could you give up something important to you if God asked you to?

God might say, "Will you give me this (habit, situation, dream) even though you don't understand why I would ask such a thing?" It could happen.

When God comes asking, what will you do?

Sacrifice is important in Christian faith. But if you sacrifice something for the wrong reasons, like in the above Scripture, it means little.

Prayer: Father, fill me with love. Without love, nothing really matters very much.

Building Up Each Other

I Corinthians 13:4, 5: Love is patient and kind. Love is not jealous or boastful or proud or rude. It does not demand its own way. It is not irritable, and it keeps no record of being wronged.

The Extra Mile: 1 Corinthians 13:4-13

What is the main thing every Christian should do for other Christians? First Corinthians 13 tells us: we are to love one another.

Love means being patient with each other, being kind, not envious. It means encouraging others, complimenting a job well done, holding each other accountable, and celebrating accomplishments.

A second way to love each other is to honor one another. Honor those who do well with words of praise. Speak highly of them to others.

Put these two together and what do you have? A loving church, who care for each other, who won't be divided in spite of the devil's attacks.

What can you do today to show love to the people in your church?

Prayer: Lord, lead me to show love to everyone, but especially other Christians.

Be Innocent

1 Corinthians 14:20: Dear brothers and sisters, don't be childish in your understanding of these things. Be innocent as babies when it comes to evil, but be mature in understanding matters of this kind.

The Extra Mile: 1 Corinthians 14

Innocent: a legal term. It means you've done nothing to get the police to come after you. Babies are innocent. They haven't grown enough to go out and do something terrible.

Most children are innocent. They not only do not do bad things, but they don't know about them, either. They wouldn't even think of doing some bad things because they don't even know what they are.

Paul says in this Scripture verse that he wants us to be "babies" when it comes to evil. Why? Because there are people who practice evil things and try to get others to do them. People who try to take away the innocence of others are evil in God's eyes.

Being a baby when it comes to evil is the only way to treat it.

Prayer: Father, when evil comes knocking, I will just lock the door.

WEEK
31

You Can't Run from God

WEDNESDAY

1 Corinthians 15:5, 6: He was seen by Peter and then by the Twelve. After that, he was seen by more than 500 of his followers at one time, most of whom are still alive, though some have died.

The Extra Mile: 1 Corinthians 15:1–11

What if you decided to run away from God? Where would you go?

You go down to the train station; he's there. You go to the bus stop; he's there too. You go to a friend's house, and there he is. You fly to another city, and God's sitting right there with you. Wherever you are, God is.

That's what Peter found out. Jesus warned Peter the night before he was crucified that he would deny he even knew Jesus three times. Peter may not have believed that it would happen, but it did, just like Jesus said.

What Peter found out, and what you need to know, is you can't run away from God. After Jesus rose from the dead, one of the first people he went to was Peter.

Prayer: Lord, it's a comfort to know you're always with me. And yet when I am embarrassed or ashamed I sometimes want to hide from you. Thank you for loving me just the same.

365 New Testament Devotions for Kids

What If?

1 Corinthians 15:14: And if Christ has not been raised, then all our preaching is useless, and your faith is useless.

The Extra Mile: 1 Corinthians 15:12–32

What if Christ didn't really rise from the dead? Is it that important? What does it really matter? After all, isn't Christian faith just keeping certain principles and truths?

In 1 Corinthians 15 Paul wrote about this very issue. He said that the resurrection of Jesus is the most important truth of Christian faith. For if Christ never rose, then . . .

- what Paul preached was useless
- our faith is useless because it's in a dead person
- Paul was a liar, because he said Christ rose from the dead
- our faith is worthless; it can't get us anywhere or anything
- none of us has been forgiven and we still have to pay for our sins.
- anyone who's died and believed in Christ is dead forever
- people should pity us because we're fools
- Christianity is a dead religion

But then Paul says, "But Christ did rise. Christ is alive. God accepted his death for our sins. He reigns forever, and we will reign with him."

Hallelujah!

Prayer: Father, because Jesus is risen I have nothing to fear.

The Mighty Men of
a Mighty Man

1 Corinthians 15:33: Don't be fooled by those who say such things, for "bad company corrupts good character."

The Extra Mile: 1 Corinthians 15:33–58

FRIDAY

Good people usually have good people as friends. Mighty people become mighty by choosing mighty people to be around them. Losers spend their time with losers. And winners win by hanging out with other winners.

Who do you hang out with? God does not always choose great people to be Christians. In fact, he tells us many times in the Bible that he didn't choose the mighty, or the wise, or the great. Instead, he has chosen the foolish, the weak, and the undesirable. However, he does not keep them foolish, weak, and undesirable. He makes them into new people who can lead, give, serve, and achieve great things in his name.

When it comes to leading people to Christ, we shouldn't overlook anyone.

But when it comes to who you hang out with and who you ally with, choose people who are wise, good, and capable. Those are the people who will help you grow. How can you begin spending time with the great Christians of your neighborhood?

Prayer: Father, help me to find a solid Christian to be friends with and to learn from him or her all that I can.

The Law of Seven

1 Corinthians 16:2: On the first day of each week, you should each put aside a portion of the money you have earned. Don't wait until I get there and then try to collect it all at once.

The Extra Mile: 1 Corinthians 16

In basketball, it's "pass, steal, and shoot."
In football, it's "run, pass, and score."
In baseball, it's "pitch, hit, and run."
In English, it's "*I* before *E* except after *C*."
Sports, games, and activities have important laws and rules. Name anything you can do and you'll soon find rules about it.

In giving of your money, time, and self, there's a similar rule: give a portion of it to God's work. In the Old Testament it was called a "tithe," a tenth. But in the New Testament, that rule does not seem to be in force. We're to give proportionately. If we have much, we give much. If we have little, we give little.

God wants you to give, especially of your wealth, not because he's poor and needs it. No, he wants you to give to learn to be generous, loving, and caring. When a person is willing to give of what's valuable to him, that's when he's truly showing he loves and cares.

Prayer: Lord, I will give as much as I can, knowing you will use it for your glory.

WEEK
31

It's for Your Comfort

SUNDAY

2 Corinthians 1:6: Even when we are weighed down with troubles, it is for your comfort and salvation! For when we ourselves are comforted, we will certainly comfort you. Then you can patiently endure the same things we suffer.

The Extra Mile: 2 Corinthians 1

Why do some Christians suffer?

Perhaps you know a boy or girl who has faced serious illness or the divorce of their parents. Maybe someone has been left back a grade in school, or didn't make the team they tried out for. All these things can hurt.

Why does God let bad things happen to his people? Why doesn't he stop such things from happening completely?

The Bible shows us over and over that God cares about our hurts. He promises one day to rid the universe completely of hurt and tears and pain. Until then, though, bad things sometimes happen to nice, decent, good people.

In 2 Corinthians 1 Paul reveals one reason that such bad things happen: so that God can comfort those people through other Christians. Did you know that? One reason bad things have happened to you is so you can be comforted by God and by other Christians. Then when bad things happen to someone you know and love, you'll know how to comfort them.

God will never let a Christian suffer alone. We may hurt. We may feel depressed. But God will be there. And he will send Christian brothers and sisters to speak kind words, offer help and friendship, and just be close.

Prayer: Jesus, help me learn to comfort those who are in distress. Let me never forget how great your love is for people who hurt.

You Start with Forgiveness

2 Corinthians 2:10, 11: When you forgive this man, I forgive him, too. And when I forgive whatever needs to be forgiven, I do so with Christ's authority for your benefit, so that Satan will not outsmart us. For we are familiar with his evil schemes.

The Extra Mile: 2 Corinthians 2

Terri sat in her seat, unwilling to look at Charla in the second row. Charla had accused Terri of writing a racist word on the wall in the girls' bathroom. Terri was not a racist, and she would never write anything like that. But the teacher decided to do an investigation. Being accused was hard enough. And now people who didn't like Terri would be questioned about her.

She walked home that day full of anger. But when she reached home, her mother said the teacher was on the phone. When Terri took the phone, the teacher said, "I'm sorry. A student told me she saw you write that word."

"Mrs. Arthur, I didn't. I wouldn't write such a thing! I don't understand why she'd tell you that I did."

"I'm sorry. But you will be suspended for one week. And when you come back, you will have to make an apology to the whole school."

Terri sank to the floor, sobbing.

What would you do if you were falsely accused? Forgiveness may be the first step.

Prayer: Lord Jesus, you were falsely accused, so you know how it feels. You never did anything wrong; yet you were executed as a criminal. You forgave those who killed you. Please help me to forgive those who wrong me.

The Veil

2 Corinthians 3:15: Yes, even today when they read Moses' writings, their hearts are covered with that veil, and they do not understand.

The Extra Mile: 2 Corinthians 3

People reject Christ for the most flimsy reasons: "I don't know enough," some say. Well, find out. "I just don't want to." What don't you want to give up? "I think Jesus was a good man, but he's not God." Lots of people say that. None of these reasons hold up.

The Bible teaches that a veil is over the eyes and hearts of people who reject Christ. They can't see. They can't accept Christ until they make a new choice. It's a sad story.

When we are born, this veil is over our eyes. God has to take it off through the power of the Spirit. When we see truly, then we begin to know God's truth through reading and studying the Bible, through prayer, and through the influence of other Christians.

What should you do about friends who do reject Christ? Pray. Keep praying. Keep being their friend. And never give up.

Prayer: Lord, I trust that as long as a person who rejects Christ is alive, there's hope in you.

Not Crushed

2 Corinthians 4:8, 9: We are pressed on every side by troubles, but we are not crushed. We are perplexed, but not driven to despair. We are hunted down, but never abandoned by God. We get knocked down, but we are not destroyed.

WEDNESDAY

The Extra Mile: 2 Corinthians 4

Dennie waited for his turn at bat. It finally came and he walked out to the batter's box. Behind him, he heard some of the guys grumble.

"He'll strike out as usual."

"We need to replace him."

"He just stinks at everything."

It was very discouraging. Dennie had made the team because there simply was no one else who tried out. He liked baseball, but he just wasn't very good at it.

He stepped up to the plate. "Please, God," he prayed, "just let me hit the ball."

The pitcher wound up. Dennie just stood there. "Strike one," the ump cried.

"'Strike two" came quickly, then two balls. Dennie still hadn't swung. He just didn't know how to judge a pitch. Finally, at a count of 2-2, he swung, and connected.

The ball stopped three feet in front of the plate. Dennie ran, but it was an easy out. He walked back to the plate saying, "Next time, a real hit."

Prayer: Lord, help me to keep trying when I'm not good at something. I won't give up knowing you're with me.

Standing Before Christ

2 Corinthians 5:10: For we must all stand before Christ to be judged. We will each receive whatever we deserve for the good or evil we have done in this earthly body.

The Extra Mile: 2 Corinthians 5

Did you know that one day you will stand before Jesus?

Every person from every age will be gathered. You will be called up to the *bema*, which is Greek for a "victor's platform." It's like the little stand that Olympic medalists stand on when they receive their medals.

Jesus will then talk about your life, what you did for him and others. Undoubtedly, he will mention many things you didn't even know about, like the money you gave for missions and how it was used to God's glory. He'll talk about that boy you witnessed to years ago, and how he became a Christian as an adult. He'll mention that lady you helped one day when her car broke down, and how she went on to do good for others because of your kindness.

Jesus will bring it all out. The whole creation will see what you did with your life. And then Jesus will praise you. This is not something Jesus does to determine whether you enter Heaven or not. Your salvation is determined by your faith in Jesus, but you'll be rewarded in Heaven for what you did with your life.

Prayer: Father, I refuse to worry. I will do good. And one day the whole world will know that I loved you and lived for you.

Choosing a Partner

2 Corinthians 6:14, 15: Don't team up with those who are unbelievers. How can righteousness be a partner with wickedness? How can light live with darkness? What harmony can there be between Christ and the devil? How can a believer be a partner with an unbeliever?

The Extra Mile: 2 Corinthians 6

The Bible warns us many times not to ally ourselves with unbelievers. Don't start a lawn business with someone who could cheat you. Don't allow a friend to cheat off your papers in school. Don't give money to someone you know will use it for wrong purposes.

It's difficult to make such decisions. A friend may be an unbeliever, but what's wrong with trusting him?

It's not that you shouldn't trust him, or think something is wrong with him. It's entrusting your life, your money, and your work to him. You must be careful to prevent him from having the wrong kind of influence in your life. If your values are fundamentally different from his, you may have difficulty making decisions together.

God wants you to make friends with nonbelievers. He wants you to hang around with them, do things with them that are fun and healthy. He doesn't want you to reject them. But he doesn't want you to let them to have control over your life.

Prayer: Lord, I will trust those people you show me to trust, and no one else.

Godly Sorrow

2 Corinthians 7:11: Just see what this godly sorrow produced in you! Such earnestness, such concern to clear yourselves, such indignation, such alarm, such longing to see me, such zeal, and such a readiness to punish wrong.

The Extra Mile: 2 Corinthians 7

In this passage, Paul refers to a situation that happened in the city of Corinth. A young man had sinned in a serious way. The Corinthians did nothing about it till someone reported it to Paul. He jumped in and confronted the problem.

But now all the Christians in Corinth were depressed, mixed up, and not sure what to do. Then Paul told them they needed to repent and experience some real "godly sorrow," sadness and guilt about doing something seriously wrong before God. That's precisely what happened to the Corinthians. They really dealt with the problem and worked hard to get everything straightened out.

God wants each of us to look straight at our wrongdoing, to feel some real sadness about it, and to have a desire to fix it.

Prayer: Lord, when I sin, show me. I will repent.

Bad Advice, Good Advice

2 Corinthians 8:10: Here is my advice: It would be good for you to finish what you started a year ago.

The Extra Mile: 2 Corinthians 8:1–11

Sam talked on the phone with his friend Len. "Well, what should I do?" he asked. "Meeker wants to beat me up."

Len said, "When you come to school, wrap your hand in a piece of chain. Then when you meet him behind the school, punch his face in."

Sam found the chain in the garage, but he worried all day that Meeker might have something worse in his hand. Finally, he went to his father and told him what might happen. His father said, "Why does this boy hate you so much?"

"Because he cheated off my math paper and I told the teacher."

"All right," his father said. "Then tell Meeker you're sorry for what happened, but if he's having trouble with his math problems, you'll be glad to help him with it."

"But what if he doesn't go for it?"

Sam's dad thought about it for a few minutes. "Then why don't you and I go meet with Meeker and his dad?"

Prayer: Father, thanks for being there to help me learn to solve my own problems and take care of myself.

Give What You Wish

2 Corinthians 8:12: Whatever you give is acceptable if you give it eagerly. And give according to what you have, not what you don't have.

The Extra Mile: 2 Corinthians 8:12–24

God wants us to give our money and our time to help others. The important thing, though, is that we give willingly. If you feel forced into it, or pushed, maybe that's a sign that you're not giving from your heart. God wants you to give from the heart. He wants you to enjoy giving. He doesn't want it to become a burden.

How much should you give? In the Old Testament, people often gave a "tithe." This was usually a tenth of whatever they earned. That means if you earn ten dollars, you give one dollar to the Lord.

In the New Testament, under Christ's rule, the tithe is not the rule. Instead, we are to give "as we prosper." This means you may want to give more than a tenth sometimes, and less than a tenth at other times.

Give thoughtfully and gratefully, and God will be pleased.

Prayer: Lord, let me give willingly. I will give from the heart, cheerfully and gladly.

Generous or Sparing?

2 Corinthians 9:6: Remember this—a farmer who plants only a few seeds will get a small crop. But the one who plants generously will get a generous crop.

The Extra Mile: 2 Corinthians 9

The Bible has a lot to say about generosity. It tells us in many places that giving of your property, money, and self will result in blessings to others and to yourself.

You probably don't have much to give at this stage of your life. A dollar here and there is probably about all you can give each week. But remember: you don't know how God will use your dollar. Maybe he'll send it to a missionary who ends up working far away with a people group who turns to Christ. Perhaps he might log that dollar for the work of a Bible translator for a people who have never had the Bible in their language. God could use it for a sports team that goes around playing other teams and sharing the gospel with their opponents.

You just never know how God will use your gifts. And ultimately, one day he will show you all the good you did with your little gifts.

Prayer: Father, let me give as much as I can and leave it all in your hands. You're an expert at making big things happen with little gifts.

The Weapons of God

2 Corinthians 10:4, 5: We use God's mighty weapons, not worldly weapons, to knock down the strongholds of human reasoning and to destroy false arguments. We destroy every proud obstacle that keeps people from knowing God. We capture their rebellious thoughts and teach them to obey Christ.

The Extra Mile: 2 Corinthians 10

Have you ever played war? There's a card game by that name. You may have played a video war game, or paintball, or laser tag, or even just run around the yard with fake guns and grenades.

We live in the middle of a war between God and the enemy, Satan. Lies and deceptions are the devil's weapons. Paul wrote that he used heavenly arguments to counter the rebellious thoughts of outsiders. The Holy Spirit equipped him to teach the truth.

Using such weapons as the truth, the Word of God, and the testimonies of those who have spoken the truth are all good ways of getting God's Word to skeptics, critics, and those who reject his gospel. Never give up on anyone, because God can use who you are and what you are to break through. Why not make a list today of the 10 most important people in your life who aren't Christians, and begin praying for them now?

The truth is a powerful weapon. It can break down walls, lies, hatred. Use the weapons of the Bible's truth and you will find some people will listen.

Prayer: Jesus, I know the truth is powerful. I will use it everywhere I go.

The Angel of Light

2 Corinthians 11:14: But I am not surprised! Even Satan disguises himself as an angel of light.

The Extra Mile: 2 Corinthians 11

He was such a nice guy. He smiled a lot. He spoke softly. And he was offering us some fun for free. Only one problem: what he was offering was drugs.

She seemed so smart. Her face almost glowed. She made everyone feel comfortable and happy. Only one problem: she was a medium and was going to help us talk to demons!

Sometimes the things Satan wants us to get involved with come in nicely-wrapped packages. The people who sell or give away these things are often nice and kind. They don't argue. They don't fight with you because they want to win you over.

The Bible says that Satan can appear as an angel of light. That means he can look like God himself when he wants to. He can look good and friendly. But in reality, he will eat you alive.

Prayer: Protect me from the enemy, Lord, but help me to fight when it's necessary.

How to Be Strong

2 Corinthians 12:10: That's why I take pleasure in my weaknesses, and in the insults, hardships, persecutions, and troubles that I suffer for Christ. For when I am weak, then I am strong.

The Extra Mile: 2 Corinthians 12

Bari was diagnosed with cancer when he was 16 years old. A friendly guy with many people who liked him, he worked as a reporter for the school newspaper and played second string on the basketball team. Many other students knew who he was, and it devastated them that this good, kind kid might die.

The cancer progressed and Bari got weaker and weaker. Soon he was bedridden. But strangely, every day, kids came to visit and Bari told them about his relationship with God. Many turned to Christ in real faith. God used Bari's weakness to change many people.

In time, Bari was so weak he couldn't even speak. But new kids came every day. A couple of friends sat with him and spoke the gospel to those who came by. They read the Bible to Bari, and he smiled and wept at various verses.

Bari went to be with the Lord at the age of 17. But many lives were influenced through his witness.

Prayer: Lord, I will never underestimate your power when I'm sick, hurting, or weak. You will use my weakness in a powerful way, if I let you.

Are You Called?

2 Corinthians 13:5: Examine yourselves to see if your faith is genuine. Test yourselves. Surely you know that Jesus Christ is among you; if not, you have failed the test of genuine faith.

The Extra Mile: 2 Corinthians 13

God has many ways to get his people walking with him. The Old Testament records how Moses was tending sheep and ended up finding Israel's God. On Mt. Sinai, Moses suddenly noticed this large bush on fire.

Moses stepped a little closer and God spoke to him. God wanted him to go back to Egypt. He wanted him to lead the Israelite people to their promised land. He wanted Moses to set his people free.

God told Moses what to do. His directions were clear. But what did Moses do? He quickly made an excuse about why he couldn't do it.

God doesn't give up easily, and he didn't with Moses. Moses became the first reluctant hero of the Bible. He didn't want to go. But in the end he went, and became one of the greatest leaders of all time.

Do you know where you stand with Christ? Are you ready to do what he tells you?

Prayer: Lord, I want you to know I will follow and obey you.

Not Made Up

Galatians 1:11: Dear brothers and sisters, I want you to understand that the gospel message I preach is not based on mere human reasoning.

The Extra Mile: Galatians 1:1–10

Joni and Molly sat together at lunch for the second time that week. Joni wanted to win her friend Molly to Christ. But it had been hard going.

"I talked to my dad about what you said," Molly told Joni as they munched on chips.

"What did he say?"

"He said the whole thing was made up," Molly answered. "It's just a story."

"You think it was all made up?" Joni asked, astounded.

"That's what my dad says."

"But what about all these years that people have believed? Wouldn't someone have found something by now to show that it's a legend?"

Molly nodded. "I guess we'll never know."

Was the gospel of Jesus made up? If it is, it's quite a lie. The disciples and martyrs since then died for believing it. Millions the world over tell the story because they've met Jesus. And history itself contains evidence.

Prayer: Jesus, I know the gospel is not made up, but some people believe it is. I will be patient with them. Please open their eyes to the truth.

Cycles of Sin

Galatians 1:20: *I declare before God that what I am writing to you is not a lie.*

The Extra Mile: Galatians 1:11–24

Anne had a problem. She told lies. Anytime she was in trouble, she made up a whopper. Sometimes she was caught. Sometimes no one found out what she'd done. But she didn't feel happy about it. Being a Christian, she knew lying was wrong.

She knew she needed to break the cycle. But how?

Jill, one of her Sunday school teachers, recommended the book of Judges. "The people kept falling into sin cycles," Anne's teacher said. "But they repented when the Lord sent them a judge."

Anne soon realized she needed someone like those judges to help her.

That Sunday in church, Anne talked to Jill again, and Jill said, "OK, every week we'll meet to pray. Then we'll talk about your week, how you did. I'll give you advice, and you'll tell me all the problem areas."

Anne was excited. The first week, she discovered telling the truth felt much better.

The second week, Jill helped her figure out ways to tell the truth always.

The third week, Anne found she hadn't told one lie.

What Jill did for Anne was "hold her accountable." That's someone who checks up on you and guides you through your problems.

Prayer: When I have problems I can't solve, Lord, I will find someone who will hold me accountable.

Crucified with Jesus

TUESDAY

Galatians 2:20: My old self has been crucified with Christ. It is no longer I who live, but Christ lives in me. So I live in this earthly body by trusting in the Son of God, who loved me and gave himself for me.

The Extra Mile: Galatians 2

Did you know that you have been put to death?

When Jesus died on the cross, in some spiritual, supernatural sense you were there on the cross with him. When he died, your old sin nature died. What's the sin nature? That's your old self, the person you were before you became a Christian. That person was prone to commit sin. That person wouldn't listen to truth, Jesus, or even his parents and friends. That person tended to do wrong things without really thinking them through.

But with Jesus, that person was killed. You now have a "new self" who is receptive to God, the Holy Spirit, parents, and others. This new self will try to do good things that make God's Word known in the world.

What about that old self? He's dead, but he's still around, like a ghost. He will try to get you to do wrong things again. But his power is broken. All you have to do is tell him to go away, and he will have to leave you in the hands of Jesus.

Prayer: I am a new person on the inside, Lord, so help me to act like it.

Doing Good Things, or Faith?

Galatians 3:11: So it is clear that no one can be made right with God by trying to keep the law. For the Scriptures say, "It is through faith that a righteous person has life."

The Extra Mile: Galatians 3

Many people today believe that getting into Heaven is all a matter of doing as much good as you can. They think when you die and get there before God, he will weigh your good deeds against your bad deeds. More good deeds, you go to Heaven; more bad deeds, Hell.

If this is the way it is about getting into Heaven, who will ever get in? Because God himself told us all our good deeds are like "filthy rags" (Isaiah 64:6). So we're in trouble with them. Also, God says we have to be perfect, like Jesus, to win Heaven. Who on earth is perfect besides Jesus?

So we're all in big trouble, unless there's another way. That's what Paul means here. He tells us we can't get salvation and Heaven by doing lots of good things. Rather, we get in by putting our faith in Christ. When we believe in him, God puts our sins on him on the cross, and they die with him. Then God transfers Jesus' good deeds to us by faith. That means, in God's eyes, we're as perfect as Jesus.

Prayer: I know believing in you, Jesus, is the key to eternal life, salvation, Heaven, and everything else. So I will stand with you.

Truly Free

THURSDAY

Galatians 4:31: So, dear brothers and sisters, we are not children of the slave woman; we are children of the free woman.

The Extra Mile: Galatians 4

Has anyone ever told you, "You can do anything you want"?

Do you believe it's true? Can we do whatever we want?

We can't fly to the moon. We can't run faster than the speed of sound. We can't just wish and become rich.

True freedom, according to the Bible, is the freedom to do what's right and good when it's necessary. Many people can't, or won't, do such things. They choose wrong ways and make wrong decisions. But when God set you free from your old life, he made it so that you can now make good and right decisions every time.

Think about what real freedom is. It's not doing anything and everything. Rather, it's the power to choose the best and right things every time. Even when we fail, we can know God will forgive us. Real freedom is living in the presence of God and knowing he is with us every moment.

That's what this verse is about. Faith in Jesus makes life better—now and for eternity.

Prayer: Lord, help me choose to do what's right every time.

Sinful Thoughts and Desires

Galatians 5:16: So I say, let the Holy Spirit guide your lives. Then you won't be doing what your sinful nature craves.

The Extra Mile: Galatians 5

All people have sinful desires: to overeat, to be lazy, to lie, to hate, to show prejudice, to be jealous, to take revenge, or to complain. There are many sinful desires we all face. None of us is immune.

How do you overcome these desires? How do you get them out of your mind and heart and live purely before God?

Martin Luther used to say that you can't stop the birds from flying over your head, but you can keep them from nesting in your hair. What he meant was you can't stop a bad thought from flitting into your mind, but you can stop yourself from dwelling on it and letting it grow.

That's the key. Through the Holy Spirit, ask God to alert you to bad thoughts. Then when they flit into your mind, refuse to think on them. Refuse to let them fester and deepen and send down roots. Don't begin to savor and enjoy them.

Paul says to let the Spirit live in you that way and you won't be overcome by sinful desires.

Prayer: Father, help me learn to say no to evil and say yes to good, for if I do I know I will find life easier, happier, and more worth living.

Don't Give Up Doing Good

Galatians 6:9: So let's not get tired of doing what is good. At just the right time we will reap a harvest of blessing if we don't give up.

The Extra Mile: Galatians 6

Do you ever feel as if doing good things for people doesn't help? They're still mean to you. Or they ignore you. Or worse, they put you down for being nice!

Sometimes it will seem as if doing good to others has no effect. No matter how many times you act nice, they're still sullen and mean.

Jesus understands how you feel. Imagine how he felt when after healing thousands of people, many of them turned on him. Many shouted for him to be crucified, even though he'd done nothing but good.

In the end, though, Jesus was rewarded for his goodness. He rose from the dead and reigns forever at God's right hand. In Hebrews 12, it even says that Jesus was able to endure the agonies of the cross because he knew the joy he would feel afterwards. In that way, he was rewarded for doing what was right for the whole world.

Prayer: Father, I know I will be rewarded for my good deeds. It might not happen today, or even next week. But I will be patient.

Chosen

Ephesians 1:4: Even before he made the world, God loved us and chose us in Christ to be holy and without fault in his eyes.

The Extra Mile: Ephesians 1

The whole class lined up on the sidelines. Then Alden and Marcus chose up teams.

Don hoped he would be chosen quickly. It was always better to be chosen first or second than tenth or eleventh. Only the poor players were chosen at the end.

Just as he hoped, Don was picked third. He ran over to Marcus's line and waited as the rest of the players were chosen.

It felt good to be part of a team and to be chosen. Don felt good all day about it, even after gym time was over.

Have you ever thought that just like we choose up teams on a playground, God chose you to be on his team? Yes, he chose you! Not last or because he had to, but because he loved you and wanted you to be on his team.

It's a marvelous thing to know you were chosen. It shows how great God's love is. He wanted to make sure you weren't left out. He wanted you to be there when that last count is made in Heaven.

So God chose you right away, from the very beginning, without looking back.

Prayer: God, thank you for picking me to be on your team. It's a great joy. Thanks especially that it doesn't depend on how good I am, but on how gracious and loving you are.

What Sin Looks Like to God

Ephesians 2:1, 2: Once you were dead because of your disobedience and your many sins. You used to live in sin, just like the rest of the world, obeying the devil—the commander of the powers in the unseen world.

The Extra Mile: Ephesians 2:1-7

Jon helped his father clean the car. They scoured the grease off the engine. They banged the rust off the tailpipe. They wiped dust off the dashboard.

When they were finished, John collected the rags they'd used and started to take them into the garage. "What are you doing?" his father asked.

"I'm gonna have Mom wash them," Jon said.

"No," his father answered. "They're too dirty. We'll have to burn them."

Jon and his dad walked into the backyard to an old barrel they used to burn trash in.

Would you want to towel yourself off after a bath with those rags? Of course not. But that's how God sees our sin—as filthy rags.

God doesn't leave our sin as rags. He gets rid of it completely through forgiveness. And then he cleans us and makes us white as snow.

You see, Jesus made a way to clean those rags of ours. He died on the cross and spilled his blood. In some incredible way, Jesus' blood makes us clean in God's sight. We don't have any dirty rags on anymore. God has made us clean all through.

Prayer: God, you are awesome! You clean the filthy rags of my sin.

Who Is Allowed?

Ephesians 2:8, 9: God saved you by his grace when you believed. And you can't take credit for this; it is a gift from God. Salvation is not a reward for the good things we have done, so none of us can boast about it.

The Extra Mile: Ephesians 2:8–22

In Dasen's school, you have to earn the privilege to go on a field trip. You have to complete your homework, show good citizenship, and sign a behavior contract before you get to go.

Some people think they have to earn their way to Heaven, but they're wrong. You don't have to do anything. When you put your faith in Jesus as your Lord and Savior he gives you the gift of eternal life in Heaven with him.

While you can't earn the gift of Heaven, you can respond in thanks for it. There's a psalm in the Old Testament (Psalm 15) that outlines things you can do to please God and show your gratitude to Him:

- Walk blamelessly.
- Do what is right.
- Speak the truth.
- Don't tell lies about other people.
- Don't wrong your neighbor.
- Keep your promises, even when they hurt you.

You are saved by faith like Ephesians 2:8, 9 says. You don't earn a place in Heaven. You can express your thanks, however, by living for God and obeying his Word.

Prayer: Lord, I want you to know how much I appreciate the gift of salvation. I will try to show my thanks by living the way you want me to.

Today, We Have a Special Message

Ephesians 3:4, 5: As you read what I have written, you will understand my insight into this plan regarding Christ. God did not reveal it to previous generations, but now by his Spirit he has revealed it to his holy apostles and prophets.

The Extra Mile: Ephesians 3:1-9

You and I are privileged. God has given us who live today a message that never existed in the time before Jesus came.

Paul wrote that God revealed to him and the other apostles and prophets of the first century the gospel and all the truth about Jesus and salvation. In Old Testament times God's people did not understand everything we know today. It all depended on the coming of Jesus.

You are special. God has given you this special message of how to be saved and go to Heaven and become his child. It's very precious. Don't scorn it, or think of it lightly, even though you may have heard it a million times. No one before Jesus ever heard it.

The truth is God has showered you with many blessings that have only come to us because of Jesus. Does that make you appreciate him more?

Prayer: Jesus, I know that without you, we are little more than nothing. But because of you we become the children of God, sent to change the world.

You're Being Watched and Studied

Ephesians 3:10: God's purpose in all this was to use the church to display his wisdom in its rich variety to all the unseen rulers and authorities in the heavenly places.

The Extra Mile: Ephesians 3:10–21

Did you know right now you're being watched and studied? Right now, angels are taking notes on your life and what you do with God's Word and the things you learn in church.

Can you imagine it? Some angel named Gabriel or Michael is sitting there next to you in school seeing how you choose not to cheat when you need an answer on a test. He's nodding when you're put in a tough spot after school with a kid who's new is being taunted by some of the bad kids. He's amazed as you sit down at lunch and bow your head and thank God before eating, even though some of the other kids snicker about it.

You're teaching angels right now about the grace, goodness, and power of God. Some of them don't even get it. But they'll watch you, and maybe today they'll learn something important.

Prayer: Father, I will always remember this: nothing I do in secret is really in secret. You and your angels are watching.

Letting It Rip

Ephesians 4:26, 27: And "don't sin by letting anger control you." Don't let the sun go down while you are still angry, for anger gives a foothold to the devil.

The Extra Mile: Ephesians 4:1–27

What can happen when you're really angry? We see a glimmer in Genesis 4:6, 7 where God said to Cain, "Why are you angry? Why are you looking so sad? Do what is right. Then you will be accepted. If you don't do what is right, sin is waiting at your door to grab you. It longs to have you. But you must rule over it."

Cain killed his brother Abel because he was jealous and angry. We see the same kind of anger in other people in the Bible: When King David's son Absalom became angry, he rebelled and almost took over the kingdom. When the apostle Paul first encountered Christians, he held the clothes of the haters of Stephen as they stoned him.

We do all kinds of wrong things when we become angry. Jesus says anger at a brother is the same as murder in God's eyes. When we call people "idiots," or "jerks," or "fools," God says we're in danger of being judged. How often do you say such things about others? Do you need to learn to curb your tongue?

Prayer: Help me not to sin by letting anger control me. Out of respect for you, Lord God, I will try to curb my tongue.

Keeping Silent

Ephesians 4:28: *If you are a thief, quit stealing. Instead, use your hands for good hard work, and then give generously to others in need.*

The Extra Mile: Ephesians 4:24–28

Matt needed some money for ice cream. He knew where to get it too: his mom's pocketbook. She wouldn't notice, and all he'd take was one dollar. He'd pay her back someday, he told himself.

Matt took the dollar. He bought the ice cream. It went down smooth and tasty. But one thing Matt forgot about. He had become a Christian the year before and he had a heavenly Father who knew what he'd done. God had to act to deal with Matt's thievery. What did God do? The very things David listed in Psalm 32 that God did to him when he sinned.

- His "body wasted away." He felt weak. He didn't have the energy he normally had.
- He "groaned all day." Inside his heart, he heard groaning and moaning. "Why did you do it?" "It's wrong."
- God's hand "was heavy on him." He felt as if a weight lay on his shoulders. It was God's hand!
- His "strength was sapped." He had no vitality, no enthusiasm. He felt dead inside.

Prayer: Father, help me to confess my sin, knowing you will forgive.

Foul Talk

Ephesians 4:29: Don't use foul or abusive language. Let everything you say be good and helpful, so that your words will be an encouragement to those who hear them.

The Extra Mile: Ephesians 4:28, 29

Jack and his friends hung out after school at the local movie theatre. Jack liked being with these boys, but one thing troubled him: they used coarse and foul language. They used every bad word he could think of.

The problem was that Jack found that he was using those words himself. Not at home or church. No, none of his Christian friends knew how bad Jack's mouth was. But with that group, he couldn't stop himself.

Do you have a problem with using foul language? A lot of young people do. We hear such words everywhere—among our friends, on TV, at the movies, in books.

God is not pleased with such talk. To take God's name in vain is the worst. When you do it, you treat God as if he were nothing.

Do you want to stop using that kind of talk? Memorize Ephesians 4:29. It tells us to stop letting that kind of talk come out of our mouths. Just stop it. Refuse to speak such words.

Prayer: Lord, let me say words that build up, cheer up, and encourage.

Grieving God

Ephesians 4:30: And do not bring sorrow to God's Holy Spirit by the way you live. Remember, he has identified you as his own, guaranteeing that you will be saved on the day of redemption.

The Extra Mile: Ephesians 4:30–32

Have you ever laughed about something you did wrong?

Have you ever told about some sin you committed like it was a joke?

Have you ever hurt someone else, and then snickered when they began to cry?

Sometimes people, even Christians, treat sin as if it were a big joke. "You should hear what Tilly did yesterday!"

But God never laughs at sin. In many places in the Bible we see how the people of Israel ran from sin to sin and only laughed. The prophets wept. They knew those people would pay for those sins with their lives.

It's an awful picture. God hurts when we sin. Our sin grieves him deeply. He weeps and cries out, "Why do they do this to me?"

Have you ever heard your mom or dad weep over something you did wrong? When we sin, people are hurt. Their lives are messed up. Sin is never funny. It always leads to pain.

Have you done things you know your parents would be horrified to learn about?

Stop! Now!

Prayer: Father, I'm so sorry for the times I have grieved you. I know that sin results in broken relationships, and I never want anything to come between me and you.

Deceiving a Parent

Ephesians 5:13, 14: But their evil intentions will be exposed when the light shines on them, for the light makes everything visible.

The Extra Mile: Ephesians 5:1-17

John's report card came home in the mail. John usually got home before his parents, so he had a plan. Get the report card. Open it. And change that D in Math to a B.

It was perfect. John got home, found the letter and went to work with his trusty pencil. When he was done, that D really did look like a B. He was happy.

His parents saw the report card, praised him for his good grades and signed off on it. All was well . . . until John's dad came upstairs to his room. He set the report card out in front of John and said, "Do you see anything odd here?"

John played dumb.

Then to John's horror, his father took an eraser and turned the B back into a D. "How did that happen?" he asked.

In the end, John confessed.

His father said, "Honesty and truth are more important than a grade, even a D."

Prayer: Sometimes I'm embarrassed or ashamed, Lord. I'm tempted to cover up my failures. But I know you see them, and you don't condemn me.

A New Song in My Heart

Ephesians 5:18, 19: *Instead, be filled with the Holy Spirit, singing psalms and hymns and spiritual songs among yourselves, and making music to the Lord in your hearts.*

The Extra Mile: Ephesians 5:18–33

Have you ever heard a song over and over in your head?

Maybe you heard it on the radio this morning when you woke up. Maybe someone sang it at school. Maybe it's an old song you heard in church.

Sometimes a song you can't get out of your mind is annoying, especially if it's a silly song, or a commercial jingle, or one you don't like.

Other times, when you have a song in your heart, you feel good, like life is all right and you have real joy.

Sometimes a song on Christian radio speaks to a problem you're having and it encourages you to trust God. Sometimes a hymn sung in worship reminds you of God's goodness, and you sing out in praise to him. When doing hard physical labor some people like to sing to help them keep moving and banish boredom.

Music speaks in different situations to different people. God gives music as a gift, and as a way to praise him. How do you make music in your heart?

Prayer: Father God, I love you so much! I'll sing one of my favorite praise songs just for you!

Put On the Armor

Ephesians 6:11: Put on all of God's armor so that you will be able to stand firm against all strategies of the devil.

The Extra Mile: Ephesians 6:1–12

Have you ever thought about being a knight in shining armor, or a lady rescued by a knight?

Here's your chance. Every Christian is engaged in a war with the devil. The enemy deceives, tempts, lies, and taunts us to get us to sin. Getting us to give in to temptation is a great victory for the enemy. As a result, we have to beware of the enemy's tricks and learn to fight against them.

How do we fight? In Ephesians 6 Paul uses the image of the Roman soldier to show us how to fight. He wants us to dress in spiritual armor. This is armor that works in the spiritual realms and can defeat spiritual forces. What is it? Telling the truth, being a good person, always being ready to share the gospel, and exercising faith at all times. Paul uses actual pieces of armor to describe these things. He also calls the Bible the "sword of the Spirit," because it can cut the enemy to smithereens.

When we wear this spiritual armor, we can defeat the enemy every time.

But fail to wear it, and you will be at the enemy's mercy.

Which do you think is better?

Prayer: Lord, help me to get that armor on every day, and no one will ever be able to defeat me permanently.

The Sword of the Spirit

Ephesians 6:17: Put on salvation as your helmet, and take the sword of the Spirit, which is the word of God.

The Extra Mile: Ephesians 6:13–24

You are in a battle for God's kingdom. All around you, fighting rages. Some spiritual forces are trying to trip you up, to keep you from doing good things, to stop you from telling a friend about Jesus. Others are encouraging you to do all those things. And in the middle of it all, the Spirit of God leads you, teaches you, encourages you, and heals your battle wounds.

In Ephesians 6, Paul lists the Roman soldier's pieces of armor and how they relate to spiritual realities. The belt holds everything together, and it's the truth. The breastplate, which protects your heart and vital organs, is righteousness, holy character, and integrity.

All the elements are defensive, except for the sword. The sword was the Roman soldier's main weapon for battle. For the Christian, the sword represents the God's Word, the Bible. It's what the Spirit uses to convict, lead, fix, and help others.

Can you use the Bible for good in your life and others? Are you memorizing verses so you know them when a situation arises? Do you meditate on them, to learn more about what they mean and how they apply?

Prayer: Lord, get me in the fight. I'm on your side always.

Sell Everything You Have

Philippians 1:21: For to me, living means living for Christ, and dying is even better.

The Extra Mile: Philippians 1

What if Jesus said this to you? "If you really want to be saved, go, give away everything you own. Then follow me, and you will have eternal life." It sounds like earning your faith by doing something, doesn't it?

But in the case of one person in Mark 10, something else was going on. This man asked Jesus what he needed to do to gain eternal life. Jesus told him to keep the commandments. The man, somewhat proudly, replied that he'd kept them all from his youth. That was impossible, but Jesus decided not to argue with him. Instead, Jesus tested the man to see if he would obey. Jesus told the man to sell everything and give to the poor.

This man turned away at that moment. He couldn't give up his great wealth to follow Jesus. Contrast him with Paul's attitude above: to Paul, every day, every moment was for Jesus.

Salvation is never based on us doing anything for Jesus, but on faith. Because we want to show our love for him, we live every day in the power, leadership, guidance, and love of Jesus. Is that where you are these days?

Prayer: Father, I see that Paul went through many bad times as a Christian. But one thing kept him through it all: your presence, love, and care. So I will depend on you too.

The Right Attitude

Philippians 2:5, 6: You must have the same attitude that Christ Jesus had. Though he was God, he did not think of equality with God as something to cling to.

The Extra Mile: Philippians 2

Have you ever been accused of having a bad attitude?

Sometimes Christians exhibit bad attitudes by complaining, putting others down, gossiping, and cutting up. But the Bible is clear that God wants us to have right attitudes.

Just what is a right attitude?

In these verses in Philippians 2 we see what God considers a right attitude. It consists of humility for one thing, not thinking you're more important than others. Jesus was God incarnate. He deserved to be worshiped by everyone he met. Yet he was humble. He didn't demand that others worship him.

In the same way, we are children of God. We will live forever. God is our friend, leader, and master. But that doesn't mean we should go around acting like we're the royal family.

Instead, we are to gladly obey God in all situations. That means doing unpleasant jobs like cleaning your dad's car or mowing the lawn with gladness, even joy. It means listening to your parents even when you think what they want is dumb or strange.

Prayer: Father, I know attitude is important. The right attitude will take me far. But the wrong one will mess things up.

Do You Have Enough Breath?

Philippians 3:1: Whatever happens, my dear brothers and sisters, rejoice in the Lord. I never get tired of telling you these things, and I do it to safeguard your faith.

The Extra Mile: Philippians 3

Psalm 150 concludes, "Let everything that breathes sing praises to the Lord."

So ask yourself this: Could you ever have enough breath to praise God, to rejoice in him, like the above passage says?

You probably think, "Sure. I can praise him easily."

But try this. Praise him first for your family, each one. Mention something specific you can praise God for about each of them.

Now go to your school. Praise God for each teacher, the principal, and the kids in your class. Stop and think of something unique to each one, and praise God for them.

OK, now think of your room. Praise God for each of the things in it: toys, games, clothes, furniture, decorations. Tell God what you like about each thing.

Tired yet? We're not done.

Praise God for your neighborhood, your community, your city, your state, and your country. Praise God for all his creation, including this planet and others. Praise God for the hope you have in the future in Heaven with him, when you'll spend eternity in praise!

Prayer: Lord, I praise you with all my heart, right now.

Don't Worry!

Philippians 4:6: Don't worry about anything; instead, pray about every-thing. Tell God what you need, and thank him for all he has done.

The Extra Mile: Philippians 4:1–7

Liz worried that kids would think her new haircut looked stupid.

Josh worried that he would get cut from the baseball team.

Sunnie was always anxious about the latest test. Would she pass?

And Gardner was never sure he was dressed properly. Would the kids laugh at him?

Worry can make a nice day feel bad. It can destroy a fun party or a happy day at school. Constant worry can paralyze you so that you can't do anything. Some people worry so much that they just stay in bed all day.

Do you worry much? If so, Philippians 4:6 is a good verse to know and memorize. It tells us not to worry about anything. The moment worry hits, pray. Tell God what you're worried about and then leave it in his hands. God's promise is that he will give you supernatural peace when you let him handle the problem you're worried about.

What are you anxious about today? Stop! Take it to the Lord and leave it in his hands.

Don't you feel better already?

Prayer: Lord, here's something I'm worried about. I will leave it with you, knowing you'll help me and give me peace.

When You Can't Sleep

Philippians 4:8: And now, dear brothers and sisters, one final thing. Fix your thoughts on what is true, and honorable, and right, and pure, and lovely, and admirable. Think about things that are excellent and worthy of praise.

The Extra Mile: Philippians 4:8–23

Clu fought many battles. In school, he faced some bullies nearly every day. He struggled to understand math. And sometimes a certain girl made him so angry! So how did Clu find peace when times were tough?

He meditated on God and his Word as he lay on his bed.

Imagine it. You're lying on your nice warm bed at home. You lay very still. But suddenly you have an itch. You scratch. You lie still again. It's not that comfortable. You switch positions. You notice it's hot.

Then the worries come: that test tomorrow, that kid who has been harassing you in the hallway, that paper you haven't started that's due next week, what you'll say to Mom and Dad if you get a bad grade.

The worries just roll around in your head, each one like a barbed tumble-weed that pokes and irritates.

What should you do? Do what Clu did: turn to God's Word. "I am with you." "Don't worry, pray." "Give thanks in everything."

You may not know where all the Scriptures are, but now is a time when you can think about them and even begin to practice them. Thank God for being with you. Pray about the things that are troubling you. Give thanks for some of the positives of the day.

Prayer: Lord, teach me to meditate on your Word so it's always in my heart.

A Wondrous Miracle

Colossians 1:16: For through him God created everything in the heavenly realms and on earth. He made the things we can see and the things we can't see—such as thrones, kingdoms, rulers, and authorities in the unseen world. Everything was created through him and for him.

The Extra Mile: Colossians 1

Imagine it! You're standing next to God, Jesus, and the Holy Spirit. They're going to do something never before seen in history. They're going to create a universe.

Jesus speaks and suddenly light pierces the darkness. It's never been seen before. You stand there, your jaw dropping. "Why, it's beautiful, Lord."

Jesus speaks again and land separates from the waters. Earth looks like a blue, sparkling gem in space.

He speaks again. This time vegetables, fruit trees, and all kinds of crops appear on the earth like a carpet. Birds, fish, and animals of all kinds swarm the planet.

Then Jesus says, "I'm not done yet." This time he does the greatest miracle of all. He creates two humans who love each other. They're perfect.

You're about to cheer, but then Jesus has you look down the centuries. One day a baby forms in a womb—your mother's. That baby is you.

Prayer: Thank you, Lord, for life, for everything. I love you.

Those Jewish Vegetarians

Colossians 2:20–22: You have died with Christ, and he has set you free from the spiritual powers of this world. So why do you keep on following the rules of the world, such as, "Don't handle! Don't taste! Don't touch!"? Such rules are mere human teachings about things that deteriorate as we use them.

The Extra Mile: Colossians 2

Food is not something we tend to think much about. Mom sets down dinner. We eat it. End of story.

Of course, each of us has preferences: steak, hamburger . . . peas?

For Jews in Old Testament times, food was extremely important. What you ate showed your obedience and faith in God. God wanted his people to be set apart from other nations, so he gave them specific instructions about what they could and could not eat. Sometimes this was hard. People just didn't understand why Jews couldn't eat pork. They weren't friendly to Jews because of such restrictions.

God doesn't ask us in our time to be vegetarians. But obedience in other matters is just as important as not eating certain foods was to Jews. Telling the truth, giving some of your earnings to the church, obeying your parents—these are ways you set yourself apart to please God.

Prayer: Lord, I won't worry about what foods to eat, but I will seek to be different from those who don't believe in you.

Forgive Like God Forgives

Colossians 3:13: Make allowance for each other's faults, and forgive anyone who offends you. Remember, the Lord forgave you, so you must forgive others.

The Extra Mile: Colossians 3:1–17

James and his friend Jackson had a problem. Jackson had stolen a couple of James's action figures. James found out and he was really mad. Jackson knew it was wrong, though, and finally he walked over to James's house with the action figures in his pocket.

"Here," he said to James when they met. "I shouldn't have done it."

James snatched the action figures out of Jackson's hand. "I thought you were my friend!"

"I am," Jackson pleaded. "I just made a stupid mistake."

"Well, we're not friends anymore. What else did you steal?"

Jackson shook his head. "Nothing. I never took anything else."

James slammed the door in Jackson's face and went upstairs. It was then that the Spirit of God went into action. The still small voice said, "God has forgiven you for doing bad things. Don't you think you should forgive Jackson?"

James thought about it. "Yeah," he finally said. He walked to the phone and called Jackson. "I'm sorry, Jackson," James said. "I forgive you. Want to come over and play?"

Prayer: Lord, I know you have forgiven me. Help me to forgive like you do.

The Power of Obedience

Colossians 3:20: Children, always obey your parents, for this pleases the Lord.

The Extra Mile: Colossians 3:18-25

When God finally moved the people of Israel to the promised land, he gave them a choice: blessing or cursing. If they obeyed God, they would be blessed. If they disobeyed, they would be cursed. Blessing meant prosperity, joy, peace, and hope. Cursing meant failure, slavery, and all kinds of real bad stuff no one wanted to think about.

Unfortunately, because of disobedience, Israel mostly got cursing.

Did you know the same principles apply to us today? God will discipline us if we disobey in order to cause us to turn back to him. That discipline can be extremely painful for some of us. Because of disobedience, Christians have lost businesses, homes, families, children, and everything dear to them.

Do you want blessing in your life? Do you want the things God longs to give you, not just the things you long for? Then obey God's Word. When it says not to cheat, refuse to cheat. When it says not to lie, refuse to lie.

Prayer: Father, let me seek your blessing every morning, noon, and night.

Better Than Texting

Colossians 4:2–4: Devote yourselves to prayer with an alert mind and a thankful heart. Pray for us, too, that God will give us many opportunities to speak about his mysterious plan concerning Christ. That is why I am here in chains. Pray that I will proclaim this message as clearly as I should.

MONDAY

The Extra Mile: Colossians 4

Paul was never shy about asking his friends to pray for him. He knew the real power of his preaching came from God through the prayers that were lifted to God for him. Can you imagine a missionary, preacher, or even a friend in school making it in life without prayer? How about you?

You don't have to spend days in prayer to get God's attention. Short prayers are just as powerful as long prayers. Prayers said when you have a headache are just as strong as when you're up and feeling great. What matters is your heart. Are you sincere? Are you in tune with God? Have you confessed any sins you may have? A right attitude can do much in God's world. He will work on behalf of a committed Christian every time.

Try to spend some time every day in prayer. You can take to God anything that concerns you. Don't worry about God hearing you. He hears all your prayers. Some you may have prayed years ago. But God never forgets.

Prayer: Thank you, Lord, that I can come to you with anything that concerns me. You are God of the universe, but you still have time for me.

Marks of a Good Church

I Thessalonians I:3: As we pray to our God and Father about you, we think of your faithful work, your loving deeds, and the enduring hope you have because of our Lord Jesus Christ.

The Extra Mile: 1 Thessalonians 1

What makes a good church? Is it powerful preaching? Is it people who show up every Sunday in large numbers? Is it the amount of money that the people give?

In this passage, Paul lists three things that made him think fondly of the Thessalonian Christians. First, it was their "faithful work." They served God where they were. They did things faithfully. They didn't do half-baked jobs, but they finished them.

Second, Paul mentioned their "loving deeds." These were people who reached out to others, gave help, and loved them heartily. They not only felt kindly toward each other, but they acted on their feelings and did good things for each other.

Third, they had an "enduring hope." This is what motivated them. They hung in there through bad times. They kept their eyes on Jesus, and Heaven.

Do those things describe you?

Prayer: Lord, I will make it my purpose to work faithfully, do loving things for others, and hold to my faith in you.

Sharing in God's Glory

1 Thessalonians 2:12: We pleaded with you, encouraged you, and urged you to live your lives in a way that God would consider worthy. For he called you to share in his Kingdom and glory.

The Extra Mile: 1 Thessalonians 2:1-12

Do you enjoy watching fireworks? Usually the display starts with simple starbursts, and then gets more and more complicated and spectacular, building to a climax at the grand finale. Everything starts firing at once. The fireworks are higher and louder, and the night sky looks like a churning cauldron of light with sparks everywhere. It's amazingly beautiful.

God's glory is his greatness, his power, and his love displayed before the world. The truth is that God's glory is something beyond description. If God showed himself to us in all his brilliance, power, and beauty, we would surely die on the spot. It would be too much. We would be overwhelmed.

We worship a God who is the greatest being in the universe. He's not just a larger version of us. He's so far beyond us we can't imagine what he is like. He is all-powerful, all-knowing, able to be everywhere at once, utterly holy, and infinitely loving.

Prayer: Father, your glory is so great, we should spend every minute of our lives worshiping you.

How We Got the Bible

THURSDAY

1 Thessalonians 2:13: Therefore, we never stop thanking God that when you received his message from us, you didn't think of our words as mere human ideas. You accepted what we said as the very word of God—which, of course, it is.

The Extra Mile: 1 Thessalonians 2:13-16

Ever wonder how we got the Bible? Do you ever wonder if one of those prophets or apostles could make up things on his own? Could he put things in the Bible that God didn't tell him? Could he throw in a joke now and then, just to make it interesting?

In the Old Testament in Numbers 22–24, we read of a king who wanted one of God's prophets to curse the people of God. Balaam knew God. He also knew he couldn't do what King Balak wanted. But because of the money involved, he wanted to try. God told Balaam not to do it. Balaam went for it anyway. God then had Balaam's mule tell the prophet what an idiot he was. In the end, Balaam could only say what God told him to say. No more. No less.

And that reveals a marvelous truth. The writers of the Bible couldn't say anything except what God told them to say. We can be confident the Bible is the Word of God because of its power and truth.

Prayer: Thank you, God, that you speak to me through your Word. It's like a personal love letter from you to me.

How Long Will You Not Answer?

1 Thessalonians 2:18: We wanted very much to come to you, and I, Paul, tried again and again, but Satan prevented us.

The Extra Mile: 1 Thessalonians 2:17–20

How long will you do nothing, God? Don't you care?"

Have you ever asked that question? If so, you're in good company. One of the Bible's prophets in the Old Testament asked that question over and over. He felt that God didn't care because God didn't answer.

He was wrong. When Habakkuk called out to God, God did answer. Habakkuk asked God why he did nothing about all the violence and sin he saw in Israel. God replied that he was doing something. He planned to raise up the Chaldeans, a vicious nation, to punish Israel.

Now Habakkuk was in a real fix. God actually was going to do something Habakkuk didn't expect or want.

Do you ever think God isn't answering your prayers?

He is. But he works on his timeline. He has good reasons for the delay.

Prayer: Lord, I believe you will do what is best at the time that is best. Help me to be patient when I'm in a hurry for you to answer my prayers.

Follow Up

1 Thessalonians 3:7: So we have been greatly encouraged in the midst of our troubles and suffering, dear brothers and sisters, because you have remained strong in your faith.

The Extra Mile: 1 Thessalonians 3

"I'm so scared Lexie's given up by now," Gracie said to her mother. Gracie had led her cousin Lexie to the Lord when she visited a month ago. But she had heard nothing from Lexie since she'd returned home. Lexie's parents didn't go to church and her father was very against Christianity.

"She's in God's hands," her mother said. "But you should e-mail her."

Gracie did, and Lexie quickly responded. "I'm so great," Lexie said. "My friend Darla goes to a nice church and I'm going with her. I really love Jesus. He's answered some prayers. I'll tell you about them when I have more time."

Gracie ran in to tell her mother. They both rejoiced, and then they prayed that Lexie would stay strong.

Prayer: Help me to encourage young Christians, Dear God. Please give me the encouragement I sometimes need.

Gone!

I Thessalonians 4:16, 17: For the Lord himself will come down from heaven with a commanding shout, with the voice of the archangel, and with the trumpet call of God. First, the Christians who have died will rise from their graves. Then, together with them, we who are still alive and remain on the earth will be caught up in the clouds to meet the Lord in the air.

The Extra Mile: 1 Thessalonians 4

One day it will happen. Joey will be standing in line at the movies, and suddenly he'll disappear before everyone's eyes.

Karly will be washing the dishes. Then, whoosh! She's gone. No more dishes to do ever again!

Ally will be getting ready for bed. Suddenly, wow! She's no longer there. There's just a pile of clothes at the end of her bed.

Have you ever thought about what will happen when Jesus comes again? The Bible says there will be a shout, the voice of an angel and the sound of a trumpet. All believers, even those who are dead, will be whisked up to Heaven. We'll meet Jesus in the air. It will be the greatest reunion of all time!

Are you looking forward to that time? It could happen in your lifetime. The important thing is that you're ready. Are you a Christian? Have you trusted Jesus with your life and soul? If you have, then you're ready.

Prayer: Jesus, I look forward to your return to earth. Help me to be ready, and to be about your work while I wait.

Take Time to Give Thanks

1 Thessalonians 5:18: Be thankful in all circumstances, for this is God's will for you who belong to Christ Jesus.

The Extra Mile: 1 Thessalonians 5

How does a person give thanks to God? Here are some ways, based on psalms written by David in the Old Testament:

- Thank God for whatever you have—your body, your mind, your home, your food, everything you have in life
- Tell others what God has done for you
- Sing your thanks in songs
- Rejoice in the good things God has given you
- Reflect on God's character qualities. Thank him for all he is
- Remember the ways God has blessed you in the past

Why not read 1 Thessalonians 5 today and put those words into practice? Begin thanking God for everything and don't stop. Then tell others what you're thankful for about him.

Giving thanks is something God wants us all to do, and learn to do with excellence.

Prayer: Lord, I want to thank you. I will express my thanks in every way I know how.

Prompts

2 Thessalonians 1:11: So we keep on praying for you, asking our God to enable you to live a life worthy of his call. May he give you the power to accomplish all the good things your faith prompts you to do.

The Extra Mile: 2 Thessalonians 1

Viva stood about to pitch the kickball, when a thought came into her head. "Make it nice and slow. You know Berta is not very good at this."

Viva was a Christian and she knew God sometimes talked to her like this. But this one seemed weird. Should she treat the other kids differently, giving the easy pitches to the not-so-good ones?

She thought about it as Berta stepped up to the plate. The girl looked a little scared, as she always did. But then Viva pitched a nice, slow, easy-to-kick roller.

Berta kicked, connected, and the ball tumbled down toward second base. She ran for first base, but was out. When she headed back to her team, she looked at Viva and smiled.

Helping a friend like that is always a good thing to do. Never cheat. Never throw a game so someone will succeed. But if it's possible to do so, give everyone a chance. It's the right thing to do.

Prayer: Lord, I'm not sure sometimes if you are prompting me to do something. I will keep trying to listen to your still, small voice inside me.

The Lawless One

2 Thessalonians 2:9, 10: This man will come to do the work of Satan with counterfeit power and signs and miracles. He will use every kind of evil deception to fool those on their way to destruction, because they refuse to love and accept the truth that would save them.

The Extra Mile: 2 Thessalonians 2

Paul wrote that at the end of human history a great event will happen. A ruler will arise who is so much like the devil that some will think he is Satan himself. This person is called the "antichrist," because he is "against Jesus."

He is called the antichrist also because he will perform miracles. He will perform signs in the sky. He will have the power to do all kinds of wonders. What these are we don't know.

Whatever he can do, though, it will be a form of deception. They won't be real miracles that change a person's life for good. They'll be the kind that lead people into evil.

After doing all these miracles and deceiving many people, he will tell the world that he is God. But God will not allow him to succeed for eternity.

Prayer: Father, sometimes I'm afraid of the future, but I know that in the end, you will protect me and you will win.

Causing Doubt

2 Thessalonians 3:3: But the Lord is faithful; he will strengthen you and guard you from the evil one.

The Extra Mile: 2 Thessalonians 3:1-9

Satan is always at work trying to lead people away from God. One of his tactics is to cause people to doubt God.

Trusting God is an awesome thing. You can't see him. Often, you can't feel him either. Situations get worse. People attack you. Nothing goes right. That's the very time Satan will tempt you to reject God.

Don't fall for Satan's schemes! Look to God. Admit you need his help. Tell him about your fears. And then plow ahead, believing God will come through, and he will. Maybe not immediately, and maybe not the way you hope, but God will do what is best.

God is worthy of our trust. Satan is a liar.

Prayer: Lord, I will always trust you. You can and will act on my behalf when you know it is best.

THURSDAY

The Lesson of the Ant

2 Thessalonians 3:10: Even while we were with you, we gave you this command: "Those unwilling to work will not get to eat."

The Extra Mile: 2 Thessalonians 3:10–12

Josh lay in bed thinking. Saturday! What a day! How nice it would be to sleep in and take it easy. Why cut two more lawns today? Why not wait till next week?

Josh thought about it. He had to act now. Lawn-cutting season would soon be over. He could always play video games. But he couldn't cut lawns in the winter. What was the lesson of Thessalonians? That he should cut lawns now while he could. He could play later.

Josh shook his head. Why did God always have to make such sense? Why did the Spirit have to speak to him right then?

Maybe because God cared about Josh, and wanted him to not become lazy.

Prayer: Lord, let me do the work you have for me when the time is right.

Keep Doing Good

2 Thessalonians 3:13: As for the rest of you, dear brothers and sisters, never get tired of doing good.

The Extra Mile: 2 Thessalonians 3:13-18

Do you ever feel like saying, "What's the use? Nothing gets better. No matter how nice I am to others, they still don't like me."

Many people struggle with that feeling. God says to you, "Keep doing right. Keep believing. Keep sticking with me. I will lead you."

Being a good person in this world isn't easy. Many times it looks like lying is the way to get out of trouble with your teacher or parents. Sometimes it seems like gossiping about kids in school, hurting their reputation, would improve yours. Often, it looks like the goody-goodies of this world get the bad deal.

But do you know what God says? Same thing: "Keep doing right. Keep believing. Keep sticking with me. I will lead you."

Doing good is not easy. It doesn't always have an immediate reward. Sometimes you will be put down or hated for doing what's right.

Prayer: Lord, I won't give up. You are with me and will bless me. I have confidence in you.

Why Jesus Came

1 Timothy 1:15: This is a trustworthy saying, and everyone should accept it: "Christ Jesus came into the world to save sinners"—and I am the worst of them all.

The Extra Mile: 1 Timothy 1

Jesus came into our world to do miracles, but they only confirmed that he had great power and was from God. Jesus came to speak wonderful words of hope that teach us how to live and believe.

This verse, 1 Timothy 1:15, tells us the main reason Jesus came: to save sinners. Every person in human history has done things wrong. Some have lied. Others have stolen. Many have cheated. A few have murdered and committed other evil deeds.

No matter how good we've been as people, though, none of us has lived a perfect life. God says everything we've done wrong must be paid for. When Jesus died on the cross, he paid the price for our sins once and for all.

Prayer: Dear God, it's hard to comprehend how the sacrifice of Jesus on the cross could pay for my sins. But I'm so grateful it did! Thank you.

Love Story: Dressing Up

1 Timothy 2:9: *And I want women to be modest in their appearance. They should wear decent and appropriate clothing and not draw attention to themselves by the way they fix their hair or by wearing gold or pearls or expensive clothes.*

The Extra Mile: 1 Timothy 2

It's all over advertising, billboards, the Internet, and everywhere else. Kids want to dress cool so others notice, but sometimes they go too far.

For some young people, the idea of dressing sexy doesn't get noticed till they're in high school. For others, it starts earlier. Some girls are in bikinis at age six.

Just because advertisers show kids dressed in skimpy or revealing clothes doesn't mean it's right. It's not. You may think that wearing them makes you look stylish, or it shows off your beautiful body. But calling attention to your body is not something you should be doing.

The Bible isn't against dressing to look nice, or even cool. It draws the line, though, at what this Bible verse is talking about. Don't be sucked in by "fashion."

Prayer: Lord, I will work at being truly cool by being kind, loving, and giving, because that's your definition of cool.

A Good Name

1 Timothy 3:7: Also, people outside the church must speak well of him so that he will not be disgraced and fall into the devil's trap.

The Extra Mile: 1 Timothy 3

Everyone is known for something. Some rock stars are well known for destroying hotel rooms, for being "loose" sexually, for doing drugs, and for getting drunk. Some actors and actresses are known for being talented but hard to work with. Some are known for the number of divorces they've gone through. Some athletes are known for being great on the field but constantly in trouble with illegal activity.

What are you known for? What's your reputation? When someone thinks of you, do they think of someone honorable and trustworthy? Are you a good worker and a reliable friend? When people hear your name do they think, "Christian"? When people see you, do they see Jesus?

Prayer: Lord, what am I known for? I will guard my reputation so you can shine through me.

You're Just a Kid!

1 Timothy 4:12: Don't let anyone think less of you because you are young. Be an example to all believers in what you say, in the way you live, in your love, your faith, and your purity.

The Extra Mile: 1 Timothy 4:1-13

Timothy had a problem. He was young, perhaps not much older than you. Paul gave him the responsibility to lead a church and help people learn to walk with Jesus. Some of these people were very old. Why should they listen to someone like Timothy? He was just a kid!

Have you ever felt like that? Why should anyone listen to you? You're only 10 years old, or 12 or 13. You're just a kid!

Don't let it bother you. God can use you and speak through you as much as any older person. Your opinions are important. If you know your Bible better than others, why not share it? Why not teach the class something you've just learned?

Never let anyone look down on you because you're just a kid. Sure, you should be humble. Don't demand to be heard. Remember that people older than you have had more life experience.

But in the end, if God decides to use you, then give yourself to the Lord completely. Don't hold back. God can work through you whether you're 4, 15, or 50.

Prayer: Lord, I will never let being young hold me back. I will get into the fight for your kingdom.

WEDNESDAY

Devoted to the Word

THURSDAY

1 Timothy 4:15: Give your complete attention to these matters. Throw yourself into your tasks so that everyone will see your progress.

The Extra Mile: 1 Timothy 4:14–16

"He reads the Bible every day, Dad," Julie said to her father one night about a boy in her science class. "He knows all kinds of Bible verses too."

"How do you know?" her dad asked.

"At the Bible study after school," Julie answered. "On Wednesdays, he started a little Bible study for us. I can't believe how well he knows the Bible. And he's only 12 years old."

"Yeah, imagine what he'll be like when he's 25."

"Or 45, like you, Dad."

If you want to stand out from the crowd, learn your Bible. How can you do this? Here are several suggestions:

- Read your Bible daily, a chapter or two
- Memorize interesting or important verses. When you find one, write it down and get it into your head
- Meditate and think about the verses and consider ways to apply them to your life

What do you think will happen when you get God's Word into your mind and heart? You will grow!

Prayer: Lord, help me to learn to read and study and memorize your Word. I want to become a person devoted to your Book.

Bad People Sometimes Have It Good

1 Timothy 5:24: Remember, the sins of some people are obvious, leading them to certain judgment. But there are others whose sins will not be revealed until later.

The Extra Mile: 1 Timothy 5

Have you ever noticed that sometimes bad people have it good? The "bad girls" are the most popular. The tough guys who don't care about school always have money and other kids hanging around them. Being bad is in. Being good is stupid.

It's not a new feeling. In fact, centuries ago, a man named Asaph noticed the problem too. It appeared to him that wicked people often made a lot of money. They had the big houses and real estate. All the beautiful girls hung around with them.

It's easy to look at the bad guys and girls and think they have it made. But one day they'll have to stand up in front of God and explain everything they did in this life, and it won't be a happy explanation: "I didn't care. I don't like your rules. I hate you. Get away from me."

God will get away. In fact, he'll send them somewhere where they can be bad all they want; alone, in darkness, with no one but themselves to be bad to.

Prayer: Dear God, help me to resist Satan's scheme to make evil attractive and exciting.

The Danger of Being Rich

1 Timothy 6:9: But people who long to be rich fall into temptation and are trapped by many foolish and harmful desires that plunge them into ruin and destruction.

The Extra Mile: 1 Timothy 6

Have you ever wished you were rich? What do you think it would be like?

Riches are a blessing. God gives riches to some people, not because they're better than anyone else, but because he chooses. He gives wisdom and intelligence and business sense so that some people can earn riches. Whatever they have is ultimately from God.

But God doesn't give riches to everyone. There's great danger in being rich, or in wanting to be rich. Some people are willing to do anything, even evil things, to get rich. For some people riches become a trap. They're never happy. They always want more. Some use their riches extravagantly and end up losing everything.

If you're rich, God tells you to be generous. And if you're not rich, don't worry about it.

Prayer: God, I can depend on you to give me the best gifts. If one of those gifts is riches, I will use it for you.

When God Calls

2 Timothy 1:6: This is why I remind you to fan into flames the spiritual gift God gave you when I laid my hands on you.

The Extra Mile: 2 Timothy 1:1-6

Have you ever felt a "nudge" from God? Maybe you're sitting in class and suddenly you feel this little voice inside telling you to say a kind word to someone. Maybe you're listening in church when God tells you to give that whole $10 you've been saving to the missions offering. It could be anything. God often nudges us to get us to do something.

God may call you at times to do something that seems unimportant. How do you know if it's God? One, the thing he asks will not be sinful. Two, what he asks will not be stupid (like standing up in church and yelling out that the Cubs will win the pennant next year). Three, it will be something that your heart wants to do.

Prayer: Lord, I know if I'm listening, you will nudge me now and then. So I will listen. You may be calling me today.

WEEK
41

What the Spirit Does in Us

MONDAY

2 Timothy 1:7: For God has not given us a spirit of fear and timidity, but of power, love, and self-discipline.

The Extra Mile: 2 Timothy 1:7–18

How does the Spirit work in us?

Some have imagined that we're like a glove. When you lay the glove on a table, it can't do anything. It has no power, no nothing.

But if you put your hand into the glove, you can make that glove do all kinds of things. Grip a bat. Pick up a pin. Make a fist.

The key to Christian living is the Spirit of God. He comes into our hearts. We're like the glove. We can't do anything for God on our own. But the Spirit works inside us. He has power.

The Spirit also produces love in us. He helps us love our family in ways we never did before. He leads us to sacrifice ourselves for them by offering to do jobs that others don't want to do. He teaches us to reach out to unlovable people and care for them.

Prayer: God, I want to read my Bible every day, but I'm tempted to skip sometimes. Let me respond to your Spirit and desire to read your Word.

365 New Testament Devotions for Kids

Pass It On

2 Timothy 2:2: You have heard me teach things that have been confirmed by many reliable witnesses. Now teach these truths to other trustworthy people who will be able to pass them on to others.

The Extra Mile: 2 Timothy 2

Even leaders as great as Moses die. But God always has a plan for the past leader to raise up and train a new leader to take his place.

This is the plan God used all throughout the Bible. Elijah had Elisha. Jesus had the 12 disciples. Paul had Timothy, Silas, and Barnabas.

God spelled out the process in 2 Timothy 2:2. Paul said that the things Timothy had learned from him he should pass on to other men and women who would be able to teach others also. There are four people or groups in that little statement:

- Paul
- Timothy
- The people Timothy taught
- The people who were taught by the ones Timothy taught

That's the process of leadership. It's like passing a baton in a relay race. You must be careful what runners you choose to pass it to. They can't drop it or the race will be lost. But if a solid pass is made, everyone wins.

Prayer: Lord, am I a possible leader in my youth group or school? Help me to find a leader, take the baton, and run.

How Do I Know?

2 Timothy 3:16, 17: All Scripture is inspired by God and is useful to teach us what is true and to make us realize what is wrong in our lives. It corrects us when we are wrong and teaches us to do what is right. God uses it to prepare and equip his people to do every good work.

The Extra Mile: 2 Timothy 3

God has many ways to tell us what he wants: the Bible, parents, a Christian teacher or friend, circumstances, or an uncle who's always saying, "Hey, you better do this, kid, or you'll die in your own blood." (Well, probably not him.)

It's never easy. How can you figure out God's will in a tough spot?

The first place to start is the Bible. That's God's Word. The Bible contains everything written that God wants us to know. According to this Scripture verse, the Bible is God's way of teaching us what is right and true, instructing us how to live, and telling us how to get to Heaven. Anything that any person says or writes in addition to the Bible may be helpful, but it is not as important as the Bible. Always start with the Bible.

Prayer: Thank you, God, for giving us your Word, the Bible. Through it you teach us what we need to know to live for you now and to be with you in Heaven someday

The Point of No Return

WEEK 41

THURSDAY

2 Timothy 4:1: I solemnly urge you in the presence of God and Christ Jesus, who will someday judge the living and the dead when he appears to set up his Kingdom.

The Extra Mile: 2 Timothy 4:1-7

What kind of behavior makes God angry? If you think about it, you may think of things like these: kids bullying others, terrorists who hurt innocent people, powerful people exploiting the weak, or leaders oppressing those they lead. God gets angry about all those people.

In fact, God assures us that he will judge people. They won't escape. One day they will all answer for their crimes. And if they never believe in and trust Jesus, they will never be forgiven.

People who do evil will get paid back in full. God will make sure of it, though it may not be as soon as you hope for people who have wounded you. What should you do about evil in the meantime? Pray for those who hurt others. Pray that God will send them the news of Jesus and open their hearts. Pray that God will comfort those they hurt. And pray that their evil will be stopped.

Prayer: Father, I pray that you will stop evil in my life and use me to stop evil in the world

When Jesus Comes

2 Timothy 4:8: And now the prize awaits me——the crown of righteousness, which the Lord, the righteous Judge, will give me on the day of his return. And the prize is not just for me but for all who eagerly look forward to his appearing.

The Extra Mile: 2 Timothy 4:8-22

"I sure wish Jesus would come soon," Becky said to her mom. "Then everything would be OK."

Have you ever wished like that? Many of us do. Whenever we're in trouble we often make that wish. When we're hurt, or suffering, that's when we wish for Jesus to hurry up and come.

Why do we have that wish? Because we who are Christians know that when Jesus comes, he will do several important things:

- He will bring peace to earth. He will get all people to sit down and stop their fighting.
- He will right every wrong. Everything anyone ever did to hurt us will be made right.
- He will be wise. He'll know how to settle problems. He'll know what to do in every situation and can tell us, face-to-face.

Won't that be a great day?

Do you look forward to Jesus coming back to earth? Do you sometimes wish he would hurry up? Many people all over the world have the same wish.

Prayer: I know, Lord, one day everything will be perfect. Help me to wait well.

Pretend Christians

Titus 1:16: Such people claim they know God, but they deny him by the way they live. They are detestable and disobedient, worthless for doing anything good.

The Extra Mile: Titus 1

Do you know kids who claim to be Christians but don't live that way? Maybe they went forward and "accepted" Christ and were baptized. They may even be able to quote Bible verses. But they steal, lie, hurt others, bully, and act as though they are rejecting God.

In the above Scripture, Paul describes such people: they deny they really know God by the way they live. You see, a real Christian's life will change as he learns and grows in faith. When they're new Christians, you can't expect them to do everything right. But if you or others teach them, they will listen. And they will apply the Bible to their lives.

No one ever becomes perfect in this world, but true Christians will continually work at becoming stronger, better, more faithful believers. They will spend time in prayer, serve in church, and do their best with what they know.

Prayer: Lord, let me never be a faker. I want to be the real thing.

Be Self-controlled

Titus 2:6: In the same way, encourage the young men to live wisely.

The Extra Mile: Titus 2

Temptations are always there: to mouth off, to criticize others, to gossip, to overeat, to take an unfair advantage, to be cowardly, or indifferent. If the devil can't get you with your tongue, he'll tempt you with laziness.

Paul's word to the young men might just as well have been addressed to everyone. Be self-controlled.

Why does Paul raise this issue? Because, when you're young you want to run wild. You want to let it all hang out. You want to just be free and go with the flow.

Do you need to work on some aspect of self-control, such as waiting your turn to speak, keeping still when it's appropriate, or not talking back to adults? Take a hint from the apostle Paul: determine to work on self-control. Ask God for power, strength, and help. Watch your tongue. Watch your discipline. And refuse to give up.

Prayer: Lord, help me to see change as I work on showing self-control.

Police Officers and Others in Authority

Titus 3:1: Remind the believers to submit to the government and its officers. They should be obedient, always ready to do what is good.

The Extra Mile: Titus 3:1-8

Benji and his friend Armand walked down the street with their baseball bats in their hands. Benji pointed to a car parked on a back street. "Watch this," he said. Then he bashed in the windshield. Armand watched, horrified.

"Wasn't that cool?" Benji asked.

Armand couldn't say anything.

"Come on, now you do it."

Armand refused. "Chicken!" Benji said. But they didn't talk about it anymore.

Awhile later, a police car stopped on the street. The officer said, "Do you kids know anything about a broken windshield near here?"

Benji said, "No, sir." Armand just looked away.

When he got home, he couldn't shake the guilt. He had to fix this. He called Benji and told him to confess. Benji cussed and said, "If you tell, I'll beat you bloody."

Armand didn't know what to do then. What would you do?

Prayer: Lord, help me to understand the reasons for laws and the importance of obeying them.

Arguing About Stupid Stuff

Titus 3:9: Do not get involved in foolish discussions about spiritual pedigrees or in quarrels and fights about obedience to Jewish laws. These things are useless and a waste of time.

The Extra Mile: Titus 3:9–15

Luis was a different kind of kid. James invited him to a Bible study he went to. He knew nothing about Luis except that he was a nice guy. But at the Bible study, Luis tore things up.

"I saw you at that dance the other day. You shouldn't dance. God is against dancing," he said one time.

No one said anything. Then he added, "And movies. You can't go to movies. They're evil."

He had a whole list: playing cards and games, going swimming with girls, and many other things. No one knew what to say, except finally James said, "Where does it say those things in the Bible?"

"I don't know. I only know they're in there," Luis said.

Other kids jumped in. "I never heard that. How do you know for sure?"

Finally, Luis got mad and walked out. "You people aren't real Christians," he said and left.

Prayer: Lord, I know Christians disagree on how to live your Word. Help me to be patient with others who don't see things the way I do and not condemn them.

Share Your Faith

Philemon 6: And I am praying that you will put into action the generosity that comes from your faith as you understand and experience all the good things we have in Christ.

The Extra Mile: Philemon

Jill sat down next to Hillary at lunch and nodded a hello. "You new?" Jill said to the pretty girl.

"I just moved here last week," Hillary answered.

Jill offered to split a bag of chips with Hillary. Over the next few days they became good friends. Finally, Jill worked up the courage to invite Hillary to her youth group.

"It's a pretty big church and there are a lot of kids," Jill explained. "Plenty of boys."

Over the next months Jill and Hillary talked a lot about faith, Jesus, and life after death. Hillary still wasn't sure she wanted to become a Christian until one day when she heard Jill praying for her. "You're praying for me?" Hillary said.

"I was praying about your family," Jill said. "I know how hard it is for you and your stepdad."

Suddenly, Hillary burst into tears. "I want what you have, Jill. I want it!"

Prayer: Father, I know sharing Jesus is more about building relationships than spitting out the truth. I will try to build relationships for your kingdom.

The Radiance of God's Glory

THURSDAY

Hebrews 1:3: The Son radiates God's own glory and expresses the very character of God, and he sustains everything by the mighty power of his command. When he had cleansed us from our sins, he sat down in the place of honor at the right hand of the majestic God in heaven.

The Extra Mile: Hebrews 1

God is spirit. He's bigger than the universe; yet he can live inside a human heart.

God is all-powerful. Yet he doesn't use his power to force us to love him; he uses it only to do good in his world.

God is all-knowing. He knows everything about you; and still he loves you.

How could this invisible, spiritual, all-powerful, all-knowing God make himself understandable to us?

Hebrews 1:3 tells us: Jesus is the "radiance" of God's glory and the "exact representation" of his nature. Jesus is God in human flesh. Jesus came to show us what God is like. When we look at Jesus in the Bible, we see God. He radiates the love and power and wisdom of God. He exactly represents everything God stands for.

If you know Jesus, you know God. Jesus makes God real to us.

Prayer: Father, Son, and Holy Spirit—I love you, God.

God's Word Is True

Hebrews 2:4: And God confirmed the message by giving signs and wonders and various miracles and gifts of the Holy Spirit whenever he chose.

The Extra Mile: Hebrews 2

FRIDAY

How do we know the Bible is true?

There are several ways. The first one is in the verse above. God did signs, wonders, and miracles, and gave gifts of the Holy Spirit to the people who wrote down his Word and witnessed for him. People knew their message was from God when they saw Paul, Peter, James, and John perform incredible feats of power. Wouldn't you be convinced if someone came to you saying his message was from God, and then he healed everyone in the hospital?

A second way we know the Bible is true is through the Holy Spirit. He confirms to us that the Bible is God's Word when we hear it. It's called the "witness" of the Spirit. In our hearts, the Spirit speaks, telling us to listen, to heed, to apply the words because they're from God.

A third way is through the millions of people whose lives have been changed by the Word. Their actions speak to the truth of what they say.

Have you sensed any of these things in your life?

Prayer: No other book is like your Bible, God. I want to know your Word and obey it.

Don't Harden Your Heart

Hebrews 3:7, 8: That is why the Holy Spirit says, "Today when you hear his voice, don't harden your hearts as Israel did when they rebelled, when they tested me in the wilderness."

The Extra Mile: Hebrews 3

Every time you hear God's Word preached, taught, or quoted, you have several choices:
- Reject it as stupid, false, or a fraud
- Accept it as God's Word and believe it
- Shrug it off like it doesn't matter

Perhaps there are even other responses. The Bible itself tells us that we can have these kinds of responses. It warns us, though, that only one response will help us, build us up, and fill us with the joy and love of God: accepting and believing it is from him.

While we can exhibit any number of responses to God's Word, we must also reckon with the truth that God may be forced to judge us for our attitude. He did that with the people of Israel in Moses' day when they rejected and laughed off God's truth. Everyone over 20 years old died in the wilderness in those days, except the few who were faithful.

God will not tolerate indifference, mocking, or shrugging off his truth. Are you ready to face him now about it?

Prayer: Lord, help me to push away the impulse of the devil to reject your Word.

God Blesses, Even When He's Angry

Hebrews 4:3: For only we who believe can enter his rest. As for the others, God said, "In my anger I took an oath: 'They will never enter my place of rest.'"

The Extra Mile: Hebrews 4:1-6

Anger is a terrible thing. When people are angry they sometimes do awful things—to their family, their friends, or others.

But what about when God is angry? Can you imagine what the all-powerful God's anger must be like? The most incredible special effects in a movie could not possibly picture it. When God is angry, the whole universe shudders.

In this passage from Hebrews, God warns the readers that they will never enter God's rest if we don't believe. God's rest is peace, joy, and tranquility; life in Heaven with no more sorrows, tears, pain, or fear.

When God speaks like this, he always does one other thing: he promises blessings to those who will repent, return to him, and believe.

No matter what you have done, no matter what mistakes you have made, God can still bring blessing into your life. God is the great fixer-upper. He can turn around your life when all you do is say, "I'm sorry. Forgive me."

Prayer: Father, I know you never act like a tyrant. You offer joy and blessing even when you are angry with us. All we need to do is repent.

Don't Harden Your Heart

Hebrews 4:7: "Today when you hear his voice, don't harden your hearts."

The Extra Mile: Hebrews 4:7–11

Have you ever been sitting in church when a small voice inside you spoke? "You need to listen to this," it says. Or "You've committed that sin."

Maybe you've been at the dinner table and suddenly you just knew God was speaking to your heart. "Help your mom with the dishes tonight." "Show your sister how to solve that math problem."

God speaks to all of us at times in our lives. He's never too loud and he never forces us to do what we refuse to do. But he will be firm. He will speak directly. He will not beat around the bush.

Have you heard God speaking to your heart lately? What is he asking you to do? Accept Jesus? Become more committed? Read your Bible regularly? Get involved in the youth group at church?

Whatever it is, you know when God is speaking. You have two choices: to listen and obey, or to harden your heart and go your own way.

Prayer: Lord, when you speak to me I will listen.

The Power of God's Word

Hebrews 4:12: For the word of God is alive and powerful. It is sharper than the sharpest two-edged sword, cutting between soul and spirit, between joint and marrow. It exposes our innermost thoughts and desires.

The Extra Mile: Hebrews 4:12–16

God's Word is powerful. Jade knew that. When she was tempted to cheat on a test, she remembered that the Bible said, "Do not lie."

Daron knew how powerful God's Word is. When he received a check from his grandmother, he remembered that the Bible said to give a portion to God, so he did.

Molly understood the Bible's power. When her friend argued with her about God, she simply quoted a verse about him that made her friend stop and think.

When you're at school this week, why not ask God to help you remember his Word when you have a need or problem? Do what God's Word says, and see if God doesn't bless you in some way.

Prayer: Lord, thank you for your powerful Word. I will read it every day.

Learning Obedience

Hebrews 5:8: Even though Jesus was God's Son, he learned obedience from the things he suffered.

The Extra Mile: Hebrews 5

Seta watched as her little brother sat at the table eating. He was making a real mess. He had food on his plate, on the floor, on his shirt, and all over his face.

"What a mess!" she said.

"We have to teach him to eat correctly," her mother said. She picked up a fork and put it in Jody's hand. He threw it onto the floor.

Mom patiently picked it up, put it back in his hand and said, "No, don't do that, Jody."

Jody laughed and threw it away again. Mom gave him a little slap on the hand, picked the fork up, cleaned it off again, and put it in his hand. She made him grip the fork, then she let go. Jody looked from Seta to Mom. Then he crinkled his lips, yelled, "No," and threw the fork into Mom's face.

Seta watched as Mom repeated this process over and over until Jody obeyed. Eventually he learned to eat without making such a mess.

Prayer: Lord, I know that discipline sometimes involves punishment. It can take a long time, but the end result is a person who listens to you and obeys. That's what I want to be.

Becoming Mature

Hebrews 6:1: So let us stop going over the basic teachings about Christ again and again. Let us go on instead and become mature in our understanding.

The Extra Mile: Hebrews 6

How do we grow up? Through instruction, teaching, practicing, and doing something over and over until we get it. Also we grow through discipline, correction, and rebuking to help us learn to do what God wants.

The believers addressed in the book of Hebrews had learned a lot over the years. But the things they learned were the basics about salvation, baptism, eternal life, and Heaven. Now they needed to learn other things.

We all have to grow up. When you first go to school, you learn the ABCs, how to count to 10, and your colors. But eventually, you have to move on, mastering math, spelling, grammar, and science.

In the same way, it's not enough to learn a Bible verse or two and think you've done it all as a Christian. There are many more things to learn about Jesus and why you believe.

Prayer: Lord, help me never to stop learning. Growing up is a lifelong process, and every day I can learn something new if I'm watching, listening, and looking.

What Jesus Does Now

Hebrews 7:25: Therefore he is able, once and forever, to save those who come to God through him. He lives forever to intercede with God on their behalf.

The Extra Mile: Hebrews 7

Some Christians worry that they'll lose their salvation. They figure that since the Christian life is hard, it's difficult to keep the faith. They're afraid they'll fall away or forget the truth.

There is one thing they might be forgetting, and you may be forgetting it too. It's not your determination. It's not your personality. It's not your commitment that gets you to Heaven. It's the fact that Jesus is in Heaven at God's right hand. And the main thing he does there is pray for Christians. He prays that they won't lose their faith. He prays about their needs. He prays that they'll never give up.

You can trust that God will get you safely to Heaven one day because of Jesus.

Prayer: Father, thank you for the gift of salvation that doesn't depend on me. Thank you for the hope I have in you.

The Day Is Coming

WEEK
43

SATURDAY

Hebrews 8:10, 11: *I will put my laws in their minds, and I will write them on their hearts. I will be their God, and they will be my people. And they will not need to teach their neighbors, nor will they need to teach their relatives, saying, "You should know the Lord." For everyone, from the least to the greatest, will know me already.*

The Extra Mile: Hebrews 8

Travis sat in his family's TV room looking disturbed and worried. "What's the matter, honey?" his mother asked as she walked in with a basketful of clothes to fold.

"There's so much evil in the world," Travis said unhappily. "I've been watching TV. And there are people angry and killing each other everywhere. People are starving in some places. And no one seems to have the money to buy stuff."

His mom sat down and began folding clothes. "You know, the Bible says that in Heaven everyone will know God and obey him. He'll put his Word in our hearts, and we'll all do what he says. There'll be no more sin, pain, or hurt."

"I know," Travis said. "But it seems like things just get worse and worse."

"Why don't you tell God how you feel? And then tell him to hurry up and come back so the world can get right again?"

"I can do that?" Travis asked hopefully.

"Sure. We can do it right now."

Prayer: Lord, sometimes I'm discouraged about how bad things are in the world. Give me faith while I wait for Heaven.

Dying Only Once

Hebrews 9:27, 28: And just as each person is destined to die once and after that comes judgment, so also Christ died once for all time as a sacrifice to take away the sins of many people. He will come again, not to deal with our sins, but to bring salvation to all who are eagerly waiting for him.

The Extra Mile: Hebrews 9

Did you know that because of Jesus you only have to die once? The book of Revelation talks about something called the "second death." This is when an unbeliever is judged and punished by going into darkness forever. They experience a second death where they will never feel, or see, or hear from God again.

But for the Christian, Jesus has made salvation, eternal life, and Heaven possible. When we believe in him, God writes our names in the "Book of Life," and works to prepare us in this life for our heavenly home.

Have you ever thanked God for that assurance? Have you ever let God know how much you appreciate his love and care? Why not do it right now?

Prayer: Lord, I want to thank for some things. And here's the list.

Lonely?

Hebrews 10:24, 25: Let us think of ways to motivate one another to acts of love and good works. And let us not neglect our meeting together, as some people do, but encourage one another, especially now that the day of his return is drawing near.

MONDAY

The Extra Mile: Hebrews 10

What if you woke up this morning and found no one at home? You go to school and no one's there! You run down the street banging on doors. But no one answers.

What if suddenly you were all alone in the world? What would you think? How would you feel? What would you do?

It would not only be scary; it would be lonely. Even with God as your best friend, you'd probably still wish for a friend who had a face and hands and skin—a human being!

God has given you friends, helpers, teachers, and relatives to be part of your life. The church is supposed to be a place where God's people come together to worship and learn about him. God doesn't want you to be like the Lone Ranger. He wants you to work with others and be with others.

Look around you. Who has God given you to keep you from being lonely in his world? God has given you a whole world of people to know, love, be friends with, and help.

Prayer: Lord, sometimes I feel lonely. Let me come to you and lean on you.

Creation or Evolution?

Hebrews 11:3: By faith we understand that the entire universe was formed at God's command, that what we now see did not come from anything that can be seen.

The Extra Mile: Hebrews 11:1-11

"People became what they are by evolution," Jack told his friend Lincoln. "It's as simple as that."

"But how do you know?" Lincoln countered. "Did anyone see it happen?"

"Fossils, my friend."

"But fossils only tell us part of the story," Lincoln said. "And there are no fossils of the intermediate forms. We don't even have a strong link between men and apes."

"OK, then what do you believe?"

"That God created everything."

"Oh, come on! How do you know that?"

Lincoln smiled and opened his pocket Bible to Hebrews 11:3. "See what this says: 'By faith we understand this.' Faith is like a sixth sense. It's like eyesight into the God zone."

Jack stared at the verse. "That's really something," he finally said. "It says you 'understand' this. That's like knowing, right?"

"Yeah."

Prayer: Father, I know evolution is a tough issue. But I will remember one thing: faith has opened my eyes to the truth. Now that I have faith, I see as you see. And that's all I need.

Little Me

Hebrews 11:12: And so a whole nation came from this one man who was as good as dead—a nation with so many people that, like the stars in the sky and the sand on the seashore, there is no way to count them.

The Extra Mile: Hebrews 11:12–40

Have you ever really looked up at the night sky full of stars? What did you think?

Perhaps you know some facts, like where the North Star is, what the Big Dipper looks like, or how close the nearest star, Alpha Centauri, is to us. If so, you have an idea of the distances involved.

For instance, the sun is 93 million miles away from earth. Alpha Centauri is 4.3 light years from the sun. A light year is approximately 980 trillion miles. That means Alpha Centauri is approximately 4,400 times farther away from earth than the sun is. And that's the NEAREST star!

Such numbers boggle our minds. But try this one: how many stars are there in the universe?

No one knows at this point, but some guess at billions of billions.

In the midst of this is you. Maybe five-foot-two, eyes of blue. Where does that put you in time and space? You could think you don't count for anything!

Yet the Bible teaches us that we are very much on God's heart and mind every day. He knows how many hairs grow on our head, how many we lose each month, and how long each one is.

Prayer: Lord, I know you are far greater, far more caring, far more loving and knowing and giving than any of us ever could imagine. I worship you.

He Worshiped, Even
When He Was Punished

Hebrews 12:5, 6: My child, don't make light of the Lord's discipline, and don't give up when he corrects you. For the Lord disciplines those he loves, and he punishes each one he accepts as his child.

The Extra Mile: Hebrews 12:1-20

In the Old Testament book of 2 Samuel, David made a big mistake. An Israelite king was not to trust in his wealth, his army, or his wisdom, but in God. God always warned all Jewish leaders that they were never to count how many soldiers they had in their army.

It seems like a small thing. But God was serious. He was the ultimate protector of his people. It was not their weapons or their power.

David, though, decided to go against God's orders and count how many young men he had for the army. God responded by telling David he had sinned. God offered David three choices. The first two were horrible, so David took the third, which called for a plague on the people. Seventy thousand people died as a result.

God's discipline hurts. But what did David do following this punishment? He went out and worshiped. He knew that loving God was better than hating him. David believed that trusting God was better than being bitter.

Prayer: Lord, I know discipline is never pleasant. Detention stinks. Being grounded isn't any fun. But parents and teachers only do this to help us learn to do right the next time. So help me to take it like a kid.

When God Comes Down

Hebrews 12:28, 29: Since we are receiving a Kingdom that is unshakable, let us be thankful and please God by worshiping him with holy fear and awe. For our God is a devouring fire.

The Extra Mile: Hebrews 12:21-29

What does God look like?

No one knows. In fact, no one can look on God's face and live, according to Exodus 33:20.

But what happens when God comes down to live among us? He did this in the days of Israel when his glory filled the temple. A shining cloud appeared in the Holy of Holies, the holiest place on earth at that time. This happened when God took up residence in the temple.

What was it like?

We don't really know. No one could step into the Holy of Holies, the inner room of the temple where God lived, except once a year when the high priest went in to make a sacrifice for the sins of all the people. What did the high priest see? Perhaps it was simply a vague cloud sitting over the ark of the covenant, which marked the site. One of the few exact descriptions we have of this presence is in Exodus 24:17: "To the Israelites at the foot of the mountain, the glory of the Lord appeared at the summit like a consuming fire."

What is a "consuming fire"? A fire so fierce and hot that it burns up everything in its path.

Prayer: God, sometimes I wish I could see you. Thank you for your Holy Spirit living in me.

The Ultimate Loyal Person

SATURDAY

Hebrews 13:5: Don't love money; be satisfied with what you have. For God has said, "I will never fail you. I will never abandon you."

The Extra Mile: Hebrews 13

Are you loyal? Can people depend on you?

For a moment, think of the average dog. Your dog will love you no matter how rich or poor you are. No matter how small or big your house, your dog will think you're the greatest. And even if you only feed him grungy dog food every day of his life, your dog will follow you anywhere.

God created dogs and designed them to be loyal the way they are. And in a small way, dogs reflect the character of their Creator. Dogs give people an example of loyalty.

God is faithful. You can trust him completely. He will never desert you, no matter how bad things get. He will never leave your side, even if you try to push him away. God's love for you is perfect, complete, and unwavering.

Do you ever wish for a loyal friend who will always stand by you? God is that friend.

Prayer: I love you, God! Thanks for never ever leaving me.

The Power of Wisdom

James 1:5: *If you need wisdom, ask our generous God, and he will give it to you. He will not rebuke you for asking.*

The Extra Mile: James 1:1–12

You don't have to know everything.

You don't have to know the chemical formula of chocolate to enjoy it. Experience teaches you that chocolate tastes great, and it slides down, oh so beautifully. If you read a recipe, would that tell you why your taste buds tingle so deliciously when you eat chocolate?

No, you just eat it. You don't have to understand all the whys. All you know is that it's good.

In the same way, God doesn't promise to tell us the answers to all our why questions: Why do troubles come? Why has this tragedy happened to me? Why am I going through this now?

Instead, God promises to give us wisdom to know how to deal with trouble. He offers us strength to overcome.

Prayer: Lord, I will try not to ask why. I will trust that you have your reasons for everything that happens, and I will trust you to see me through.

WEEK
45

The Blessed Person

MONDAY

James 1:13: And remember, when you are being tempted, do not say, "God is tempting me." God is never tempted to do wrong, and he never tempts anyone else.

The Extra Mile: James 1:13–27

Sin tricks us. It tells us that whatever it wants us to do is OK, that no one will mind, and that it's fun.

After sin gets us to that step, it then moves further. It gets us to join up with others who do the same thing. It gets us to ally ourselves with people who commit the same sin and to agree with them.

But sin isn't satisfied there, either. It pushes us to one last stage. That's when we get into our little group and taunt everyone else who won't commit the sin we're doing. It gets us to mock and scorn and throw abuse at them. It gets us to think they're weenies and jerks and scaredy-cats.

Do you see the progression? It can happen so easily, before we've even thought about it. A friend might tempt us to do something wrong. We do, and the next thing we know we go out there and try to get other kids to do the same thing. This is a very bad thing, and God warns that when we become "sin evangelists" we're in great danger.

Has this happened to you?

Prayer: Lord, I know there's only one way out of a sin problem: confess my sin and turn away from it. Here's one sin I confess: _____.

Actions Always Are Louder Than Words

James 2:14: What good is it, dear brothers and sisters, if you say you have faith but don't show it by your actions? Can that kind of faith save anyone?

The Extra Mile: James 2

Words are so easy. You can say you'll do something and everybody's happy. But what if you don't do it? What if you walk away, thinking, "They're happy, so I won't actually do it."

That's a bad way to be, but a lot of people are like that. They make promises they don't keep. A lot of people may be counting on those promises. When politicians make certain promises, people may vote them into power because of those promises. But if that politician doesn't do what he promised, watch out! He may lose the next election!

A person who keeps his word and his promises has integrity. It means that we live up to what we say in public. If you say you're gentle and you'll never yell when you get angry, you'd better not be caught yelling at your little brother. If you say you'll be there for the class next Sunday, but don't show up, people will think less of you.

Do what you say you believe, and people will believe you will always do what you say.

Prayer: Lord, if I make a promise, I will keep it. People are watching.

Jealousy in the Crowd

James 3:14: But if you are bitterly jealous and there is selfish ambition in your heart, don't cover up the truth with boasting and lying.

The Extra Mile: James 3:1–13

Cindy was angry. Gwen had received the Clement Award—a prize given to the best student in her class. It wasn't that Cindy wasn't a good student. She was. It wasn't that people didn't think well of her. They did. It was just that Gwen got the award, and Cindy didn't.

So Cindy began criticizing Gwen. "Have you ever seen the way Gwen waves her hands when she's speaking? She looks like a windmill." "Have you ever noticed who Gwen hangs out with—a bunch of losers!"

Oh, jealousy! How it can rage!

Cindy went around speaking all kinds of nasty things about Gwen, and soon people were putting down Gwen too. The few who were loyal to her weren't listened to. In time, it took a lot of work for Gwen to clean up her reputation.

Prayer: Father, I know jealousy is an ugly emotion, but I confess I'm jealous sometimes. Help me to find my value in what you think of me, and not in comparing myself with others.

The Choice of Wisdom

James 3:17: But the wisdom from above is first of all pure. It is also peace loving, gentle at all times, and willing to yield to others. It is full of mercy and good deeds. It shows no favoritism and is always sincere.

THURSDAY

The Extra Mile: James 3:14–18

Say someone who loves you came to you and said, "You are an important person to me. I want to give you a choice of one of three things. Whichever one you ask for, I will give you."

What are the choices?

1. All the riches you could ever want: enough to buy a great car, a huge house, have fantastic parties, and live anywhere you want.
2. Amazing power. You could become President of the United States. You could win all the great prizes on earth.
3. Wisdom: the ability to know what is the best and wisest decision in any situation.

Which would you choose?

Only one person in history was given such a choice. King Solomon chose the third, wisdom. God was so pleased with that that he threw in riches and power anyway.

Prayer: Jesus, I will choose wisdom by studying your Word and learning your truth.

Why God Doesn't Answer

James 4:3: And even when you ask, you don't get it because your motives are all wrong—you want only what will give you pleasure.

The Extra Mile: James 4:1-5

Temple prayed and prayed. But he didn't get that new minibike.

Sean spent a long time on his knees. But God didn't let him go to Disney World.

Paige asked friends at church to pray. But her complexion didn't improve.

Why does God say no to some prayers? James reveals one reason in James 4:1-3. He tells us first we do not have because we do not ask. If we learned to ask God for more, maybe he would answer more. Then James says we ask and do not receive because we ask with wrong motives. We just want something for ourselves. It's selfish.

Prayer: Lord, help me to avoid selfish prayers. Let my desires be your desires so I ask for the right things.

Don't Forget God!

James 4:6: But he gives us even more grace to stand against such evil desires. As the Scriptures say, "God opposes the proud but favors the humble."

The Extra Mile: James 4:6–17

What are the most dangerous times in life? The good times, fun times, when everyone is happy. Hard to believe, but it's true.

Why? Because during happy times people start to forget God. They party so much, they forget to pray. They have more money, and giving 10 percent of more is tough. They're having so much fun they forget to go to church.

You say, "I won't forget God. How could I forget my best friend?"

It happens. Your life gets going so well and suddenly God doesn't seem so important. "God? Yeah, he's around here somewhere."

So what does God do? He sends hard times to get people back to doing what really matters.

Where are you today? In the middle of good times? Are you remembering the Lord? If so, pray that God will say, "Now we can let the good times roll" instead of, "Better send them some bad days so they remember me."

Prayer: Lord, I will never forget you, no matter how good things are. I will worship you with my whole heart.

The Complaining Crowd

James 5:9: Don't grumble about each other, brothers and sisters, or you will be judged. For look—the Judge is standing at the door!

The Extra Mile: James 5:1–14

Do your parents ever tell you that you complain too much? "Stop that whining!" "Will you quit it with the put-downs?" "If I hear another complaint, I'm going to scream."

Complaining comes naturally to most of us. We don't like this. We don't like that. Did you know that God, like our parents, hates complaining? Ultimately, complaining says, "God, you haven't treated me right. You've been mean. I'm not putting up with it." God gets very tired of people shouting complaints into his ear about everything.

What should we do instead? Try praising God. Try thanking him. Try telling him how much you appreciate his world and the ways he's blessed you. "Lord, thank you for my . . . *ahem* . . . little sister."

What might happen if we try that? God might just bless us more!

Prayer: Jesus, I have to stop complaining. Help me to become aware when I do start complaining, so I can stop. Teach me to be thankful in everything.

The Blame Game

James 5:19, 20: My dear brothers and sisters, if someone among you wanders away from the truth and is brought back, you can be sure that whoever brings the sinner back will save that person from death and bring about the forgiveness of many sins.

The Extra Mile: James 5:15–20

"Hey! Who left the dirty dishes on the table?"

"Not me," said the brother.

"I didn't," said the sister.

"They made me do it," said the little brother. "They wanted me to play!"

Ever get into one of those situations? Everybody gets blamed, including the dog, cat, and hamster.

Like Adam and Eve blamed others for their sin in the Garden of Eden, so we blame others today. What does God want us to do about it? Look at the verse above.

Admitting when you've done something wrong is the first step toward God's love and blessing. When we see someone else wandering from the truth, like the passage says, stop them. When we confess our sins, we always find God willing to forgive. It's when we try to hide them that God is not pleased.

Prayer: Lord, next time I make a big mistake, there are some ways I shouldn't handle it. Instead, I will accept the consequences, and go on and do better next time.

The Greatest Mystery of All

1 Peter 1:16: *For the Scriptures say, "You must be holy because I am holy."*

The Extra Mile: 1 Peter 1

TUESDAY

"Holy mackerel!"
"Holy cow!"
"Holy cannoli!"

We say all kinds of things using the word *holy*. Some of them are not very nice and no one would print them. But what does "holy" really mean?

In the Bible, to be holy meant to be utterly separate, utterly different, reserved only for God's personal use. For instance, in the temple all the utensils and pots were considered holy. That meant they could only be used in the temple, nowhere else. Your mom probably has some "holy" dishes she only uses at special times of the year.

Because God is holy, when we sin, he is displeased. But when we accept Jesus, all that sin is forgiven—past, present, and future. When we become Christians, God sees us as if we were Jesus himself.

How does it feel? If you've trusted Jesus, you belong to God. He never sees you as a crummy, ugly sinner. He sees Jesus, who is holy and good through and through.

Prayer: Jesus, teach me to be holy. I will let you have your way in my life.

Give Me Milk

1 Peter 2:2, 3: Like newborn babies, you must crave pure spiritual milk so that you will grow into a full experience of salvation. Cry out for this nourishment, now that you have had a taste of the Lord's kindness.

The Extra Mile: 1 Peter 2:1–20

Have you ever been around a newborn baby? Do you have one in your house right now?

What does that baby want? Basically three things: to have his diaper changed; to be held and cuddled; to drink milk. Of the three, mostly milk. Babies want it all the time. Mom has to get up at all hours of the night because that kid is screaming for milk. "Give me milk!" his wails say. "I want milk!"

So Mom wearily pulls herself out of bed and goes to the baby's bedroom.

God wants us to be like that baby in one way. Do you see what it is from 1 Peter 2:2? It's that we crave spiritual food, that is, reading the Bible, walking with Jesus, discovering all the great promises of God, and overcoming sin.

When we crave spiritual food like that, God gives it to us, like milk to a baby.

Prayer: Help me to get spiritual food, Lord. Don't let me forget I'm a Christian. I will remember who I am so I can be who you want me to be.

By His Wounds

1 Peter 2:24: He personally carried our sins in his body on the cross so that we can be dead to sin and live for what is right. By his wounds you are healed.

The Extra Mile: 1 Peter 2:21–25

What exactly did Jesus do for us? Look at these words from the Scripture:
- Carried our sins
- Wounded
- Healed

It doesn't sound pleasant, does it? But what does it mean?

Because God is holy, righteous, and just, some penalty must be paid for sin. Whether the sins are "small" like little lies or nasty looks, or "big," like hateful words, cheating, and stealing, they must be paid for. How are they paid for?

In Old Testament times, God required a blood sacrifice for sin. His people offered sheep, bulls, and goats as burnt offerings to God. The gruesome, bloody sacrifices were a vivid reminder to the people of the seriousness of their sins. But that system was only temporary.

God provided a final sacrifice to pay for all sins from that point on. This is where Jesus came in. He stepped in between us and God. He said, "I will die in their place." Jesus died on the cross, and God the Father accepted that payment as the blood sacrifice for all people.

Why did Jesus do this? Because he loves us.

Prayer: Thank you, Lord, that you have forgiven me for everything and given me eternal life.

True Beauty

1 Peter 3:3, 4: Don't be concerned about the outward beauty of fancy hairstyles, expensive jewelry, or beautiful clothes. You should clothe yourselves instead with the beauty that comes from within, the unfading beauty of a gentle and quiet spirit, which is so precious to God.

The Extra Mile: 1 Peter 3:1–8

Do you like you?

Do you enjoy being who you are?

Many young people struggle with self-image. They want to be beautiful, noticed, number one, the center of attention. When they don't get it, they feel as if their world has died.

But real self-esteem begins with self-respect. You can accept yourself for who you are, flaws and all. Your essence is your personality, not your looks. Few of us can ever be truly beautiful as it's defined in today's world. But all of us can be beautiful in God's eyes because of our loving, joyful, and gentle personalities.

When you realize that who you are is what is lovable, not your lips, cheekbones, or hair, you can be happy with yourself and others. Outer beauty can fade, but a truly loving person is beautiful forever.

Prayer: Lord, I know real beauty and good looks are inner, not outer. Work on the inner me, and the outer me will be fine.

Revenge

1 Peter 3:9: Don't repay evil for evil. Don't retaliate with insults when people insult you. Instead, pay them back with a blessing. That is what God has called you to do, and he will bless you for it.

The Extra Mile: 1 Peter 3:9-14

Matt thought about it constantly. Jacob had led some of Matt's enemies down to his tree fort. They had destroyed it. Matt felt betrayed and horribly angry.

He thought about simply cornering Jacob after school and beating the tar out of him. Matt could bring along a couple other guys to make sure Jacob didn't get the upper hand.

Or maybe he should wait for a while. Wait till Jacob didn't suspect it anymore. Then strike, and really hurt him.

But Matt was a Christian. He knew all about forgiveness and kindness and love. He felt that what Jacob had done surely deserved the worst.

Matt struggled deep in his heart about it. But one day he thought of a way he might solve the problem and get rid of his own anger too. He invited Jacob to help him build a new tree fort that everyone could share.

Jacob was amazed when Matt spoke to him about the idea. He was ready for Matt to slug him. He decided Matt was sincere, and a friendship was saved.

Prayer: Father, help me never to repay evil people with evil. I will give a blessing instead.

Having All the Answers

WEEK
46

1 Peter 3:15, 16: *Instead, you must worship Christ as Lord of your life. And if someone asks about your Christian hope, always be ready to explain it. But do this in a gentle and respectful way.*

SUNDAY

The Extra Mile: 1 Peter 3:15–22

Many Christians pride themselves on having all the answers. Name a problem, and they have a Bible verse for it. Share with them a difficulty, and they know just what God says about it. Sometimes such people are right. Sometimes they're wrong. But one thing is for sure: they're not usually very nice about it!

Do you know the answers?

Maybe you've even searched your Bible. Maybe you've talked to your minister or youth leader about your problem. But you can't seem to find the answer.

You know what? It's OK to be confused. It's OK not to know what to do sometimes. It's OK to feel pushed and shoved and not know which way to turn. It's OK to just trust that God will show you the truth soon and that you will be able to explain it to others.

That's what God asks all of us for: trust. When we trust him, everything else begins to fall into place.

Prayer: Jesus, I won't worry about having all the answers because I know you have them. If I am sincere and gentle, people will listen.

365 New Testament Devotions for Kids

331

Surprising Your Friends

1 Peter 4:4, 5: Of course, your former friends are surprised when you no longer plunge into the flood of wild and destructive things they do. So they slander you. But remember that they will have to face God, who will judge everyone, both the living and the dead.

The Extra Mile: 1 Peter 4

Sierra gazed at her four friends.

"What is wrong with you?" Valry asked.

"You became different," Zell said flatly.

"All I've done is believe in Jesus," Sierra said, trying to be honest without overwhelming them.

"But you won't do anything anymore," Zell said. "And we have a club."

"And enemies," Valry added.

"We may need to punch someone out," Zell added. "And you're the best puncher."

It was really tough. Sierra knew and loved her friends. But she also loved Jesus, and she knew she couldn't live now like she used to.

She nodded. "I'll pray about it," she said and walked away. All her friends stared on in horror.

Prayer: Jesus, I know becoming a Christian doesn't mean suddenly everything in life will be easy. In some ways, it may be more difficult. So I will look to you to lead me.

Real Humility, Real Service

1 Peter 5:5: And all of you, serve each other in humility, for "God opposes the proud but favors the humble."

The Extra Mile: 1 Peter 5

Sometimes kids will be involved in a "slave day," a fundraiser in which they offer to do odd jobs for someone in exchange for financial support for a project or mission. Have you ever been someone's "slave"?

Jesus served us as a slave. He laid down his life for us. He served us from the moment he arrived to the moment he left. One passage in Philippians 2 says that he became a servant, a slave, for us.

No one really wants to be a slave. But God wants you to go out of your way to serve others. He wants you to commit your life to helping, giving, loving, and listening. He wants you to be so committed to him that you'll do whatever he says. Are you up to it?

Prayer: Lord, I will serve you all my life, because I love you so much.

How to Make Sure

2 Peter 1:10: So, dear brothers and sisters, work hard to prove that you really are among those God has called and chosen. Do these things, and you will never fall away.

The Extra Mile: 2 Peter 1

Do you ever wonder if you're really a Christian? Do you ever doubt that you are saved? Do you ever worry that you won't be in Heaven with Jesus for eternity?

Here are three questions you might want to consider to figure this out:

• Do you ever feel that God talks to you and assures you? If so, that's the "witness" of the Holy Spirit in your heart. He will assure you that you belong to God.

• Do you have a desire to lead a good life and please God? You wouldn't have that desire if God did not put it in you.

• Are you growing in your relationship with Christ? Do you believe in him right now? If so, then you are his.

God never wants any of us to be worried about his love for us. Second Peter 1:10 tells us to make certain about God's call on our lives. Why not make sure today by answering those three questions?

Prayer: Lord, let me know I'm yours in ways I could never think of.

False Prophets

2 Peter 2:1: But there were also false prophets in Israel, just as there will be false teachers among you. They will cleverly teach destructive heresies and even deny the Master who bought them. In this way, they will bring sudden destruction on themselves.

The Extra Mile: 2 Peter 2

"Satan is a myth," Paco said to Junior. "No one believes in him anymore."

"Then where does evil come from?" Junior asked, thinking he'd won the argument.

"Bad people. There are lots of them."

"So bad people cause all the temptations around there?"

"Most of them. Others come by accident."

Junior was stumped. "But what about the Bible?" he asked.

"The Bible is full of myths, like Satan," Paco said. "No one believes it anymore, except dumb people."

"So I'm dumb?"

"If you really believe it."

Prayer: Father, I know there are false teachers everywhere. If someone tells me something is untrue and I know the Bible says it's true, either that person is ignorant or he's a false prophet. I will avoid his teachings.

The End of the World

2 Peter 3:13: But we are looking forward to the new heavens and new earth he has promised, a world filled with God's righteousness.

FRIDAY

The Extra Mile: 2 Peter 3

Many people are afraid of the end of the world. Some thought January 1, 2000 (Y2K) would be it. Best-selling books have told us about terrible things that will happen at the end of time. They scare many people. Do you ever worry about such things? Could the world end today or sometime soon? What if it ended while you were asleep or doing something wrong?

God doesn't want you to worry about such things. Yes, the world will end. Yes, Jesus will come back in power and glory. But if we trust Jesus, he will be with us no matter what happens in this world.

God is going to rid the universe of this sinful world and create a new one in which righteousness dwells. There will never be any sin again.

When we live in fear, we often do strange and stupid things out of fear. We might run away from home or tell a lie or steal. When we know we are loved, though, we will give our best.

That's what God wants—our best. Our best love, our best worship, and our best commitment.

Prayer: Lord, I never have to be afraid again. And if I ever am, I will just remember you have everything well in hand.

365 New Testament Devotions for Kids

Confess Those Sins

1 John 1:9: But if we confess our sins to him, he is faithful and just to forgive us our sins and to cleanse us from all wickedness.

The Extra Mile: 1 John 1

Janette knew it was wrong to scream at her sister Carrie the way she had. It was just so frustrating to try and make a four-year-old understand she couldn't play with her stuff. Janette had tried calmly warning her little sister. She'd gone to her mother and had her talk to the little girl. But this was too much. Carrie had just about destroyed Janette's dollhouse that their grandfather had made for her.

Janette felt bad all through dinner. When bedtime came, she knew she should apologize, but Carrie didn't seem to notice. She just acted like she always did.

Finally, taking a deep breath, Janette knelt down by her bed. She told God she was sorry for the outburst. She asked him to help with Carrie so that her dollhouse didn't get ruined. And she admitted she had a bit of a temper and needed some help there.

Before bed, Janette went to Carrie's room and apologized to her too.

What a good feeling!

Prayer: Lord, I confess my sins every day, and if possible, the moment I sin. I know you will always forgive.

Angry No More

1 John 2:12: My dear children, I am writing this to you so that you will not sin. But if anyone does sin, we have an advocate who pleads our case before the Father. He is Jesus Christ, the one who is truly righteous.

The Extra Mile: 1 John 2:1–14

Do you ever feel as if God is always angry with you? Your conscience yells at you, "You didn't do this. You did that. That was wrong." Your inner voice screams at you, "You're worse than nothing. You're a loser," or "God is ashamed of you. You've made him really angry."

Are those the kinds of words that go through your mind?

Stop! God is not angry at you at all. He doesn't even feel irritated with you. And he certainly doesn't think you're a loser. He loves you. God could never turn against you or turn away from you. He is with you to the end, and when the end comes, that's only the beginning.

Isn't that amazing? Start resisting those feelings that God is mad at you. That's a trick of the devil.

Prayer: I believe you love me, Lord, and you'll never reject me when I come to you and ask for forgiveness.

Peer Pressure

I John 2:15, 16: Do not love this world nor the things it offers you, for when you love the world, you do not have the love of the Father in you. For the world offers only a craving for physical pleasure, a craving for everything we see, and pride in our achievements and possessions. These are not from the Father, but are from this world.

The Extra Mile: 1 John 2:15–29

"Come on," Jesse said. "No one's going to find out."

"You're just a big chicken," Harrison told his friend Matt.

"Everybody's doing this," Jeannie said to Becky.

"It's just a little thing," Ally told Martha. "Your parents won't mind."

Have you ever heard one of these come-ons? They usually appear in the form of a taunt, or a put-down, or even a threat. Your friends think you're a "sissy" or a "weenie" or a "nerd" because you won't do what they do.

Peer pressure is a powerful thing. It can get us to do things we would never do on our own. King Solomon did that. He listened to his many wives and became an idol-worshiper.

Peer pressure can make even the wisest people give in to sin.

Is anyone trying to persuade you to do something you know is wrong? What can you do to deal with them? Run, hide, confront, or just ignore them—or something else?

Prayer: Lord, I won't give in to those who want to get me to sin. You are with me. So I will run, if necessary.

We Will Be Like Him

1 John 3:2: Dear friends, we are already God's children, but he has not yet shown us what we will be like when Christ appears. But we do know that we will be like him, for we will see him as he really is.

The Extra Mile: 1 John 3

Have you ever thought about what it will be like in Heaven with Jesus? What kind of body will we have? What will we be like?

First John 3:2 gives us an inkling. We will be like Jesus.

What was Jesus like after he was resurrected? Some things you might remember. For one thing, Jesus could appear out of nowhere. Apparently, he could go through walls.

For another thing, people sometimes didn't recognize him at first. Perhaps he didn't look exactly like he did on earth. He was in a glorified body. Maybe he was handsomer, stronger-looking, more robust and perfect than ever before. So he did look a little different. But when he spoke, when he talked with the disciples, they knew him immediately. His personality shone through the glory.

In the same way, our personality will shine through everything when we are in Heaven. People will know us by who we really are inside. We will live in powerful, spiritual, glorified, heavenly bodies.

Prayer: Thank you for my earthly body, Lord. Even though I don't like some things about it, I know you created me and you are good. I'm looking forward to having a glorified spiritual body in Heaven.

Shield and Reward

1 John 4:4: But you belong to God, my dear children. You have already won a victory over those people, because the Spirit who lives in you is greater than the spirit who lives in the world.

The Extra Mile: 1 John 4

We have enemies. Right now, they're thinking up ways of messing up our lives. Imagine that you can you hear the conversation.

"I'll tempt him with video games," says one. We'll call him Rumbuzzer.

"I'll make her discouraged," says another, Lunkgeezle.

"I'll get him to flunk his English test," adds a third, a particularly smelly one named Limburgergarlic.

These enemies think up great ways to mess you up. But they also have a problem: our powerful God. He has placed a shield, like a sci-fi force field, around us. God won't let anything get through to wreck you. Isn't that cool?

Satan can't get through it, unless God lets him. And of course, God will only let him if he knows we can pass the test.

Think about it. God is in charge. He loves you. The shield is in place. We can do anything in this world for God, and Satan can't touch us.

Isn't that amazing?

Prayer: Jesus, I want to get out there and do something great for you, so lead me.

Eternal Life

1 John 5:11, 12: And this is what God has testified: He has given us eternal life, and this life is in his Son. Whoever has the Son has life; whoever does not have God's Son does not have life.

The Extra Mile: 1 John 5

Have you ever wondered what we'll be doing for all eternity? Eternal life is a long time. Even in a normal human lifetime people can get bored. Will we ever get bored in Heaven?

Let's imagine how it could be. First off, we'll begin the process of learning everything we can about God. We'll know him personally and intimately. Over time, we'll come to understand every aspect of his personality and majesty. That will be one mighty task.

We may also get to know everyone else in Heaven. There'll be so many wonderful saints to interact with, we'll find joy in them.

After that, perhaps we'll learn new things, like playing the violin, doing a cross body block in soccer, or painting a masterpiece. Things that were impossible for us on earth will be commonplace in Heaven, and ever better.

There are many other things we could say. But you can believe it—Heaven won't ever get boring or stale. There will always be something new to do and see and learn. God's going to make the greatest experience of life.

Prayer: Jesus, I know Heaven will be the greatest thing any of us could experience, so I will look forward to it.

Deceivers

WEEK 48

2 John 7: I say this because many deceivers have gone out into the world. They deny that Jesus Christ came in a real body. Such a person is a deceiver and an antichrist.

FRIDAY

The Extra Mile: 2 John

Have you ever met a deceiver?

They often speak well. They seem smart. They know their stuff. But they're deceivers. They are pawns of Satan meant to derail us from following Jesus and living for him.

How can you tell a deceiver? They will say nice things about Jesus, but also the wrong things. Like, "Jesus was just a great man. He gave us wonderful words to live by, but that's about it." "Jesus came to show us a better way to live, but all that stuff about miracles and dying on the cross was just made up." And the worst of all: "Jesus was a great teacher. He knew the truth, just like Buddha and Mohammed knew the truth."

The one thing a deceiver won't do is admit that God came in human flesh as Jesus. They'll never say Jesus was God incarnate—fully human and fully God.

Prayer: Lord, I believe that you are the Christ, God in the flesh, and my Lord and Savior.

True Friends

3 John 15: Your friends here send you their greetings. Please give my personal greetings to each of our friends there.

The Extra Mile: 3 John

What makes a true friend? Is it the cool things you do together? Is it because she has a pool in her backyard, or because he throws great parties? Is it because she is popular, and you want to be too?

People look for different things in friends. In the Old Testament we read about the relationship of David and Jonathan and we see several things that made their friendship great and beautiful.

For one, Jonathan and David spent time together. They shared their real feelings and thoughts. They let each other know if they were afraid or worried.

Second, they loved each other enough to help even when it was danger-ous. Jesus said that a true friend will lay down his life for his brother (see John 15:13). David and Jonathan were willing to do the same for each other.

Third, they enjoyed each other. They had fun together. They did "wild" things. They went on adventures. They had a good time together.

Look for the right qualities and you may find a friend worth having.

Prayer: Thank you, God, for the stories of true friends in the Bible. Thank you for my friends. Here's what I appreciate about each of them.

Life Without God

Jude 8: *In the same way, these people—who claim authority from their dreams—live immoral lives, defy authority, and scoff at supernatural beings.*

The Extra Mile: Jude 1–20

What would life be like without God? For one thing, there would be no food. God created all the different foods of the earth. Without God, all food would disappear.

Without God we would have nothing to drink. You're thirsty. You need some soda, or water, or some apple cider. But guess what? There is none.

Friends? Forget them. There aren't any. You're utterly alone. You have no one to talk to, no one even to complain to. For without God, there are no friends. He invented them. And by the way, no family either.

No entertainment. TV, movies, or video games—would that be the killer for you? Worse still, no beauty, joy, peace, security, or contentment; they've all disappeared without God.

Prayer: Lord, every good thing I have or know comes from you. Let me never forget that I need you desperately.

Presenting You

Jude 24: Now all glory to God, who is able to keep you from falling away and will bring you with great joy into his glorious presence without a single fault.

The Extra Mile: Jude 21–25

Do you ever worry about committing a sin so big that God lets you go? Are you ever scared that you could blow it so badly that you forfeit Heaven? These are normal worries Christians face at one time or another. The best place to go for answers is always the Bible. Here in Jude 24 we find one answer.

Jude was a half-brother of Jesus. He was a son of Joseph and Mary who came after Jesus was born. When Jesus started his ministry, Jude and other family members didn't believe Jesus was the Messiah. In fact, they thought Jesus might be crazy (see Mark 3:21).

But after Jesus rose from the dead, one of the first people he appeared to was Jude's other brother, James. The whole family at that point came to faith.

Over the years, Jude probably struggled with the same worries as you. Could he fail so badly that God gave up on him? So Jude wrote his letter to help people with that problem. He says a mighty thing, too: God is "able to keep you from falling away."

Prayer: Father God, I want to love you and be faithful. Keep me from falling away.

The Glorified Jesus

Revelation 1:13, 14: And standing in the middle of the lampstands was someone like the Son of Man. He was wearing a long robe with a gold sash across his chest. His head and his hair were white like wool, as white as snow. And his eyes were like flames of fire.

TUESDAY

The Extra Mile: Revelation 1

What does Jesus look like?

In all of the Bible we don't have anything to help us understand what Jesus looked like on earth. We only know that he was "despised and forsaken" and that no one thought he was anything special, looks-wise.

But in Revelation, John describes the risen Jesus. He meets with Jesus in Heaven so he can write the book of Revelation. There he sees Jesus. Look at what he describes:

- He wears a robe reaching to his feet. It has a golden sash around the chest.
- His head and his hair are pure white.
- His eyes are like a blazing fire.
- His feet are like glowing bronze.
- His voice is like "the sound of many waters."

How do you picture Jesus?

Prayer: Jesus, I can't imagine what it will be like to see you face-to-face, but I'm looking forward to it. Help me by the way I live to give others an idea of what you are like.

Lost Your First Love

Revelation 2:4: "But I have this complaint against you. You don't love me or each other as you did at first!"

The Extra Mile: Revelation 2

Jana stood in the church office stacking boxes. Mrs. Langer came in and asked, "Jana, could you run down to the Sunday school office and get some new envelopes for me? We're out."

Jana nodded, put up one more box, and then hustled down. On the way, her little brother stopped her. "Jana, could you come home now? Jacquie's sick. And the baby is tearing everything up. Mom had to go to the hospital to see Grandmom, and Dad is at the bar."

"You can't bother me now, Davie. You can do it. Just put the baby in the playpen."

"Please, Jana. It's too hard for me."

She gave him a push. "Just go."

The little boy turned around, and with hunched shoulders walked out.

Jana started for the stairs. On the way, her pastor met her. He said, "I heard your little conversation, Jana. I know our church is important to you. But I want you to go find a Bible now and go read Revelation 2:4. And then come and tell me what you think of it."

Prayer: Father, I realize it's easy to lose your first love. So I will take a look at what's important. If I need to make some changes, I will make them.

Be an Overcomer

Revelation 3:5: All who are victorious will be clothed in white. I will never erase their names from the Book of Life, but I will announce before my Father and his angels that they are mine.

The Extra Mile: Revelation 3

The Christian life is a battle. An overcomer is a fighter.

Armies of the night surround us. They want to kill us, to destroy us, to wipe us out of existence.

But we have a king who cannot be defeated. Jesus our Lord commands the armies of God. And he will not allow us to go down to the dirt.

Do you ever feel as if it's a losing battle? Do you ever wonder if things will ever get better in your life?

The battle is real. The enemies of God tempt, distort, deceive, taunt, coax, and do everything they can to lead us into sin. What parts of your life are the most difficult? Taming your tongue? Being disciplined? Not giving up when things get tough?

The Spirit of God will give you the help you need. Call on Jesus for power, for greater faith, and for determination. He intends to get you through to the end, whole and joyful.

Prayer: Make me an overcomer, Lord. I will trust you for the battle.

THURSDAY

Lavishing God with Your Best

Revelation 4:10, 11: The twenty-four elders fall down and worship the one sitting on the throne (the one who lives forever and ever). And they lay their crowns before the throne and say, "You are worthy, O Lord our God, to receive glory and honor and power."

The Extra Mile: Revelation 4:1-8

On Glenn's tenth birthday his parents went all out. They took him to Disney World. They bought him a minibike. They rained down a bunch of games for his PlayStation. They took him out to dinner where he ordered his favorite foods. And that night, he went to the best movie he'd ever seen.

Glenn was so amazed, he said to his mom afterwards, "Why did you do that?"

"Well," his mom answered. "We've never really lavished love on you like that. So we decided to do it this time."

Lavished. That's an interesting word, isn't it? It means to "give in abundance."

Sometimes people today complain about how much money Christians put into church, missions, buildings for worship, and for God. But when it comes to God, do you think any expense should be spared? Shouldn't we go "all out"? Shouldn't we "lavish" God with our best?

Prayer: Lord, show me how I can lavish my love on you today.

God Is Worthy

Revelation 4:11: "You are worthy, O Lord our God, to receive glory and honor and power. For you created all things, and they exist because you created what you pleased."

The Extra Mile: Revelation 4:9–11

The king sat on his throne with his best adviser at his right hand. Into the room stepped a man, bald, with his cap in his hand. The adviser motioned to the man to step forward and then he said to the king, "He is a good man. He is worthy to be heard by you."

The President received the couple from Pakistan. As they sat down to dinner, a member of the Cabinet leaned down to whisper, "They speak well. Be open. They are worthy of America's gifts."

Worthy. Interesting word. What does it mean? It means that something or someone has the value to be prized and kept secure. It means that the people in question have made a good mark on the world and they deserve our highest respect and honor.

In Revelation 4:11, we see some fantastic creatures crying out that God is worthy to receive glory and honor and power. Not only should God receive those things, not only does he have a right to those things, but to all eyes, he is worthy of those things. It is good and right and honorable to give him glory and honor and power because he deserves them.

Prayer: You are worthy, Lord, to receive my love and worship.

Honoring Jesus

Revelation 5:13: And then I heard every creature in heaven and on earth and under the earth and in the sea. They sang, "Blessing and honor and glory and power belong to the one sitting on the throne and to the Lamb forever and ever."

The Extra Mile: Revelation 5

Can you think of anyone who deserves to be worshiped? Some movie star hero-type who beats the baddies? A ballplayer who hits the most home runs each year? The President of the United States? A great preacher who captivates his audiences and leads many people to Christ?

All these people might deserve to win awards, be honored in public, and even make lots of money. But worship them? No way! Alas, many people do worship such people. But there is only one person who is truly worthy of worship: Jesus.

He saved the world from Hell and sin.

He showed us how to live rightly.

He spoke words that give us hope and joy.

Really, who else has done such things?

Prayer: Jesus, how can I possibly put into words how much I love you, and how grateful I am for all you've done for me. Even eternity in Heaven won't be long enough to give you all my worship.

The Great Day of Wrath

Revelation 6:16, 17: And they cried to the mountains and the rocks, "Fall on us and hide us from the face of the one who sits on the throne and from the wrath of the Lamb. For the great day of their wrath has come, and who is able to survive?"

MONDAY

The Extra Mile: Revelation 6

Do you ever wish evil leaders and dictators will be dealt with once and for all? Do you ever look around at some of the evil done in the world, such as abortions, murders, wars, and destruction and wish God would hurry up and do something?

The truth is God is doing something. He's been doing something all through human history. God is in charge of history, and those who despite him and harm his people will not only face God at the judgment, but will face his discipline now in this world. There are more than one hundred wars going on in the world right now. Do you think God isn't at work in the lives of world leaders?

One answer is the above passage. This is what happens to evil people, leaders and everyone else, when God speaks.

Prayer: Lord, I know no matter how bad it looks right now, you are in charge of history. You will make everything right on your timetable.

Cheated and Robbed?

Revelation 7:14: Then he said to me, "These are the ones who died in the great tribulation. They have washed their robes in the blood of the Lamb and made them white."

The Extra Mile: Revelation 7:1–14

Have you ever been cheated, robbed, or had family members who were? It can be a terrible experience. One lady came home to her home to find someone had entered and gone through all her clothing. She felt as if she had been assaulted. She ended up throwing all those clothes away, as well as many other things. She also felt extremely unsafe and anxiety struck constantly.

What does God say to such Christians? It comes down to a word he uses often: trust. "Trust me," God says. "I will deal with those thieves and robbers. Look to me for help and strength. I will provide it."

God wants us to know that he is on the side of people who are hurt, oppressed, and broken. He assures us that he is with us when we face disaster, robbery, and put-downs.

No matter how bad it looks, God is on your side. Can you trust him to act on your behalf? Can you look to him to bring victory from the burned-out ashes?

Prayer: I trust you, Lord. So lead me and fill me with your Spirit.

Never Again

Revelation 7:16, 17: "They will never again be hungry or thirsty; they will never be scorched by the heat of the sun. For the Lamb on the throne will be their Shepherd. He will lead them to springs of life—giving water. And God will wipe every tear from their eyes."

The Extra Mile: Revelation 7:15–17

During World War II, over six million Jews were murdered by the henchmen of Adolph Hitler. Many of those Jews went to their deaths without fighting back or trying to resist. They died in submission and terror. So Jews today have a saying: "Never again!" This is a promise that never will they go to their deaths without fighting tooth and nail every step of the way.

God also says "never again" about some things. Our world is a hurting planet. Millions starve. There is pain everywhere. Diseases destroy the bodies of even the young. Hatred, racism, and terrorism abound.

But God cries out, "Never again!" When he creates the new Heaven and earth, never again will there be hunger. Never again will there be thirst. Never again will there be disease or tears or murder or hatred. Never again!

Prayer: Jesus, though things may look tough right now, help me to trust that one day all will be peace.

Terrors Coming

THURSDAY

Revelation 8:13: Then I looked, and I heard a single eagle crying loudly as it flew through the air, "Terror, terror, terror to all who belong to this world because of what will happen when the last three angels blow their trumpets."

The Extra Mile: Revelation 8

There are many ways to motivate a person. One is to be nice, to explain how it is, and to show the way. Another is to take the person in question by the collar and haul him along till he gets it and comes along on his own. Finally, there's the method God uses in the book of Revelation: terrors!

All through human history people have decided to follow God because of his gentleness, kindness, and compassion. But sometimes people have had to hit rock bottom and come to the end of themselves before they turn to God. The Bible gives examples of times God punished his people in order to get them to turn back to him.

In Revelation we read that at the end of time, God will have enough of our stubbornness and complaints, so he's going to bring in the heavy guns: plagues, earthquakes, strange beings with awful powers, signs in the heavens, waters turned to blood, raining death from the sky. During that time many people will turn to God in faith. They'll be convinced. "I'd better become a Christian, or I'm dead," they'll be saying.

But it's always better to say that before all these bad things happen.

Prayer: Lord, I see that when it comes to getting people to believe, you will use any means possible to motivate them. I believe, Lord; show me how to help others to believe.

Supernatural Beings

WEEK 50

FRIDAY

Revelation 9:7, 8: The locusts looked like horses prepared for battle. They had what looked like gold crowns on their heads, and their faces looked like human faces. They had hair like women's hair and teeth like the teeth of a lion.

The Extra Mile: Revelation 9

This is a description of some of the strange beings God will release into the world in the last days to try and save some people. Some scholars believe these "locusts" are actually demons from the pit of Hell or judging angels. Whatever they are, they're powerful and their sting hurts worse than anything. Anyone who gets stung by them will have intense pain like the pain from a scorpion's string for five months. They will actually wish to die, and God won't let them. No one on earth will die for that whole period.

While we don't know what these things are or how they will actually look to the naked eye, we do know God will send these beings into the world. Why? To wake people up. God wants to make them see the errors of their sins and motivate them to turn to Christ.

Why such terrible pain? Because nothing else has worked. And God loves his people too much to let them perish, even if it means hurting them in this world to save them for the next.

Prayer: God, your love is so great that you will stop at nothing to turn those you love back to you. I thank you, Lord, for turning me back to you.

365 New Testament Devotions for Kids

A Heavenly Secret

Revelation 10:4: When the seven thunders spoke, I was about to write. But I heard a voice from heaven saying, "Keep secret what the seven thunders said, and do not write it down."

The Extra Mile: Revelation 10

As John wrote the book of Revelation while Jesus told him the things that would happen in the last days, he came to this portion. It was called "The Seven Thunders." There have been the Seven Seals earlier, and then the Seven Trumpets. Later, there will be the Seven Bowls. Each one of these were judgments on the world for rejecting God and Christ. They were all designed to get people to repent and turn back to God.

We don't know what the Seven Thunders will be. John was not allowed to write about them. What could they be? Are they judgments so terrible we would faint if we knew them ahead of time? There are many things they could be, but many interpreters believe they are judgments so terrible that the world will stand in stunned shock at each one, and many people will come back to God through faith.

Whatever they are, you can be sure the thunder will be loud and unmistakable. It will say one thing: repent and believe the gospel of Jesus. Many people will believe, and one of the greatest revivals in human history will occur.

Prayer: When you have a secret planned for the future, God, I know I'd better listen up. You have something important to say.

The End of the World

Revelation 11:3: And I will give power to my two witnesses, and they will be clothed in burlap and will prophesy during those 1,260 days.

The Extra Mile: Revelation 11

This verse from Revelation concerns the end times, when Jesus comes back and God rules the world. Two witnesses will be sent to earth. Some scholars believe these two are Moses and Elijah because they didn't complete their ministries when they were on earth. Others think they might be Enoch and Elijah because they are the two people in human history who went to Heaven without dying first.

It doesn't much matter who these people are. What matters is what they will do. They will point people to the living God. And millions will be converted to faith in Jesus because of their witness.

While the idea of the end times might be scary to you, it is nothing to worry about if you're on God's side. He wins, so you're on the winning team.

Prayer: Father, I know you love me and will take care of me, so I will trust you to the very end.

Satan's Rebellion

Revelation 12:3, 4: *I saw a large red dragon with seven heads and ten horns, with seven crowns on his heads. His tail swept away one-third of the stars in the sky, and he threw them to the earth.*

The Extra Mile: Revelation 12

We don't know a lot about Satan from the Bible. We know he tempted Adam and Eve and drew them into sin. We know he tried to destroy Job and prove Job would curse God if God didn't bless him. But Job stuck with God, and proved that even when God lets bad things happen to faithful people, they continue to trust him.

Satan also tempted Jesus in the wilderness in Matthew 4, and he also entered Judas Iscariot to make him betray Jesus. From other passages we know Satan is a liar, deceiver, accuser, tempter, and all-around hater of God.

The passage above, some believe, refers to Satan leading a third of the angels to follow him. This may be true; we can't be completely sure. What we do know is that Satan will do anything to hurt and destroy us.

Prayer: Lord, Satan only has power as long as you allow him to. You are greater than Satan and can stop him with a word.

Dragons!

Revelation 13:4: They worshiped the dragon for giving the beast such power, and they also worshiped the beast. "Who is as great as the beast?" they exclaimed. "Who is able to fight against him?"

The Extra Mile: Revelation 13

Sara stepped into the car. "I'm sitting in the front," she said to the other kids. No one thought much about it as they all piled in.

At the zoo, Sara told them, "Follow me; I'll show you the best animals first."

Later in the afternoon, when everyone was going home from the trip, Sara instructed the driver, "Let me off first. My mom wants me home right away."

Have you ever known a person like Sara? They always have to be first. People have to step aside so they can pass. They want the best seats at the ball game, and the most recognition for anything they do.

The dragon in this verse represents Satan. And Satan loves to be first. That's the main thing he wants. He longs to take God's place. He wishes that God would fade away and he could step in. Satan will always demand to be first until the very end when God throws him down for good.

Watch yourself. It's easy to want to be first, to be number one, to be worshiped. Don't start complaining and making little demands and pushing everyone aside like Sara.

Prayer: Lord, I will learn to wait, give others first place, and love even the unlovable.

Worshiping the Beast

Revelation 14:9, 10: Then a third angel followed them, shouting, "Anyone who worships the beast and his statue or who accepts his mark on the forehead or on the hand must drink the wine of God's anger."

The Extra Mile: Revelation 14

John recorded his vision of the last days on earth in the book of Revelation. He described how an antichrist, someone who will pretend to be Jesus, will come to earth. He will demand that everyone follow him, love him, and, most of all, worship him. To make sure that everyone will do this, the antichrist will make everyone take a "mark" on his body (perhaps on the forehead or the hand). Anyone who doesn't have this mark will not be able to buy or sell anything anywhere on earth.

Christians will never take this mark. It signifies that you belong to Satan. It means you will ultimately be judged with the sentence of Hell.

No one knows what this mark will be until it appears. Then it will be obvious to any Christian what it is. How will such Christians survive in such a world? The antichrist will kill many of them. But those who survive will be supported and helped by God himself. In fact, many more people will become Christians because of what they've seen God do in the lives of his children.

Prayer: I can't understand all the details of what will happen in the last days, Lord. I'm not even sure I'm supposed to. But I know enough to say I want to be on your side. I will remain faithful to you; I need your help to not be led astray.

Joy Unspeakable

Revelation 15:2: *I saw before me what seemed to be a glass sea mixed with fire. And on it stood all the people who had been victorious over the beast and his statue and the number representing his name. They were all holding harps that God had given them.*

THURSDAY

The Extra Mile: Revelation 15

You may have read the last few devotions from Revelation with a lot of fear. "Could I take the mark?" You might ask yourself. "What would I do if I live in this time?"

While many teachers today believe horrible things will happen during this time of trouble, God has promised to be with his people, lead them, and supply them no matter how difficult it might seem. Even though the antichrist will hunt and kill Christians, God promises to get all of them safely to Heaven.

And look at what these people are doing when they get to Heaven, according to the above passage. It's a party!

Prayer: Father, what a party we'll have in Heaven some day. And you'll be the guest of honor!

When God Gets Angry

Revelation 16:1: Then I heard a mighty voice from the Temple say to the seven angels, "Go your ways and pour out on the earth the seven bowls containing God's wrath."

The Extra Mile: Revelation 16

Do you wonder why God takes it? People curse his name all the time. Yet God just takes it. Murderers walk the street looking for new victims. Sometimes they're caught, sometimes not.

Children bully their brothers and sisters. Parents beat their kids up. Mothers and fathers swear at each other.

Do you ever wish God would just haul off and smack some of these people into the middle of Hell? That day is coming. God is going to show his real anger at sin and rejection and people putting God down. He's going to let everyone know how he really feels. He will haul off and give a lot of sinners a stiff right to the jaw!

The book of Revelation reveals the story of what God will do at the end of human history. All the anger he's been stuffing all these years he will let out. He'll show bad people just how bad he can be to them! It won't be a pretty sight. But it will happen.

Prayer: Lord, I'm sorry you have to see so much sin in the world, especially the sins I've done. Forgive me for these.

Ten Kings

Revelation 17:12: The ten horns of the beast are ten kings who have not yet risen to power. They will be appointed to their kingdoms for one brief moment to reign with the beast.

The Extra Mile: Revelation 17

Some people believe a 10-leader group of peoples and nations will rule the world in the last days. While we don't know who or where these kings will come from, it's probable they will the leaders of the 10 most powerful nations on earth at the time. They will all support, adore, and worship the antichrist or Satan himself.

While much of that is speculation, we can be sure of one thing. When these things start to happen in the world, the world will know it. Christians who are living at that time will know exactly what this kingdom is all about, and they will reject it. They will read the book of Revelation like they're reading today's newspaper. The events in Revelation, though mysterious, vague, and cloudy right now, will be perfectly clear then. This will be God's primary way of convincing people he is God and he knew the end from the beginning.

Revelation was written around AD 95. So it's been around almost 2,000 years. And it predicts things that happen in the last days. When you see the events of Revelation happening, be ready.

Prayer: Lord, I know you don't want me to be afraid or discouraged. You know the future, and I'm safe in your hands.

The Greatest City of All Time

SUNDAY

Revelation 18:10: They will stand at a distance, terrified by her great torment. They will cry out, "How terrible, how terrible for you, O Babylon, you great city! In a single moment God's judgment came on you."

The Extra Mile: Revelation 18

In the last days, the greatest city on earth will be Babylon. It will have taller buildings, more majestic architecture, and every great thing, the ultimate symbol of the powers of the world. It will be the capitol of the antichrist and the center of everything: government, commerce, and entertainment, like Paris, Tokyo, New York, and Bejing all thrown into one.

But it will be evil, and God will destroy it in a single moment. Think of the great power it will take to do that. God is great, and because of his great power, he is worthy of respect, love, loyalty, and worship. What is valued in this life must come to an end to start the next.

Prayer: I love you, God. I want the day to come soon when I can be forever with you.

Jesus Comes Back

Revelation 19:11: Then I saw heaven opened, and a white horse was standing there. Its rider was named Faithful and True, for he judges fairly and wages a righteous war.

The Extra Mile: Revelation 19

What does the good guy always do in the old westerns? He wears a white hat. He rides a white horse. And he rides off into the sunset after fixing all the problems in the world.

That's not exactly how Jesus will come back. But one part is true. He will be riding a white horse. The book of Revelation says that Jesus will be called Faithful and True, and he will bring justice.

Jesus is different from any other leader in all of human history. He's faithful. He will never be disloyal. He will never give up on his people. He will always do what's right.

He's also true. He speaks the truth. He won't tell us lies. He won't make promises he doesn't keep. He lets us in on all the secrets of God and history.

Last, he's just. He will bring in perfect justice. Racism will end. Murder and strife will be stopped. Abuse, hatred, anger will all be halted in their tracks.

It will be a glorious day.

Jesus is coming. Look forward to it. And be ready.

Prayer: Father, I plan to be watchful and to obey you.

Endless Lists

Revelation 20:12: *I saw the dead, both great and small, standing before God's throne. And the books were opened, including the Book of Life. And the dead were judged according to what they had done, as recorded in the books.*

The Extra Mile: Revelation 20

It's the start of class. The teacher opens his grade book and starts reading off names. Students respond, "Here!" "Present!" "Accounted for!" and other creative ways of saying they're there. It's the teacher's way of seeing who showed up for class.

One day, God will take attendance too. He has a number of books, but one very special one is called the "Book of Life." In this book God has recorded the names of every person in human history who believed in him and in Jesus.

Can you imagine going down that list? Statistics experts tell us that there are over 680 million "born again" Christians in the world today. These are just the ones who are alive now. There are many times that number who, through the ages, have believed in God. Can you imagine God going through that list?

Maybe you can't, but it won't be boring. Everyone will be listening for his name and the names of those he or she loves. Everyone will listen too for the names of famous people in history. It'll be the greatest attendance call of all time.

How do you know if your name is written in the Book of Life? There's only one way: put your faith and trust in Jesus. Have you accepted his payment for your sins? Have you repented and been forgiven?

Prayer: Lord, I want to be there among the millions in Heaven praising you.

No More Pain or Crying or Death or Sorrow

Revelation 21:4: He will wipe every tear from their eyes, and there will be no more death or sorrow or crying or pain. All these things are gone forever.

The Extra Mile: Revelation 21

What are the worst things that have ever happened to you? Some kids your age would mention losing a loved one, suffering from a serious illness, flunking a grade in school, or having unfulfilled dreams.

Every person on earth has gone through a lot of pain and hurt throughout life. When we hurt, no one can just whisk a wand over us to make it all better. Even when Jesus healed people in the Bible when he walked on earth, those people didn't have pain-free lives after that. All of them died one day. And they probably all saw many loved ones die too.

But one day, death, pain, suffering, and sorrow will be all over. One day God intends to bring about a new world where all is well. No one will ever sin again. No person will ever hurt another in thought, word, or deed. You will never be alone, or rejected, hated, or put down ever again.

Can you imagine such a world?

You'd better. It's coming. And it will be amazing.

Prayer: Jesus, I know Heaven will be one amazing thing after another, forever and ever and ever.

Visible God

Revelation 22:4, 5: *And they will see his face, and his name will be written on their foreheads. And there will be no night there—no need for lamps or sun—for the Lord God will shine on them. And they will reign forever and ever.*

Revelation 22:1-5

Wouldn't it be nice when we're in a tight spot if Jesus just appeared out of nowhere and stood in front of us? If a bully cornered us we could just shout "Jesus!" and he would appear, maybe with a whip in his hand, no less!

It's a nice fantasy. But since Jesus ascended into Heaven, he hasn't appeared on earth. Still, many of us think if Jesus were just here with us in the flesh, we'd do so much better.

During the exodus, God appeared in a pillar of cloud by day and a pillar of fire by night. The Israelites saw God every hour of the day. They knew he was there, watching, listening, and helping. And what happened? The Israelites wanted something better. Can you imagine it? God was there all the time and they were tempted to go back to Egypt with their idols. How dumb!

God is invisible, but he's with us wherever we are: in a football game, at the mall, in class, in the darkest or scariest place you've ever been. He's there. That's a bit better than an idol, don't you think?

Prayer: Lord, I see that you are with me everywhere now, but one day I will see your face. Incredible!

The Way to Fame and Glory

Revelation 22:12: *"Look, I am coming soon, bringing my reward with me to repay all people according to their deeds."*

The Extra Mile: Revelation 22:6-12

August was president of the sixth-grade class. Everyone thought he was so cool.

Sharry made it on the cheerleading squad. People talked about how pretty she was all the time.

Gareth hit a home run in the last inning of a big Little League game. He got his name in the paper for that one.

Nikki, though, never made a mark, never got her name in lights. She wanted so much to be somebody, to be important, for people to think she was pretty and cool and smart, but hardly anyone ever noticed her.

One day while studying her Bible she found Revelation 22:12. It told her that one day God would reward her for her good deeds. It promised that God would bless her in ways she could never imagine.

Nikki thought about it. OK, she would look to God. She would do good—not in order to get her name in lights, but just to please God. She became a steady worker.

Prayer: Lord, I know one day I will stand before you. What you give me will be far greater than being on the honor roll, getting my name in the paper, or being on TV.

Out of Egypt, Into Canaan

SATURDAY

Revelation 22:13: *I am the Alpha and the Omega, the First and the Last, the Beginning and the End.*

The Extra Mile: Revelation 22:13, 14

Have you ever noticed how God likes to put beginnings and endings in our lives like bookends? You start out on earth; you end up in Heaven. You were once a sinner; now you're a saint.

They're like bookends. You're born, and one day you die. You enter a contest, and one day you win something. It's amazing how many things in life have beginnings and endings.

But did you know God IS the beginning and the end? He's everything before and after, and in between. That's one good reason to get to know him better.

Prayer: God, I will study your Word and learn all I can about you, and it still won't be everything there is to know.

Living a Lie

Revelation 22:15: Outside the city are the dogs—the sorcerers, the sexually immoral, the murderers, the idol worshipers, and all who love to live a lie.

The Extra Mile: Revelation 22:15, 16

Jeff's father sat across from him at the dinner table. "Mr. Bresser called me today at the office. He said you and his son Brad were playing with firecrackers out behind their house."

"Yeah, we were," Jeff answered honestly.

"You know they're illegal?"

"Yes."

"Why did you do it?"

"I don't know. We just wanted to have some fun."

"Where did you get them in the first place?"

That was the tricky issue. Jeff knew his father would hit the roof if he told him the truth—he'd gotten them from a kid at school. So he decided to lie. "Grandpa had some left over from last year."

Jeff's dad nodded. "Well, then I guess I'll have to talk to Grandpa about this!"

Oh no. Oh no! Now Jeff was really in trouble.

His dad did call his grandpa and eventually the truth came out. He had lied, a worse thing to do than playing with firecrackers.

Prayer: Jesus, I will try always to tell the truth, because you have shown me mercy in the past.

Last One

Revelation 22:17: The Spirit and the bride say, "Come." Let anyone who hears this say, "Come." Let anyone who is thirsty come. Let anyone who desires drink freely from the water of life.

The Extra Mile: Revelation 22:17–21

Are you thirsty? Have you ever been thirsty? It starts with a little dryness in your throat. Soon, it burns a bit. In time, it's like your whole mouth and throat are on fire. "Water," you say. "I need water."

Then you see a store up ahead. You start running. You open the door. Water!

You grab a bottle, pay for it. And then you drink.

Ahhhhhhh.

Spiritual thirst is like that too. You sense things aren't right in your life. Then you start to wish for something better. "There has to be more than this." Gradually, you learn about answers to some of the great questions: Why are we here? What's life all about?

Then one day you find out about Jesus. "Come," he says. "I will quench your thirst."

What do you do?

Prayer: Lord, I will follow you forever. Don't let me go.

Use these pages to track your progress in reading this book and the Bible. Use the space provided to write down what you pray for, and note God's answers.

I read this week's devotions (check box)　　　Date completed

❑ Week 1 　　　＿＿＿＿＿＿＿＿＿＿
❑ Week 2 　　　＿＿＿＿＿＿＿＿＿＿
❑ Week 3 　　　＿＿＿＿＿＿＿＿＿＿
❑ Week 4 　　　＿＿＿＿＿＿＿＿＿＿
❑ Week 5 　　　＿＿＿＿＿＿＿＿＿＿
❑ Week 6 　　　＿＿＿＿＿＿＿＿＿＿
❑ Week 7 　　　＿＿＿＿＿＿＿＿＿＿
❑ Week 8 　　　＿＿＿＿＿＿＿＿＿＿
❑ Week 9 　　　＿＿＿＿＿＿＿＿＿＿
❑ Week 10 　　　＿＿＿＿＿＿＿＿＿＿
❑ Week 11 　　　＿＿＿＿＿＿＿＿＿＿
❑ Week 12 　　　＿＿＿＿＿＿＿＿＿＿
❑ Week 13 　　　＿＿＿＿＿＿＿＿＿＿
❑ Week 14 　　　＿＿＿＿＿＿＿＿＿＿
❑ Week 15 　　　＿＿＿＿＿＿＿＿＿＿
❑ Week 16 　　　＿＿＿＿＿＿＿＿＿＿
❑ Week 17 　　　＿＿＿＿＿＿＿＿＿＿
❑ Week 18 　　　＿＿＿＿＿＿＿＿＿＿
❑ Week 19 　　　＿＿＿＿＿＿＿＿＿＿
❑ Week 20 　　　＿＿＿＿＿＿＿＿＿＿
❑ Week 21 　　　＿＿＿＿＿＿＿＿＿＿
❑ Week 22 　　　＿＿＿＿＿＿＿＿＿＿
❑ Week 23 　　　＿＿＿＿＿＿＿＿＿＿
❑ Week 24 　　　＿＿＿＿＿＿＿＿＿＿

DEVOTIONAL JOURNAL

DEVOTIONAL JOURNAL

- ❏ Week 25 _____
- ❏ Week 26 _____
- ❏ Week 27 _____
- ❏ Week 28 _____
- ❏ Week 29 _____
- ❏ Week 30 _____
- ❏ Week 31 _____
- ❏ Week 32 _____
- ❏ Week 33 _____
- ❏ Week 34 _____
- ❏ Week 35 _____
- ❏ Week 36 _____
- ❏ Week 37 _____
- ❏ Week 38 _____
- ❏ Week 39 _____
- ❏ Week 40 _____
- ❏ Week 41 _____
- ❏ Week 42 _____
- ❏ Week 43 _____
- ❏ Week 44 _____
- ❏ Week 45 _____
- ❏ Week 46 _____
- ❏ Week 47 _____
- ❏ Week 48 _____
- ❏ Week 49 _____
- ❏ Week 50 _____
- ❏ Week 51 _____
- ❏ Week 52 _____
- ❏ Week 53 (1 day) _____

I praise, you, God for

These are ways you have blessed me, God. Thank you!

Dear God, I pray these things for my family

I thank you, God, for these friends

_____   _____

_____   _____

_____   _____

_____   _____

_____   _____

Please help my friends by

_____

_____

_____

_____

_____

_____

Dear God, I need your help!

_____

_____

_____

_____

_____

_____

_____

_____

_____

_____

Please help these people, God

Please help these people, God

_____

_____

_____

_____

_____

_____

_____

_____

_____

_____

_____

I'm sorry, God